NEW
FORCES
IN AMERICAN
BUSINESS

An Analysis of the Economic Outlook

New York   Toronto   London

NEW
FORCES
IN AMERICAN
BUSINESS

for the '60s by Dexter Merriam Keezer

AND

WILLIAM H. CHARTENER

DOUGLAS GREENWALD

ROBERT P. ULIN

E. RUSSELL EGGERS

MARGARET K. MATULIS

McGRAW-HILL BOOK COMPANY, INC.

NEW FORCES IN AMERICAN BUSINESS

FIRST EDITION

CONTENTS

1097787

INTRODUCTION   vii

CHAPTER ONE   1

The Operation Laid Out

CHAPTER TWO   15

*Prospects for Sustaining
a High Level of Business Investment*

CHAPTER THREE   48

Research—Key to Growth and Stability

CHAPTER FOUR   70

The Changing Consumer Market

CHAPTER FIVE   90

The Fateful Art of Marketing

CHAPTER SIX   124

Government's Expanding Role

CHAPTER SEVEN   149

*Will There Be Enough
and Rugged Enough Competition?*

CHAPTER EIGHT   174

Prospects of Avoiding
Disastrous Price Inflation

CHAPTER NINE   200

Are Agriculture's Aches Contagious?

CHAPTER TEN   213

U.S. Business and the World Overseas

CHAPTER ELEVEN   237

The Last Round-up

APPENDIX I   247

Development of the McGraw-Hill
Index of Manufacturing Capacity

APPENDIX II   256

Special Problems in Income Distribution

APPENDIX III   262

Improvements in the U.S. Economic Intelligence

APPENDIX IV   267

Special Aids for Small Business

INDEX   273

The Questions and the (Short) Answers

Has the American economy got what it takes to sustain the remarkable record of growth and stability which it has made since World War II?

—Is the American economy of the late fifties simply bigger than the economy of the late forties or thirties, or does it have a basically different character, and hence a different and better prospective performance?

It is to these consequential questions that the following discussion is primarily addressed.

Lest the suspense be excessive, our answers are stated at the outset. They are that:

1. Short of some cataclysmic development, such as an atomic world war, the American economy has undergone basic changes since its catastrophe of the thirties which give powerful support to the expectation that relatively steady growth and prosperity will be the general rule, rather than the nervously embraced exception to the rule, over the next decade, and

2. While it remains preponderantly a business economy and, to this extent, is the same kind of economy we had in the thirties, there have been institutional changes of such scope and magnitude as to make it a basically different economy, with new driving forces, from that of earlier decades.

A SOMEWHAT PHILOSOPHICAL NOTE— IT CAN BE SKIPPED

You will observe that the answers to the questions raised at the outset have been phrased quite affirmatively. There

are no ifs, ands or buts about them. This is partly because
we are confident enough that the answers are correct as
stated. But it also is because we are business, rather than
academic, economists.

In the nature of his calling, it is the privilege of the academic economist to weigh the pros and cons of any given
economic question—and then, if he wishes, to retire from the
field leaving the answer, if any, to be provided by his lis-
teners. In fact, this process frequently has attached to it the
intellectually laudatory label of open-mindedness.

The business economist, however, enjoys no such leeway
for detached expression. He works for people who must make
decisions. And if he does not learn it quickly, he soon will
be told that a take-off on a course of action cannot satis-
factorily be made from a teeter-totter. "Tell me," he will be
asked, "what in your best judgment is going to happen. I'll
forgive you if events prove you wrong. But I won't tolerate
you if you simply ask me to weigh the pros and cons. It's
your job to do that and give me the result."

It is out of a habit bred of business necessity that we state
our conclusions affirmatively. It is not because of any inbred
dogmatism. We are as fully aware of the qualifications and
limitations as our academic brethren. But we put the conclusions first and boldly, with the qualifications to follow.
The academic economists are privileged to reverse the process if they see fit, and they generally do. Sometimes we envy
them—a little.

OUR POINT OF VANTAGE

Our answers to the questions posed at the outset are the
result of group operations by the Department of Economics
of the McGraw-Hill Publishing Company. This department
acts as a central economics staff for both the management of

the company and its periodical publications. In this capacity it is continuously and intensively concerned with the future course of American economy, a subject on which it regularly reports to its McGraw-Hill associates.

The department is in a better position than that occupied by some economists to get glimpses of important changes in the American economy. We have as neighbors and colleagues more than 600 industrial and business editors of forty industrial and business publications. Between them they have both a rather intimate and current knowledge of what is going on in a large part of the American economy, and they are very cooperative in alerting us to important new economic developments as they find them.

In the nature of our business environment, we do not have as much time for reflection on what we find out as that afforded to many economists in universities and research establishments. In this regard we occupy a sort of halfway house between the hurly-burly of periodical journalism and the detached calm which is attributed, at least, to the university cloisters. Much more than incidentally, it is a location where our privilege of assessing the passing and coming economic scene objectively is quite as good as it is in the academic world, in the judgment of members of the department who have spent many years as college and university faculty members.

We are, however, sufficiently detached from the never-ending race to keep up with the news of the day to have the privilege of:

1. Doing our best to sort out the economic developments which have potentialities of profound effects from those which may simply be flashy, and

2. Trying to put important developments in a broad perspective which permits a careful judgment of their effects on the future operation of our total economy.

And in the nature of our operation we must do all of this in simple English prose. Neither our associates nor our audience permit us to report our findings "partly in English and partly in algebra," a method currently characteristic of a remarkably large share of the discussion in professional economic journals.

REPORTS FROM THE FRONTIERS

In the chapters that follow we have exercised our privileges in the straightforward manner indicated, partly in the normal course of operations and in part as an extracurricular operation. Some of the material presented was originally assembled for a dozen lectures on the postwar American economy and its prospects which I had the honor of giving at the Salzburg (Austria) Seminar in American Studies. However, the lecture notes were lost in transit home, so that share of the material has not been rehashed. It has been entirely reassembled and largely supplemented.

That the writing done in this process has been done by several people is manifested by variations in style which there has been no attempt to edit away. The substance of what is written, however, finds at least enough general agreement among those identified as participating in it to escape such ultimatums as "I absolutely refuse to be associated with anything as silly as that!" Among economists this might be construed by some as virtually complete and angelic unanimity.

With the exception of E. Russell Eggers, all of those listed as authors of this volume are present members of the McGraw-Hill Department of Economics. After he made his important contribution to the work while one of us, Mr. Eggers left us to join the economics staff of the Chase Manhattan Bank, where our Department of Economics has a thriving alumni chapter, composed preponderantly of vice-presidents of that great banking institution.

An attempt to list all those who have given us useful lifts with this book would extend this introductory note to inordinate length. However, it would be positively remiss not to mention Martin J. Kohn, a member of our Department before he became an Intelligence Research Specialist in the Office of Research and Analysis for Sino-Soviet Bloc, Department of State. He gave us decisive critical help at numerous points.

At one time or another in the development of the final product we also received and were helped by critical observations we solicited from William Diebold, Jr., Director of Economic Studies, Council on Foreign Relations, Inc.; John K. Libby, Kuhn, Loeb & Co.; Pierre A. Rinfret, Vice-President and Director of the Economics Department, Lionel D. Edie & Co., Inc.; Charles W. Smith, Senior Consultant, McKinsey & Co., Inc.; Ted H. Steeg, Publications Division, McGraw-Hill Publishing Co., Inc.; and Richard L. Waddell, Marketing Editor, *Business Week.* We thank them very much, as we do Anne M. Keezer for giving the manuscript some editing and the benefit of a strictly lay reaction. We're also very grateful to Mrs. Edna Cochrane for helping to monitor the myriad of changes of one kind or another in the manuscript as it moved along the way to publication.

The findings and conclusions here in no way reflect any attitude or policy on the part of our employer, the McGraw-Hill Publishing Company. While we are continuously engaged in making economic studies for the company and its publications, the fact that we make them does not give these studies any status as expressions of company or publication policy.

For our findings we do not claim infallible contact with the ultimate in economic verity. Our observations are those of outposts on the economic frontier, and a clearer and later view of the full development may call for reassessment, at least in detail. We do, however, hope that our associates in the business world will not ignore the sort of developments we both envisage and document at the risk of missing great opportunities for their enterprises. To our academic confreres and those in the field of research, we submit our findings and impressions as something in the nature of a careful field report, for such amplification, refinement or perhaps even correction, as their meticulous assessment of the report should make possible.

In pursuance of this general frame of mind, we have enthusiastically collaborated with a number of university faculty members in making material assembled through our field studies of business investment available to them for scholarly analysis and for factual checking of theoretical work.*

In making these studies we guarantee that there will be no disclosure of individual company figures. No one has ever had occasion to question the validity of the guaranty. With such limitation, the results of our studies present a wealth of valuable material for research scholars. Further removed than we from the distraction of actual business operations and with more time available for contemplative and painstaking analysis, university scholars have the opportunity to join us in making further advance upon the ultimate truth than either of us can make separately.

By such collaboration there is a chance to make the best

---

* For example, see "Expectations, Plans and Capital Expenditures, A Synthesis of Ex Post and Ex Ante Data," a paper delivered at a joint meeting of the American Economic Association, the Econometric Society and the American Statistical Association, December 1953 by Robert Eisner of the University of Illinois; and "Plant and Equipment Expenditures Surveys: Intentions and Fulfillments," Cowles Foundation Discussion Paper #17, Oct. 26, 1956, by Robert A. Levine of Yale University.

of two worlds—the world of direct but careful and orderly economic observation where we operate and the world of meticulous scholarship reserved to the economists in universities and research establishments. American economics is desperately in need of such cooperation and cross-fertilization. It is our hope that this volume will make a considerable contribution to this process.

Dexter Merriam Keezer

CHAPTER ONE

The Operation Laid Out

Since the end of World War II the American economy has made a remarkable record of both growth and stability. In contrast to the depression which many economists expected to follow four years of war, and business based on war, our output of goods and services has more than doubled since 1939 and has increased more than two-fifths since 1948 (a year that may be regarded as the peak of the "postwar" boom).*

In rebounding from its most recent setback (in the brief recession of July 1957 to April 1958), our economy gave perhaps its most remarkable demonstration of vitality and long-run growth potential. From the low point of $433 billion early in 1958, gross national product increased to approximately $476 billion by mid-1959. Noting the speed of this advance, business forecasts for 1960 began to be phrased in terms of a "half-trillion-dollar economy." And indeed the stock market —impatient for such a development—reached a level by early 1959 that implied considerable confidence in the achievement of further business growth in 1960 and beyond.

Is this renewed growth in business activity simply a speculative upturn in the old up-and-down business cycle? Or is it part of a longer-term growth trend that is more soundly based? The fact is that for more than a decade now, eco-

---

* These comparisons and others that follow in this chapter are in terms of the gross national product in constant (1958) prices, from the dates shown to the second quarter of 1959.

nomic growth has been remarkably sustained. As the chart indicates, in only two years during the postwar period (1949 and 1958) has it departed more than 4 percent from a straight line of growth. And over this period the employment of the nation's labor force has ranged from 92.5 percent to 97.5 percent of the total, with employment falling below 94 percent of the total labor force only for brief periods.*

Can we maintain this record of growth and stability for another decade?

Gross National Product

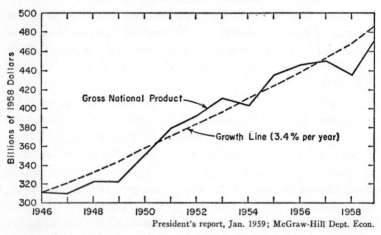

President's report, Jan. 1959; McGraw-Hill Dept. Econ.

Since the end of World War II, our economy has grown steadily. In physical terms (as measured by the gross national product adjusted for price changes) growth has averaged about 3.4 percent annually. This is a rate of growth about one-sixth higher than the long-term rate of growth since 1909.

A CATALOG OF FEARS

The record from 1946 to date has been compounded in large part of elements related to war-making, past and

---

* For amplification see statement by Dexter M. Keezer in *Federal Policy for Economic Growth and Stability: Papers Submitted by Panelists Appearing Before the Sub-committee on Tax Policy,* Joint Committee on the Economic Report, Nov. 9, 1955; p. 1.

prospective. Enormous backlogs of demand, built up during the rationed years of World War II, sped the economy on its postwar course and called for much expanded production. Also, continuous participation in a cold war with the U.S.S.R. and participation in a shooting war in Korea have played no small part in keeping the economy booming.

The part which past and potential wars have played in propelling the American economy since the end of World War II seems to many people an ominous portent for its future. One fear is that if our prayers for something really resembling peace were answered, it could only be at the expense of a severe letdown of the economy. For example, in his book, *Turning Point toward Peace,** James P. Warburg remarked that "If the cold war were suddenly to end, we should find ourselves paralyzed by a major depression before plans could be devised to drain off our surplus production into a program of creative foreign aid and investments."

Another fear which grips many others is that our downfall will be propelled by excessive demands of organized labor, with more monopoly power than wisdom or experience to exercise their demands with adequate restraint. The sequence envisaged here is one of excessive wage exactions, followed by insupportable price increases and then a crash.

There are those who share this fear of a sequence of insupportable price increases, to be followed by a crash, but they see another set of culprits. The parties playing the satanic role in their vision of impending economic disaster are the great business firms, which they see overriding the restraints of competition and paving the way for depression by too greedy exercise of monopoly power.

There are others who agree that a soaring price level will be our undoing, but who find that the leading horseman of the economic apocalypse is government, and primarily the

* Current Affairs Press, New York, 1956; 56 pages.

Federal government. By spending more and more that it does not collect in taxes, they see its inflationary deficits doing us in.

But if the Federal government does collect the taxes to pay its mounting bills, at least by prevailing methods of taxation, there are those who see it promoting not merely a temporary but a chronic state of economic collapse by the paralyzing force of excessive personal and business taxation. Why knock yourself out with work and enterprise if the government cuts itself in as a major and often the principal financial beneficiary? More and more the answer is that there is no reason, in the view of those who share the fear of creeping and indeed galloping paralysis from taxation. For example, in its monthly letter of July 1956, the First National City Bank of New York remarked, "The present steep progression (of income taxation), as personal income levels rise, will progressively suffocate the economy as a whole just as it already is suffocating opportunities for the singularly gifted and skilled individual."

Another worry is that the American farmer has produced such an abundance that, left to sell it in relatively free markets, his sagging prices and income put a depressing, and for politicians particularly disturbing, drag on the economy —the sort of drag which contributed greatly to economic disaster in the thirties. But when prices are propped up by billions of dollars in price supports by the Federal government, as they are now, there are those who simply see the seeds of economic disaster—via inflation—transplanted, but not destroyed.

But perhaps the most pervasive of all fears about the American economy is the idea that a build-up of producing capacity, on the scale that has occurred in recent years, must sooner or later sink us under an overload of surplus producing facilities. This theory has gained special support from those who point out that the 1958 recession was heavily weighted with a decline in business expenditures on new plant and equipment, and that as the recovery progressed in 1959 there continued to be a notable lag in this important sector. Since there has developed in recent years a substantial difference between the amount of industrial capacity in place and the amount actually utilized (a ratio varying from 70 percent to 85 percent during 1958 and early 1959), and since the development of surplus capacity has in economic theory, and in historical fact, played a key role in business downturns, we shall find it necessary to deal at length with this special fear in Chapter 2.

This by no means exhausts the catalog of fears that our economy is riding for a major fall—fears invigorated, of course, among those of the older generations by memories of the Great Depression of the thirties. Still another fear is that we lack the know-how in the realm of economic management to keep our almost unbelievably complex economy on an even keel once it starts to disintegrate in formidable degree. This fear is, of course, nourished among the elders by recollection of:

1. The confident assurances of eminent economists that we had attained a new plateau of sustained prosperity when we were in fact on the brink of the greatest of depressions, and

2. The butchery performed on the body politic and economic by those parading as competent economic surgeons as we went over the brink.

When surrounded by such a thicket of fears, all of them embraced by at least some intelligent people, it may seem daring to entertain the belief that there is solid nourishment for the hope that none of them will be fulfilled in devastating degree. And it may seem positively foolhardy not only to entertain but to proclaim the view that over the years ahead, say over the next decade, general prosperity will be the general rule in the U.S.

Perhaps it is a bit brave to proclaim this view. Certainly some exercise in faith is necessary, for in the very nature of the case only time can tell the full story. But if, as we find to be the case, our economy has acquired key elements needed to sustain its postwar pace of growth and stability for years to come, it is only the part of prudence to get that probability popularized, instead of remaining the captives of obsolete economic terrors. Indeed, the neglect of this probability can be extremely costly to individuals, business firms and to the nation. One of the powerful allies of our Russian Communist adversaries is the widespread fear in the uncommitted countries that the American economy is chronically in peril of another disastrous plunge into a great depression like that of the thirties.* It is an ally which we believe proper appreciation of the powerful underpinnings of sustained prosperity in the United States would largely disarm.

BUMPS AND BOTTLENECKS

Lest it appear that we believe that the American economy is not merely knocking at the gates of the Elysian fields but is most of the way inside, some qualification may well be needed here. When we visualize the American economy as "steadily sustaining a high level of prosperity," we do not see it traveling along an ascending slope with the monotony of perfect smoothness. This would be altogether too much to expect of an economy which derives its great driving power largely from a process of putting into gear the energies,

---

* This fact was powerfully driven home to me by the line of questioning I encountered in India in 1958, in the course of conducting a series of seminars on the American economy, under the auspices of the United States Information Agency.—D.M.K.

and with them the inevitable mistakes, of myriads of free people and the enterprises they operate. If this process did not result in some ups and downs in business, we would have left the realm of economics and entered the realm of the miraculous.

Indeed, we would not feel that our expectations of the American economy over the years ahead had been blasted if as much as 6 or 7 percent of our labor force, or even more, were occasionally unemployed for periods measured in months. We know it is sometimes suggested that when unemployment reaches 5 percent of the labor force the time has come for the government to make massive moves designed to reduce it. But in an economy where the labor force can vary by more than 4 million persons (as it did in the first six months of 1957) very considerable changes in unemployment may take place as the result of relatively slight changes in business conditions. Also, in an economy undergoing a technological revolution of the magnitude of that now in process and prospect in the United States, there may be considerable bottlenecks in the relocation of workers with skills made obsolete rapidly by the very sweep and speed of technological change. We would not, therefore, be surprised or upset in our general economic expectations if there were spurts of unemployment above the 6 or 7 percent mark —a possibility which argues strongly for generous unemployment compensation, both on economic and humane grounds.

However, while we anticipate continuing ups and downs of the economy within the general limits indicated, it is our confident expectation that we shall not at any time in the decade relive anything like the economic nightmare of the thirties. Then, at the depth of the depression, approximately 25 percent of the labor force was unemployed, and other key indices of economic well-being were even further depressed. In happy contrast, we visualize the clear possibility, to be documented in the pages that follow, that general and expanding prosperity will be the rule over the next decade, and that the occasional ups and downs will not be severe enough to prove significant exceptions to this rule.

OUR ROUTE IN BRIEF

The developments which support our confidence in this conclusion involve every phase of the economy—from the gleam in the eye of the worker in the research laboratory, which is the prelude, often remote, to capital investment, to the final phase of ultimate consumption. Following another method of slicing up the total economy, the developments affect the sectors of government, of consumption, of investment.

As is true to the point of pain for the economic analyst, developments which have added great new strength and stability to the American economy are interlaced in complex patterns which cut through and across different sections of the economy. For example, the force of research and development by American industry, for which the current expenditure of over $9 billion annually constitutes perhaps the most dramatic aspect of the American economy, moves in one direction to shape both the pattern and tempo of business investment and in another direction to remodel the processes of production and distribution. Thus, it is difficult to deal with any of these new developments in a tolerably comprehensive way without having a considerable amount of overlap. We shall, however, do our best to avoid it.

Historically, business investment has been the most unstable element in the American economy. It also has been a primary, most economists would say *the* primary, source of growth. Hence, we shall start our detailed analysis by looking at business investment in new plant and equipment to see if there are new elements at work which promise:

1. To increase its stability, and

2. To stimulate the urge to keep investment expanding steadily.

We shall find that there are such elements, among them the driving force of rapidly increasing expenditures for research and development, the development of longer-range planning of investment and relatively well lubricated machinery for generating investment funds. They are elements so powerful and pervasive that if the process of business investment were carried out in a self-contained compartment we might confidently expect that its role as a disastrous disturber of the economic peace would be simply an aspect of history, rather than a matter of deep contemporary concern. But, of course, we recognize that business investment is not carried out in either a vacuum or an isolated compartment. In the last and not very remote analysis, it depends for both its expansion and its stability on what consumers do by way of buying the goods and services produced by the plants and equipment which the investment provides.

So from the prospects for expanding and steadily sustained capital investment, we turn to a consideration of the prospects of a steadily expanding volume of consumption over the next decade. This will, of course, involve us in such matters as population growth, income distribution and, by no means least, the arts of marketing.

As it is constituted today, government (national, state and local) plays a powerful, and can play a decisive, role in determining the course of both growth and economic stability. It can do so in two ways: (1) by exercise of its power to make the rules governing economic activity, including the rewards to be permitted, and (2) by the manner in which it handles its operations as a consumer of goods and services—of which it now takes about one-fifth of the nation's total. Indeed, fluctuations in the volume of these operations have at times in the postwar decade been a major contributor to economic instability.

So to round out an appraisal of the prospects of the American economy for growth and stability, we must deal with what the government is doing to shape the nation's economic course. These operations will take us into such matters as the relationship between defense expenditures and prosperity, the over-all policies of government in promoting full employment (as directed in the "Employment Act of 1946"), the success of monetary policy in restraining price inflation and the adequacy of Federal antitrust law enforcement.

In connection with our discussion of government, we shall pay our respects to what economists have termed the "built-in stabilizers" in our economy, since most of them have been creations of government. They include such diverse arrangements as unemployment insurance and steeply progressive income tax rates, each of which in its own way tends to mitigate the forces of business fluctuations, at least in their first impact. And we shall, of course, be equally mindful of what have recently been and promise to continue to be important economic *unstabilizers*, such as the lack of firm throttles on both consumer credit and the accumulation of business inventories.

In traversing the broad segments of economic activity— those of business investment, consumption and government —which we have blocked out, we shall either explicitly or by clear implication take account of all of the fears for the future of our economy which have been catalogued, as well as others to be encountered along the way. So far as perhaps the most haunting and harrowing fear of all is concerned— that of World War III with atomic weapons—we shall simply assume that war will not occur in the span of years to which we are addressing ourselves. We also assume that no change in domestic politics will be so sweeping as to alter the present determination of both major parties to maintain a strong defense establishment, and to conduct that defense within the framework of a general economic policy that rules out wild inflation. On any other assumptions, an analysis of the prospects for economic growth and stability becomes a hopelessly bootless exercise.

We are also making the assumption that over the period with which we are concerned our economy will not be hamstrung by shortage of basic resources. If the time span we had in mind ran over several decades, rather than roughly a single decade, this is an assumption which probably should be subject to very close scrutiny, especially on the important question of whether the water supply will hold out. But for the shorter period, the assumption can be defended as tolerably in touch with the prospective facts.

And even for the longer run, there are people of technical competence who feel that basic resources will not be the limiting factor in shaping the course of economic prosperity and growth. For example, Franklin Lindsay, who writes with authority, concludes that "the resources of the world are sufficient to support a population of many times present levels and standards above those of today." *

In conclusion we shall (1) summarize our more detailed findings on developments in the economy which support the expectation that it will extend over the next decade the extraordinary record of growth and stability which it has made in the past decade, and (2) reiterate our conclusion that these developments are so basic in character that they

* In a report of the "Planning for Non-Renewable Resources," prepared for the panel on United States Economic and Social Policy, organized by the Rockefeller Brothers Fund, 1957.

make our economy something fundamentally different from
the economy of the twenties.

WHAT IS LEFT OUT

Having stated our conclusions we shall not be offended if
you feel that we have not said the absolutely last word on
the very large and formidable subject at hand. For one
thing, we shall be aware that we have scarcely tipped our
hats to, let alone treated definitively, some of its crucial aspects. For example, one of the key considerations in gauging
the business outlook for the years ahead is the prospective
capacity of corporate management to do its job with an
effectiveness commensurate with its importance. We make
the cheerful assumption that, thanks to striking advances in
its effectiveness in recent years, corporate management has
what it takes. We do not document the basis for this good
cheer, and not least for want of technical capacity to do it.

Among other omissions perhaps we should note that we
are not dealing with our prospects for sustained growth in
broadly philosophical terms. Whether steadily sustained
prosperity will make us either happier or more righteous is a
question beyond the scope of our explorations and reflections.
So, for the most part, is the question of whether or not we
are directing our productive efforts to ends which are as
uplifting culturally as they should be. This is a question which
drove John Kenneth Galbraith to a point of distraction where
(in his discussion of "The Affluent Society") he cast aside
"the conventional wisdom" and proposed that we stop worry-
ing about having enough and steady enough production and
concentrate on what he would regard as a worthier distribution of its fruits.*

In a volume, *Making Capitalism Work*, which we published
in 1950 as the result of a cooperative departmental effort

* See Chapter 5 for a brief discussion of this point of view.

such as that which has gone into this volume, we dealt at some length with our conviction that a successful business system is peculiarly compatible with our basic political and personal freedoms.* But no such broad, and important, philosophical excursions are made in this volume.

Finally, we are not going to tell here what will happen to the stock market. Despite the increasing importance of stock investment as an outlet for savings—as evidenced by the increase of more than 6 million since 1952 in the number of persons owning stock †—the fluctuations in stock prices caused by current trading on the exchanges remain a matter primarily for discussion by the investment analyst rather than the general economist. This is so, despite increasingly widespread stock ownership, because the number of shares actively traded in today's market is much smaller than the total number held as savings.‡ Also, the volume of trading is much smaller in relation to national income than it was in the 1920s and involves far less credit, either of individuals or of financial institutions. For example, in 1929 the total dollar volume of stock market transactions was twice that of the national income, compared with only 9 percent of the national income in 1958.

As a result, the close interrelationship between the stock market and business activity which existed in the 1920s does not apply today. Even if stock prices were to crash with a speed approaching that registered in 1929, most of our present business structure would probably remain unscathed. Accordingly, the fear of a stock market debacle is one that we are not exploring in any detail in the pages that follow.

* McGraw-Hill, New York, 1950, Chap. 9, "The Companionship of Capitalism and American Ideals."

† Third Census of Shareowners, Share Ownership in America, New York Stock Exchange, 1959.

‡ There are 5 billion shares of stock listed on the New York Stock Exchange, but only a few million are traded each day. *Ibid.*, p. 13.

We shall, however, in the next chapter, deal extensively with the basic *economic* factor that was most important in the 1929 debacle, underlying the weakness in both general business and stock prices—namely, the development of surplus producing capacity in industry. In particular, we shall dwell on recent developments that make it unlikely that this will again lead to a collapse of business investment. On the contrary, we advance what seem to us convincing reasons why both capital investment and general business activity can be sustained at high levels in the years ahead.

If, having explored with us the foundations for our good cheer about the economic prospects of our nation over the next decade, you retain a little trace of skepticism, we shall not feel that we have failed entirely. In fact, we feel that, within limits, an attitude of skepticism serves a constructive purpose in an economy propelled primarily by individual initiative. If everybody were to believe that everything is going along swimmingly all the time, a constructive element of restraint in the conduct of business would be missing. But we shall be surprised, and disappointed, if you do not agree that our findings support a cheerful view of the prospects of the American economy over the next decade, rather than the pervasively pessimistic view that in the economic field we are living on dangerously borrowed time.

CHAPTER TWO

Prospects for Sustaining a High Level of Business Investment *

Investment is the key to both short-run stability and long-term growth. If a rate of investment high enough to maintain full employment—historically about 16 to 17 percent of the Gross National Product—could be maintained indefinitely, we would have achieved both stability and a reasonable guaranty of sustained long-term growth. Unfortunately, however, the rate required to maintain full employment is not maintainable. This is the dilemma.... *A boom level of investment, maintained for several years, causes the stock of capital to increase so rapidly that further investment eventually becomes unprofitable. It is this that sounds the death knell of every boom.*

*   *   *

These observations, with which Professor Emeritus Alvin H. Hansen of Harvard University led off a statement to the Joint Congressional Committee on the Economic Report on "Federal Tax Policy and Economic Growth," succinctly block out the problem to be considered in this chapter.†

* Some of the substance of this chapter appeared in *The Harvard Business Review* for January–February, 1957.

† Professor Hansen's observations are presented in the volume, *Federal Tax Policy for Economic Growth and Stability,* Hearings before the Subcommittee on Tax Policy of the Joint Committee on the Economic Report, Congress of the United States, 84th Congress, First session, Pursuant to Sec. 5(a) of Public Law 304, 79th Congress. December 5, 6, 7, 8, 9, 12, 14, 15 and 16, 1955. U.S. Government Printing Office, Washington, D.C., 1956. Italics

The question is whether the American economy can sustain for the next decade a high level of business investment in new producing facilities, as it has for the past decade. In this chapter we go at the question primarily in terms of how production requirements promise to influence demand for capital equipment, and the prospective financial capacity of our business firms to meet this demand. Consideration of the question of whether there will be enough consumption to sustain a high level of capital investment by business comes later.

There is no doubt, of course, that investment is *a* key, if not *the* key, to both growth and stability. There would be neither, of course, if consumption, which accounts for about two-thirds of the nation's total volume of business, were to fold up. But consumption of itself does not necessarily result in growth which, in almost any of the going conceptions of it, involves increasing the volume of goods and services. In contrast, capital investment, through its capacity to provide better products and processes, makes a key contribution to growth as well as being a key element in stability, or the lack of it.*

---

were added by the authors to emphasize the last sentence of the above quotation.

In making his observations, Professor Hansen was dealing with the total of gross private domestic investment, including residential, commercial and industrial construction, nonfarm producers' durable equipment, farm construction and equipment, and net changes in business inventories. In this chapter the discussion is concerned primarily with *business* investment in new producing facilities, which includes only industrial and commercial construction and nonfarm producers' equipment. This is a more limited segment of investment than that with which Professor Hansen was concerned but to which it seems clear he would also apply the observation quoted.

* "There is a line of economic theory which holds that a dollar of capital investment plays a much more crucial role in the creation of prosperity or the lack of it than a dollar of consumer expenditure because, with multiplying force, it is spent and respent many times in the complex process of creating capital goods. It is not necessary, however, to embrace this theory to accept the proposition that business investment in new producing facili-

While it could be argued that he was moving toward the edge, Professor Hansen was also on safe ground historically in emphasizing the failure to maintain a high level of capital investment in the past. The record since the end of World War II, shown by the chart on this page, tarnishes a bit the proposition that it is not possible to maintain a high level of investment for a sustained period without overdoing it and

Expenditures for New Plants and Equipment

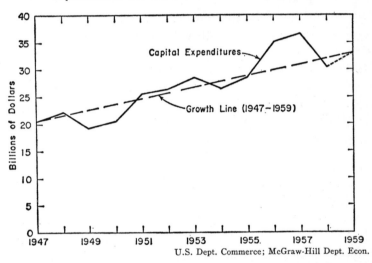

U.S. Dept. Commerce; McGraw-Hill Dept. Econ.

The dollar volume of capital expenditures maintained a relatively stable growth throughout the postwar period with the exception of 1956 (when the unusual rise was partly due to price inflation) and the compensating decline in 1958.

ties is a key ingredient of prosperity. This is the case if for no other reason than that about one-fourth of our industrial workers, and by and large the best-paid industrial workers, are engaged in producing and installing capital equipment. Their employment is obviously a key ingredient of prosperity, as it is also a key ingredient of economic growth and the improvement of levels of living." From a paper on "Economic Stability and Growth" by Dexter M. Keezer, contained in the volume *Federal Tax Policy for Economic Growth and Stability*, papers submitted by panelists appearing before the Subcommittee on Tax Policy, Joint Committee on the Economic Report, Congress of the United States, Nov. 9, 1955, p. 9, U.S. Government Printing Office, Washington, D.C., 1955.

bringing on a collapse. Actually it has been done since 1947.
As the chart indicates, expenditures for new plant and equipment in 1958 dropped more precipitously from those of the
previous year than they had in any year since 1947. But
the decline, which was arrested after twelve months, was
neither sharp enough nor prolonged enough to invalidate the
proposition that a high level of business investment in new
plant and equipment has been sustained since the end of
World War II.

It is true, however, that historically capital investment has
gone by fits and starts, with valleys of despair in between.
And it is also true that, against this historical background,
there is room for argument that the high level of capital
investment in the postwar period has simply been stretched
out to fill an especially big gap created by World War II
and the depression preceding it, with the collapse to come
along later to be outsize, too.

NEW ELEMENTS SHAPE BUSINESS INVESTMENT

We submit, however, that there are now new elements
shaping business investment in the United States which
promise to make it possible to sustain it on an expanding and
relatively even keel over the decade ahead, thus extending
the postwar record of economic growth while eliminating
what has been a major if not the most important single contributor to disastrous ups and downs of business. As they
affect prospective need of more and better capital equipment to meet production requirements, these elements include:

1. Striking shrinkage, relatively, in the hours of labor available
   to meet the production requirements of a rapidly expanding
   population, thus creating a scissorlike pressure for more capital
   equipment.

2. A formidable backlog of overage and antiquated facilities that must be replaced if we are to make the required gains in industrial production.

3. An increasingly heavy requirement for investment in industrial equipment to:
    a. Cope with the increasing difficulty of obtaining industrial materials such as crude oil and iron ore, and
    b. Prevent or eliminate community hazards, such as pollution of air and water by industrial operations, and reduce the risks of injury on the job for workers directly involved in these operations.

Perhaps most important, both in terms of the need for capital equipment and the incentives for installing it, is the assurance of a continuing flood of designs of new and better products, processes and equipment from research and development laboratories. Coupled with business competition, these new developments create their own new and special need for capital equipment. They are, in fact, largely responsible for what can perhaps be termed a new industrial revolution in the field of production. Moreover, they offer strong and demonstrated profit incentives to get in on this revolution.

In terms of our ability to fill expanding requirements for capital investment in a steady and orderly way, the new elements are:

1. A broad development of long-range planning of business investment in the last decade, in dramatic contrast to the earlier business practice of making capital investment on a short-term and opportunistic basis.

2. More assured and better balanced sources of funds with which to carry out a steadily increasing investment program. In particular, the increase in tax-free depreciation allowances promises to be a strongly sustaining force for business investment over the next decade.

In this chapter, we shall expand on these new elements in the outlook for business investment in new plant and equipment, dealing first with the needs and incentives for a high rate of investment and later with the new elements of stability.

It is reserved for a subsequent chapter to deal broadly with the prospect of having enough people, people equipped with sufficient purchasing power, and people possessed of the desire to do what is necessary in the decisive area of consumption to create a steadily expanding economy. At this point, consideration of the population prospect is limited to one aspect of it which sharply points up the necessity of increasing investment in new producing facilities at a rate outstripping the growth in population, if we are merely to maintain our present standard of living, let alone increase it.

NEED FOR GREATER PRODUCTIVITY

Our population as a whole is growing rapidly and promises to continue to do so in the years immediately ahead. But it has been growing even more rapidly at the extremes of youth and old age. Continuation of this process is also the prospect for the years ahead. Since 1930, the arts of prolonging human life have worked such wonders that people 65 years of age and over have jumped from 5 percent to 8.6 percent of the total population; and by 1968 they are expected to constitute no less than 9 percent of the total. Youngsters under 15 years of age were 29 percent, but if current trends in the enterprise of producing infants continue, they will constitute 32 percent a decade hence.

The net effect, of course, is a telescoping from both ends of the part of the population conventionally considered in the working age group—that between the ages of 15 and 64. Where it was 65 percent in 1930, the prospect is that this age group will account for 59 percent of the population in 1968. In the interim there may well be some lengthening of the normal span of working life at the upper end, but it is likely as not to be more than offset by a shortening of the span of working years at the lower end as a result of increased educational requirements. Thus, the clear prospect is that over the next decade the nation's labor force will decline substantially in relation to the amount of work to be done.

Also, unless past trends are to be violently reversed, we shall not only have proportionately fewer workers on the job as we move through the next decade, we shall have them on the job for less time per day and per week.

Each decade since 1930 we have cut the workweek by an average of three hours. Unless this process is to be terminated —an operation that would require the subduing of extremely powerful forces—the average workweek will continue to decline in the years ahead and by 1968 can be expected to be about two hours less per week than it is today.

When the prospective decline in the percentage of the nation's population in the work force is compounded by the prospective decline in the amount of time this work force is likely to be on the job, a very formidable imbalance is struck between production requirements and the manpower to meet them. If we are to provide the *present* level of goods and services per capita a decade hence, the nation's total output, to be divided among about 32 million more people, must be increased by 18 percent. But over this same period the prospect is that the manhours of labor actually worked will increase by only about 13 percent.

If during the next decade we are to do *better*, and have an increase in goods and services per capita, like that of the past decade, our national output must be stepped up accordingly. Indeed, by 1968 we must be producing 36 percent more as a nation than we are now. And as noted above, our relatively

smaller labor force and the shorter workweek will compel us
to accomplish this 36 percent gain with only 13 percent more
human effort as measured in terms of manhours.

This is simply another way of saying that we must step
up our investment in capital equipment, both absolutely and
relatively. Some gain in output per manhour can undoubtedly be obtained by better organization and direction
of production, but the bulk of it must come from more and
better tools.

Even with better tools, in the years ahead there is no
guarantee that we are going to match the increase in output
per manhour we have had since the end of World War II.
There have been periods when we haven't done as well and
few, very few, when we have done better. During wars and
depressions we have done very poorly; only in the decade
1919–1929 did we do better. The point is that we must strive,
against what may seem like rather long historical odds, to
achieve a relatively high rate of increase in productivity from
here on.

Therefore, the fact that we require an increase of 36 percent in national output to maintain the rate of increase in
living standards that we have had since World War II should
go far to assuage the fear that we cannot maintain a "boom
level" of investment in new and better producing facilities
without having our economy sunk by an overload of such
facilities. Such an increase in output cannot be accomplished
with the manhours likely to be available unless we do maintain a high level of capital investment.

AGING EQUIPMENT MUST BE REPLACED

There is another element of major importance, in the com-
position of our industrial establishment, which operates to
reduce the danger of too much capital investment over the

years ahead. This is the element of wear, antiquity and obsolescence in our present industrial plant and equipment.

In 1958, our department conducted a survey to establish the magnitude of this accumulated obsolescence. We asked a large sample of manufacturing companies, and experts in other industries, "What would be the cost to replace all obsolete facilities with the best new plant and equipment?" It turned out that it would cost $95 billion, broken down among major segments of business as follows:

Manufacturing and Mining	$34.3 billion
Petroleum Industry	5.3
Transportation and Communications	18.4
Electric and Gas Utilities	12.0
Finance, Trade and Services	25.0
Total: All Business	$95.0 billion

Our inquiry into the state of American business plant and equipment, in terms of antiquity and degree of obsolescence,* also disclosed that less than one-third of it is modern, in the realistic sense of being new since 1950. Yet the years 1950–1958 comprise a period when rapidly changing technology has made older equipment obsolete in many key lines of industry. Consequently, the old age of our equipment means a general inability to perform according to the best industrial standards.†

* The results of the study were presented in full in a report "How Modern Is American Industry?" by the McGraw-Hill Department of Economics. This report provided the broad factual foundation for "Plan '59," a cooperative undertaking in which all of the McGraw-Hill magazines explored the state of the equipment in their various industries and what might be done to speed the process of getting it up to date.

† One of the main reasons for industry's failure to carry out an aggressive replacement program during the postwar period is that, because of inflation in the prices of new plant and equipment, the depreciation reserves calculated on the basis of prewar prices fell considerably short of replacement

This general finding is supported by checks on the state of equipment in specific industries. In its 1958 census of metal-working equipment *American Machinist,* a McGraw-Hill magazine, found that three out of five metalworking machines in the United States are over ten years old, and many of the tools industry now uses are of 1939 or earlier design. Our own inquiry disclosed that about two-thirds of the nation's freight cars are more than ten years old. It also showed that less than half the capacity to process chemicals, rubber or petroleum is new since 1950, a period which has seen revolutionary development of automatic controls for these process industries.

Something of the significance of the degrees of obsolescence indicated can be gained from these facts: on the average, a 1958 metalworking tool is about 54 percent more productive than one that could be purchased in 1948. A combination of new freight cars and modern freight yard equipment can reduce operating costs up to 50 percent. New instruments that automatically direct the flow of chemical (or other raw material) processes, can often reduce costs enough to pay back the cost of the controls in one year. These savings are rarely possible in older plants.

In the light of the high level of investment in new plant and equipment which has been maintained since the end of

---

costs. Early in 1957 it was estimated by Dr. George Terborgh, director of research of the Machinery and Allied Products Institute, that the annual depreciation allowances of U.S. business were probably falling short of actual replacement costs by about $6 billion a year. (*Capital Goods Review,* No. 29, February 1957, published by the Machinery and Allied Products Institute.) Although this gap between depreciation allowances and replacement costs continues to be a problem for many companies, there have been encouraging developments in the field of depreciation—discussed later in this chapter—that have made this, relatively at least, a less formidable barrier to modernization in the years ahead.

World War II, it is hard for many people to believe that an increasing proportion of our industrial establishment is becoming obsolete. However, for what in many ways is our most basic industrial equipment—that for metalworking— the successive censuses taken by *American Machinist* over the past decade clearly establish the fact of increasing obsolescence. In its 1949 census *American Machinist* found that 43 percent of the nation's machine tools were over ten years old. The census of 1953 disclosed that 56 percent of our machine tools were over ten years old. And the 1958 census— a monumental study covering 157 types of equipment in 5,800 metalworking plants—found that no less than 60 percent of our machine tools were at least ten years old. The 1958 *American Machinist* census also located about 400,000 machine tools, or about one out of five in the nation's total of about 2.2 million, which were more than 20 years old— authentic antiques in a period which has seen tremendous change and advance in the design of these tools.

The problem presented by aged and obsolete producing equipment is, of course, much more formidable for an industrial economy that has been in process of extensive development for a long period, such as that of the U.S., than it is for an economy just moving into a massive industrial development such as that of the U.S.S.R. With our far larger and older industrial establishments we need a much larger proportion of our capital investment to cope with worn-out and antiquated equipment than does the Soviet Union. Conversely, a far larger share of the Soviet investment outlay is available for expansion with what is, in the nature of the case, up-to-date equipment. This fact is reflected in the following rough breakdown of capital expenditures in the U.S. and the U.S.S.R., for the years 1950–1955, the latest years for which relevant comparable figures are available.

| | U.S.A.* | U.S.S.R.** |
	percent	percent
Expansion	47	90
Replacement and Modernization	53	10

Failure to appreciate the relative advantage enjoyed by a fast-growing young economy in keeping its industrial establishment up to date and failure to gauge the adequacy of our capital investment, accordingly, could obviously have disastrous consequences for our country in the contest for primacy in industrial power which is somewhere near the core of our struggle with the U.S.S.R. The fact of our relatively high investment requirements to cope with industrial wear and tear, old age and obsolescence also should have a comforting bearing on the fear that by maintaining a high level of investment in new plant and equipment we shall be speeding our way to economic collapse.

SOME INVESTMENT ADDS NO CAPACITY

In addition to investment that is required to maintain productive efficiency, most industries face steadily rising expenditures to maintain adequate sources of raw materials. The steel industry provides a case in point. In order to replace the original Mesabi Range iron ore, which was developed at a cost of $20 to $40 per ton, the industry has recently been investing in facilities to process lower-grade ores, such as taconite, for which the investment cost comes to about $50 per ton of annual capacity. The exacting requirements of

* McGraw-Hill survey of Business' Plans for New Plants and Equipment.
** Estimated from the *Economic Survey of Europe in 1955*, United Nations, pp. 198–200.

modern steelmaking are such that in the future *all* ores may have to be processed to insure a high degree of purity and uniformity. Even though high-quality imported ores will ease the problem to some extent, the industry will continue in the foreseeable future to face relatively high costs for domestic ore development and processing.

Likewise, as the oil companies are under the necessity of going deeper and farther for their oil, the amount of capital investment per unit of oil recovered mounts. The capital investment needed to produce a barrel of oil in the United States now amounts to about two and one-half times more than it did fifteen years ago. There have been comparable increases in the investment required per unit to secure supplies of other key industrial materials such as copper and sulfur. For U.S. industry as a whole the increased difficulty of obtaining basic materials accounts for perhaps as much as $2 billion of its investment over the past five years. And the problem involved promises to become more, rather than less, burdensome.

The fear that our economy will be sunk by an insupportable load of business investment can be still further eased by taking into account the mounting requirements of business investment to provide safer and more pleasant working conditions and to prevent or overcome the pollution of our water and air as a result of industrial operations. The latter increase is due in part to more community-minded administration of industrial processes involving the disposal of noxious waste materials. It is also due to more rigorous community pollution regulations; and the more complete enforcement of the regulations already on the books, points in the direction of much heavier expenditure in the years ahead. When, for example, the City Attorney of Houston, Texas, obtained a court injunction to secure compliance with the city ordinance against air pollution, it was estimated that compliance with the regulation would cost chemical companies in that city alone about $6 million. For industry as a whole it is estimated that expenditure to eliminate pollution of air and water totaled about $750 million in 1958.

Business investment to prevent or eliminate pollution, it should be stressed, does not eventuate, except incidentally, in greater producing capacity. The same thing is essentially true of investment to offset old age and wear and tear, and of investment to overcome the increased difficulty of obtaining some of our key industrial materials. None of these types of business investment imposes the threat of adding too much producing capacity. On the contrary, their primary purpose is simply to overcome previous damage to and deterioration of our economic establishment.

The same thing is true, in some measure, of an expanding volume of business investment to provide greater safety and convenience for workers engaged in hazardous occupations. A considerable part of the investment for this purpose, estimated at about $2 billion a year currently,* is reflected in a compensating, or more than compensating, increase in the volume of production or in lower cost of production. But a part of it simply reflects adherence to higher humanitarian standards through what, so far as any increase in the resulting output of goods and services is concerned, is nonproductive business investment.

When account is taken of such elements in the outlook for business investment as those which have been reviewed, the controlling fact seems to be that we *must* maintain a high level of capital investment not only for the sake of our domestic prosperity, but also for the sake of our national security, and to provide increasingly decent working conditions and community living standards.

* Estimated by editors of McGraw-Hill technical magazines.

PRESSURE FROM RESEARCH

But granted the long-range need, have we got the immediate incentive to promote such a high level of investment? In all of its ramifications, this question involves the whole range of economic life and, in one way and another, constitutes the subject matter of this entire volume. But in terms of the immediate pressures to maintain a high level of investment with which we are concerned here, one of the most crucial considerations is the prospect for a continuation of the technological revolution which has played such a major role in the postwar surge of capital investment. Along with it goes the scarcely less crucial question of whether, if it should continue, this technological revolution would be essentially a disturbing or a stabilizing force.

In the following chapter, devoted to research and development and its economic impact, these questions will be dealt with at some length. Here only short answers will be given, by way of rounding out the broad framework of the outlook for investment in new plant and equipment. The prospect is that the pace of the technological revolution will not only be maintained, but that it will be accelerated. This prospect is provided primarily by the tremendous outlay being made by American industry for research and development (over $9 billion in 1959) and the plans to make even larger outlays in the years ahead (almost $11 billion in 1962).*

There is also the prospect that the continuing and expanding technological revolution in the United States will add some important new elements of stability to the economy as a whole. It is true, of course, that in some dimensions the introduction of new products and equipment and the at-

---

* *Business' Plans for New Plants and Equipment, 1959–1962,* a survey made by the McGraw-Hill Department of Economics, 1959, p. 12.

tendant capital investment is an economically disturbing process. The introduction of improved industrial equipment involves shifting of work forces and sometimes reduction of the number of production workers. New products which replace existing products, in whole or in part, have similar effects in the course of churning up markets and marketers where they are introduced.

But research and development spawn new products and even new industries, the very diversity of whose fluctuations in sales and production tends to create offsets and hence, for the economy as a whole, a stabilizing effect. Also, the timing of the end-product results of industrial research and development—in products, processes and equipment—still tends to be shaped by forces generated in the laboratory rather than the market place, and thus to have potentialities of providing counterweights for ups and downs of business originating in the market place. We have more to say on relationships between industrial research and development in the next chapter.

RESEARCH AND NEW CAPACITY

Here, however, it should be remarked that when the record is fully analyzed it will probably be clearly seen that the continuing "boom" in research and development accounted in major degree for what many sophisticated observers found the remarkably brief decline of expenditures for new plant and equipment in the recession of 1957–1958. For several years the "boom" in investment in new manufacturing plant and equipment had been creating a widening gap between manufacturing capacity and the amount of it being used for current production. As the chart indicates, this gap had been brought into sharp relief by comparison of the course of the Federal Reserve Board's index of manufacturing pro-

duction and the course of the McGraw-Hill index of manufacturing capacity, created and maintained by the McGraw-
Hill Department of Economics.*

When such a substantial gap between manufacturing
capacity and industrial production opened up in 1957, it was
the widespread expectation of careful students of previous
declines in investment in new plant and equipment that the

Capacity and Production in Manufacturing

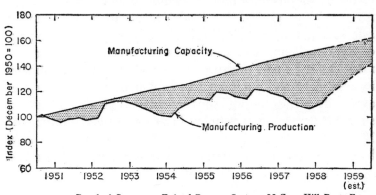

Board of Governors, Federal Reserve System; McGraw-Hill Dept. Econ.

Since the end of the Korean War in early 1953, manufacturing capacity has expanded
faster than production. The widening gap in December 1953 was a factor in the 1954
business recession. And in December 1957, a very wide gap between production and
capacity foreshadowed the more severe recession of 1958. However, rapid expansion
of consumer spending narrowed the gaps in both 1955 and 1959. Since the expansion
was largely in demand for new products, industry has continued to need additional
plants and relatively large amounts of new equipment.

* It can be safely asserted that this is the best index extant of the manufacturing capacity of the United States, if for no better reason than that it
is the only comprehensive index of this kind. But analytical work and cross-
checks from more limited indices of manufacturing capacity have indicated
that the McGraw-Hill index has much more affirmative virtues than this and
is, in fact, a very significant measure of manufacturing capacity in the United
States. Both on this account and because the index is a tool of major importance for business and economic analysis—a fact recognized by its inclusion in the January 1959 Economic Report of the President to the Congress—an account of the development of the index and a critical appraisal
of it are presented in Appendix I.

decline which started in the fourth quarter of 1957 would
be much longer and much more severe than it turned out
to be. A full arraying of the reasons why the brevity of the
decline upset this expectation will certainly include the fact
that consumption showed a remarkable resistance to decline.
At no time in the recession did it drop more than one percent
below the peak it reached in the fall of 1957. Also, as indicated subsequently, credit can also be expected to be given
to the development of and adherence to long-range business
investment programs. But it also seems to be a relatively
safe speculation that, in the final analysis, the speeding up
of the development of new products, processes and equipment created a new pressure to move ahead with investment
in new plant and equipment to exploit these developments
as rapidly as possible, and thus contributed notably to cutting
short the decline in investment in new plant and equipment.
By reference to historical patterns this decline might have
been expected to run several years rather than the period of
about 12 months it actually did run.*

* For a full discussion of this point see Robert P. Ulin, "Does Excess
Capacity Mean Recession," *Challenge*, March 1958, pp. 49–53. This article
states in part (p. 53):

"As recently as 1956, a McGraw-Hill survey showed that manufacturing
companies, on the average, prefer to operate around 90 percent of capacity
—which allows only a 10 percent cushion for emergencies.

"However, the growing interest in long-range planning, research and
development has undoubtedly had some effect; a few years ago the average
preferred rate might have been close to 100 percent. And in the industries
where markets are growing and technical advance is rapid, there is an
increasing tendency on the part of the more progressive firms to accept
lower operating rates as one of the costs of continuous development.

"Thus the concept of capacity itself has changed. Whether a given facility
is truly in excess does not depend solely on its being idle. If the product it
makes is obsolete, then its capacity is not merely excess; it is useless. If, however, machines are kept because they might be needed in an emergency,
then this temporarily unused capacity is fulfilling a function in a long-range

In particular, the desire to install new cost-cutting devices as rapidly as possible contributed notably to cutting short the decline in investment in new plant and equipment. So did the necessity for "tooling up" to introduce new products for the consumer market, ranging from new types of packaged foods to the new "economy-size" automobiles. While none of these expenditures compared in size with the expansion of basic facilities undertaken by many companies in 1955–1957, opportunities to introduce new products and install

sense and can be justified on the same terms as insurance. Thus, the presently unused capacity of one-fifth [in January 1958] is not such a dangerous factor in the economy as it would have been a generation ago."

All Unused Capacity Is Not "Excess"

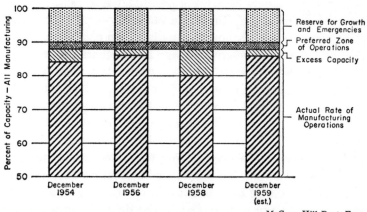

McGraw-Hill Dept. Econ.

According to McGraw-Hill surveys, most companies do not want to operate at 100 percent capacity. They prefer an operating rate of 88–90 percent, which allows some older facilities to be kept in reserve for emergencies and some new plants to be used for experimental output of new products. Thus, the amount of truly excess capacity has not been as large as commonly supposed. Actual manufacturing operations have been close to the preferred rate except during general business recessions, and in 1959 capital expenditures increased while manufacturing operations generally were below 90 percent of total capacity.

cost-cutting methods were of sufficient magnitude in 1958–1959 to encourage an increase, or "turn-around," from the recession level of capital investment. In future years, as research programs expand, this influence will be even stronger.

RESEARCH AND INVESTMENT INCENTIVES

The future development of new products and processes, as the result of research, is particularly important in terms of incentives for investment because it provides the most compelling sort of reasons for risking a firm's money on new plant and equipment. One of these is the opportunity to capture a new market—or to head off a competitor who is invading a present market. Present-day competition, in many industries, is largely in terms of product quality, so that when research shows a way to offer a markedly superior product, most companies will move immediately to capitalize on this advantage, even if relatively large investments are required. In some cases, research develops completely new products so that a company may acquire (for a time, at least) a market entirely for itself. An example is the development of new synthetic fibers (with "wash and wear" or other attractive properties), for which large capital investments in new facilities were made even during the 1958 recession.

This example points up another key feature of new products, which is that they usually carry very high profit margins. When a company is first in the field, it can set a relatively high price (which may be justified by the large investment required in research effort and plant facilities) and hope to earn a high return—far higher, in most cases, than on standard products for which markets are intensely competitive. There is, therefore, every incentive to take quick advantage of new product developments by the construction of new plant capacity. Similarly, a new cost-cutting process offers a quick return on investment and will usually be adopted without delay.   1097787

It is still too early to assess the full effects of increased research and development on over-all corporate profit margins, but the experience of 1958 is significant. After declining to an annual rate of $32 billion during the recession, corporate profits before taxes increased to an estimated rate of forty-five billion dollars in the fourth quarter, with a rate approaching fifty billion dollars in prospect in the course of 1959. In reporting on this development, as regards their individual companies, a number of company presidents have credited the improvement in profits to the installation of new processes and the introduction of new products—trends that are expected to continue. Thus, the spread of research and development provides not only technical incentives for a high level of investment but profit incentives as well.

TREND TO LONGER–RANGE PLANNING

Granted, as it now should be, that our national interest requires a high level of capital investment over the next decade and granted, for the moment, that there are and will be effective business incentives to do the same thing, what is there to keep this demand for capital goods from bobbing up and down in response to developments, such as changes in sales and sales prospects and shocks to business confidence, as it has done in the past? One reason is that there has been a broad development of longer-range planning of business investment in the United States. This development has potentialities, some of them demonstrated, for getting the handling of business investment away from the quick start-and-stop process, shaped by short-run market and political developments, and putting it on a basis and in a perspective running over a period of years.

The broad scope of the development of longer-range planning of business investment in the United States in recent years is clearly indicated by the results of the surveys of Business' Plans for New Plants and Equipment conducted by our McGraw-Hill Department of Economics. When we inaugurated these surveys twelve years ago only a handful of the cooperating companies could give us any estimates of their expenditures for new producing facilities running beyond the current year. This year (1959) about 90 percent of the companies covered by the survey—and it was a far larger number of companies than was covered by the survey twelve years ago—could give us estimates of their investment in new plant and equipment running three years ahead.

A part of the explanation of this striking increase in long-range planning of business investment in new producing facilities is to be found in the increasingly complex technology of investment in these facilities. More time is required to design, produce and install ever more complicated—and more productive—equipment. For example, the Bell Laboratories will have been occupied on the job for almost a decade when an experimental central telephone exchange equipped with electronic switching devices is ready for experimental operation in 1960.

Still more of the explanation of the growth of long-range planning of business investment is to be found in the increased business use of long-range economic projections—of such indicators as gross national product, or disposable income—as the starting point for sales and production objectives. Based largely on past experience, such projections show promise of great growth for the American economy over the years ahead. While they remain to be convinced that these growth potentials will be attained by a relatively smooth and steady ascent, American business leaders are increasingly disposed to be ready to capitalize on them with adequate producing facilities, provided through a long-range program, even at the expense of having some excess capacity from time to time. And—perhaps the most important part of the explanation—these leaders increasingly recognize that it is both good business and good economic policy to do everything within their power to iron out disruptive ups and downs of business investment and thus make a key contribution to keeping the economy as a whole on an even keel.

There is, of course, nothing automatically self-enforcing about a long-range program of investment in new plant and equipment. Such a program is obviously subject to some modification both in magnitude and direction of expenditure and in the timing of it, in response to changing competitive, financial and general business conditions. But the very fact that there is such a plan, to which it is the purpose of the company to adhere as closely as possible, provides an important element of stability in the investment program.

Although we have yet to devise a way to prove it conclusively to the confirmed nonbeliever, it is our conviction that the widespread prevalence of long-range business investment plans during the 1957–1958 business recession accounted very considerably for what, in historical perspective, was the remarkable brevity (about a year) of the decline in this type of investment. With the further development of well-conceived long-range plans of investment, the stabilizing influence can be expected to become more pervasive.

WILL ADEQUATE FUNDS BE AVAILABLE?

But if even the best laid long-range investment plans are to be carried out successfully, one of the conditions that obviously must be fulfilled is that the necessary funds be available. So there is occasion to consider whether there have been any developments that give promise of providing the flow of funds required for the steady maintenance of a high level of capital investment. This is another of those questions which, in all of its ramifications, involves all phases of the economy. Profits from business operations provide the principal incentive for business investment in new plant and equipment and a major source of the funds to carry out the investment; and profits and prospects of profits reflect a myriad of economic arrangements including rates of taxation fixed in legislative halls, wage rates determined over bargaining tables and bargains made over consumer counters, any detailed discussion of which must be deferred to subsequent chapters.

Here, however, it is happily possible to point to one development of major importance which greatly increases the prospects of having a flow of investment funds sufficient to sustain steadily a high level of business investment in new plant and equipment. This is the great increase since the end of the war in the proportion of total capital investment by business which can be met by annual depreciation allowances. How much this proportion has increased since the end of World War II is indicated by the chart on this page.

Growth of Depreciation Allowances

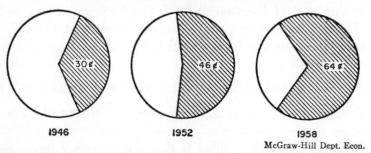

1946   1952   1958

McGraw-Hill Dept. Econ.

Depreciation allowances have increased substantially since 1945, now accounting for about two-thirds of every dollar of corporations' capital expenditures. Rapid amortization and the change in methods of calculating of depreciaton have contributed to the increase.

There are two major reasons for this increase. One is found simply in the fact that the high post–World War II level of business investment in plant and equipment has built up a large base against which to charge annual depreciation. The other is the more liberal governmental provision for the accumulation of depreciation reserves, first in pursuance of the accelerated amortization program adopted during the Korean War crisis to stimulate construction of defense facilities, and subsequently as a result of the methods for computing depreciation allowances authorized by the Internal Revenue Code of 1954. More recently, in the small business legislation passed in 1958, Congress introduced a new provision for additional depreciation allowances in the first year after equipment is purchased. *

At the end of World War II, there had been a period of about fifteen years of virtual starvation of business investment in new producing facilities, first as a result of the great depression and then as result of war. This left U.S. business with a very low stock of capital equipment (about $120 billion) subject to depreciation. But since then, investment has gone forward at the high level already reported, and at high prices. The resulting accumulation of high-priced capital facilities is now helping to generate depreciation allowances at a high level, both absolutely and in relation to current replacement requirements.

Moreover, the average *rate* at which depreciation is charged against new facilities has been increased by recent changes in accounting procedures, which in this case depend largely on what are ruled acceptable procedures for income tax purposes. To encourage provision of facilities needed for defense, or defense-supporting, lines of production, the Federal government inaugurated a program of accelerated amortization for tax purposes during the Korean War. This

* This new provision is described in Appendix IV.

program was continued at a reduced pace through 1957 but at present applies only to a few, highly specialized defense facilities, so far as new investment is concerned. In pursuance of the program, production facilities with a total value of over $36 billion have been certified for five-year amortization, which is a rate considerably faster than is normally permitted. The maximum speed-up allowed has been recovery of the full investment in five years, though on the average only about 60 percent of the total cost is covered by the five-year privilege. (The remainder must be depreciated under one of the normal depreciation methods.)

Another share of depreciation reserves, but a share that is increasing, is accounted for by use of the liberalized provisions for computing depreciation allowances introduced in the 1954 Internal Revenue Code. Detailed discussion of the monumentally complicated provisions is not in order here beyond taking account of the fact that, by taking advantage of them, a business can recapture through depreciation allowances almost 50 percent more of the investment in new producing facilities during the first half of their useful life than it could before the provisions were adopted.

FUTURE FLOW OF FUNDS

In anything remotely resembling a normal course of events, the proportion of new business investment represented by depreciation allowances will not increase in the next decade as it has in the last. The very magnitude of the postwar investment in new plant and equipment—about $340 billion since 1945—now in the process of being depreciated points to this conclusion. Furthermore, the special five-year amortization program is now running out. But, given relative stability of prices for new capital equipment—an assumption which we shall argue later is not fanciful—and barring unfavorable revision of the legal rules governing the calculation of depreciation allowances, there is reason to believe that the proportion of business investment represented by depreciation allowances will remain about the same over the years ahead as it is currently.*

This means that depreciation allowances can be counted upon, as they are currently, to provide a major part of the funds for investment in new producing facilities. It is true, of course, that a company is under no compulsion to spend that share of its earnings which it sets aside as depreciation reserves for new producing facilities or anything else. It is also true that a depreciation allowance does not become a reality simply by being allowed by the taxing authorities. The money to make it a reality obviously must be earned before being set aside—a point which some accountants enjoy laboring. But in practice, depreciation allowances, being a first claim on earnings, are almost always earned and almost always reinvested in new facilities. For example, the 1954 McGraw-Hill Survey of Business' Plans for New Plants and Equipment indicated that 90 percent of all manufacturing companies usually spend their entire depreciation allowance on new plant and equipment.

When these depreciation allowances represent a major proportion of the business investment in new producing facilities, as they now do and promise to continue to do, the structure for this investment is strengthened accordingly. In 1957, with $20 billion of depreciation allowances, American corporations had to draw only $13 billion from retained earnings and the sale of new securities combined to finance total investment of nearly $33 billion in new facilities—an all-

* This is the conclusion reached by George Terborgh as part of the process of very carefully making "A Ten-year Projection of Corporate Internal Capital Funds in Relation to Projected Requirements for New Plant and Equipment," *Capital Goods Review*, November 1955.

time record-breaking total. The share financed by depreciation allowances was even larger in 1958. And again in 1959
and the years ahead, depreciation allowances, their adequacy
enormously increased in the postwar decade, promise to play
a dominant role in sustaining a high level of capital investment if prices remain relatively stable. Indeed, the Annual
McGraw-Hill Survey of Business' Plans for 1959 indicates
that these allowances, which amount to $22.8 billion in 1959,
will increase 20 percent by 1962.*

Of course, if price inflation were again to pick up the
momentum it has gained at times in the postwar period, it
would speedily erode depreciation allowances and make
them progressively less adequate. It could take industry
back to the situation that prevailed in the earlier postwar
years when, because of rapidly rising prices, depreciation
allowances supplied only a small proportion of the funds
needed to buy new plants and equipment. However, we
shall argue in a later chapter that there are good reasons to
believe that the upward course of prices will not get out of
hand in the next decade.

Moreover, recent discussion of the depreciation problem
among private and government experts has focused strong,
and increasingly favorable attention, on new accounting
methods to make depreciation allowances more adequate

---

* Annual allowances for depreciation are in part arbitrary figures, determined by tax regulations and accounting conventions, rather than precise
measures of the actual rate of wear and tear and obsolescence. They include
both accelerated depreciation allowed to stimulate investment and "retarded"
depreciation calculated at unrealistically low rates. Depreciation accounting,
indeed, is to the layman a forbiddingly complex and mystical operation,
because of the many (and sometimes conflicting) functions it performs. In
this chapter, the function of depreciation as a major source of funds for
business investment has been stressed. But depreciation is also a systematic
way of accounting for costs of wear and tear, a means of recovering past
costs of investment in producing facilities and, sometimes, merely an inviting
device for claiming a tax deduction.

under inflationary conditions. While discussion of any of these reforms (or the whole subject of depreciation for that matter) has the unfortunate attribute of doubling almost perfectly as a high-powered soporific, what is done along this line can have a major bearing on the course of American business. Hence, some of the principal reform proposals are indicated in the paragraphs which follow.

One of these proposals, identified with Maurice E. Peloubet, a leading public accountant, is to allow companies that install new equipment to take a special one-year depreciation deduction equivalent to the difference between accumulated depreciation on the old machine and the actual (higher) cost of replacement. This would, in effect, make up for any inadequacy of depreciation funds caused by inflation. The special deduction would not, of course, increase the total depreciation a company could take over the life of the equipment, but it would provide more tax-free money when it is most needed—at the time new equipment is installed. Introduction of such a plan might well be timed for a period when rising costs of capital equipment seem to be having adverse effects on new orders for capital goods.

DEPRECIATION AS A STIMULANT

The use of accelerated depreciation methods to stimulate capital investment once business generally has entered a decline is obviously a more difficult course of therapy. Nevertheless, the amounts of investment stimulated by the special wartime five-year depreciation allowances (and similar experience in Canada and Sweden with peacetime acceleration) suggest that, even under much less favorable conditions, we might expect to see some result from this type of tax concession. In a severe recession, the wartime formula might not be the best one. Few companies would wish to reduce their reported earnings as sharply as was done by five-year amortization. However, other improvements in depreciation procedure might well be introduced to stimulate lagging investment.

One plan which has been suggested, for a time when new incentives are needed, is the "bracket system" which has already been tried out successfully in Canada. Under this plan, companies would not be required to demonstrate any particular "useful life" for a particular piece of equipment to be depreciated. Instead, all productive equipment would be assigned to 14 broad categories, and in each the depreciable life of equipment would be significantly shorter than is now allowed in the United States for tax purposes. By eliminating much of the red tape now involved in obtaining Treasury approval for depreciation rates, and by recognizing the relatively fast pace of obsolescence for most types of equipment (without requiring proof in specific cases), this tax reform would—in the opinion of many experts—provide a strong incentive for more rapid replacement of machinery and buildings.

The "bracket system" also would make it possible to increase depreciation allowances quickly and substantially in response to a downturn in demand for capital goods. This could be done by a simple ruling that for a specified period—say one or two years—all new investments could be depreciated at, say, twice the usual rates for their respective brackets. Conversely, during a period when excessive investment is helping push up prices of scarce resources, the respective rates could be slowed down as an investment deterrent. Such changes would have to be reserved for really critical periods of recession or inflation, since frequent changes would upset long-range planning. But the point made here is that emergency stabilizers can, if necessary, be devised.

The appeal of any scheme of larger depreciation deductions, of course, depends upon the existence (or prospect) of taxable income from which deductions can be taken. Hence, as has been suggested, increased depreciation would not offer a very strong incentive for increasing capital investment if a severe economic collapse should bring profits down to a very low level. Likewise, the incentive to invest would be weak if the investment did not hold the promise of a profitable return in the future. But if this book succeeds in its purpose, it will demonstrate adequately that these are unlikely eventualities in the years with which it is concerned.

HOW IT LOOKS IN ALGEBRA

If we were to follow a vogue which currently has a large following among college and university economists, we would now reduce our observations to an equation of solemn and imposing mien. We would let

$\Delta I =$ the prospective increase in business investment in new producing facilities

$c =$ the increase in the ratio between labor cost and the cost of plant and equipment

$r =$ the recent rate of increase in expenditures for industrial research and development

$X =$ the investment needed to take care of future population growth

$Y =$ the investment needed to offset the accumulated inroads of industrial antiquity and obsolescence

$Z =$ the increase in the needs for safety provisions and pollution control

$p =$ the growth of long-range planning

$C =$ industry's capacity to produce goods and services

$R =$ the average operating rate

$M =$ the (slow) increase in manhours of labor available to industry

D = the rise in funds from depreciation allowances
P = the prospective increase in business profits
T = the always-present bite of the tax collector out of these profits

The increase in investment, ΔI, would be directly proportional to c, r, $(X + Y + Z)$, p and $(D + P - T)$, and inversely proportional to $C(1 - R)$ and M. From this arrangement it would then follow that

$$\Delta I = cr \left[\frac{(X + Y + Z)^p}{C(1 - R) + M} \right] + \Sigma(D + P - T)$$

For those who, from experience acquired in their school days, tend to associate the use of algebraic symbols largely with things which are proved (Remember *Quod Erat Demonstrandum?*) or at least provable, such a demonstration might create the impression of closer companionship with the truth than the same thing said in words.* But such a companionship would be so illusory that we do not propose to give it any mysterious aura of validity by symbolic exposition.

Nor, returning to plain English, do we wish to imply that the maintenance of a high level of business investment in the years ahead has the status of inevitability. There is no doubt about the element of rapidly increasing need of such investment. There is no doubt that there will be increased stimulation of such investment through research and development. And there is the prospect of improved capacity to command the necessary financial wherewithal to sustain a high level of investment. But all of these would, of course, come to naught without the maintenance of a level of consumption sufficiently high to take off the production made

* For discussion of this point see "Mathematics: Logic, Quantity and Method" by David Novick in *The Review of Economics and Statistics*, Vol. XXXVI, No. 4, November 1954, pp. 357–358.

possible by a high level of investment. So, in a subsequent chapter, we shall address ourselves to the prospect that such a level of consumption can and will be maintained over the next decade. As we move toward consideration of this prospect we shall, in the next chapter, take a closer look at the role, present and prospective, of research and development, how this role is being performed, and its economic significance.

In the meantime, if this chapter has done the work cut out for it successfully, it has demonstrated that Professor Hansen's generalization about the impossibility of maintaining a high level of private capital investment, with which the chapter was opened, may be well along the road to being obsolete—a development which would surely gratify him greatly. Developments of the type detailed give promise that in the years ahead business investment in new producing facilities will be maintained both at a high and relatively stable level, as it has been in the past decade.

CHAPTER THREE

Research—Key to Growth and Stability

In 1959 American industry is spending over $9 billion on scientific research and development. This is research performed by private industry only. Including the several billions spent by government laboratories, universities, scientific associations and private research organizations, the grand total is about $12.5 billion—two and a half times the sum spent on research in 1953.*

Spending on this massive scale is enough to create a major industry overnight. In one sense, research and development *is* an industry—the "industry of discovery," as Professor Sumner Slichter of Harvard University has aptly called the current efforts in industrial research. And it is an industry whose achievements will determine the outlook for new capital investment—in fact, the outlook for much of the U.S.'s growth and prosperity—in the years ahead.

This chapter, therefore, deals with research in an economic—as opposed to a scientific—setting. It considers the research "industry" as one key to general economic growth and stability. And it attempts to answer some basic questions about the research boom. For example:

* Although the contributions of government and university research are obviously important to scientific advance, our concern here is with research as an economic and business stimulus. Hence it is with the $9 billion private research that we shall be dealing hereafter. As we note later on, almost half of the research *performed* by private industry is paid for by the Federal government under defense and atomic energy contracts.

1. What striking developments—both in new consumer products and methods of production in industry—are likely to come out of the research boom?
2. When did the amazing surge in research spending start, and who plays the major role in this industry of innovation?
3. How much economic growth do we get from industrial research, and is it a stable pattern of growth?

First, let us look at the growing importance of research in today's economy. To the military expert, research has recently become the key to national defense. To the scientist, it is the accelerating "breakthroughs" in such exciting new fields as solid-state physics and chemotherapy. The presi-

Research and Development, 1945–1959, 1962

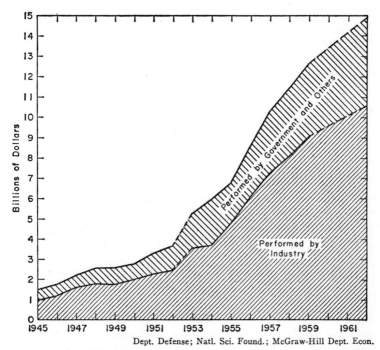

Dept. Defense; Natl. Sci. Found.; McGraw-Hill Dept. Econ.

Total expenditures on research and development have increased by leaps and bounds in recent years. The dollar volume of R&D work performed by industry has grown tremendously since the end of World War II.

dent of a large corporation knows that more and more of his company's sales are coming from new products. An economist might think of the recent revisions in economic theory that relate research to levels of income, employment and investment.*

To Wall Street, research budgets are a good explanation of why capital and profits have been flowing to certain industries. Even Madison Avenue—in its campaigns to sell swept-wing autos or filter-tipped cigarettes—is standing on the edge of the research boom.

All these developments, together with the multi-billion figures on research spending, testify to the growing impact of research on today's economy. But the really dramatic nature of the research boom can be stated more simply: Today's research will change the way a family lives tomorrow—how people communicate, where and how they travel, what they eat and wear. In industry, research is unlocking new sources of energy, revolutionizing methods of production, changing the very structure of industry itself. For the economy as a whole, research on today's massive scale removes the traditional limits on economic growth—a given supply of land, raw materials, labor and skills—and in their place sets what Dr. Vannevar Bush once called an "endless frontier."

In more specific terms, we can predict a number of business developments that are literally scheduled for the next few years as the result of applied research and product development that is now underway. Out of the research now reaching a commercial stage will come an increasing flow of new materials—such as new plastics, metallic alloys and ceramics—for use in both consumer goods and capital goods. In consumer goods especially, the new materials will make

* See, for example, James S. Duesenberry, *Business Cycles and Economic Growth*, McGraw-Hill, New York, 1958, pp. 218–219 and 225–239.

possible rapid changes in styling and packaging. In capital goods, we can expect faster, more compact machines and great improvements in the automatic control of machinery. As a result of these developments, which are already in progress, it seems safe to predict that over half of all capital expenditures in 1965 will go to make new products or install new machines that were not on the market in 1958. The flow of new products and new processes, from advanced research to commercial testing, is already reaching these proportions.

SOME HINTS ON THE FUTURE

Looking further ahead, no one knows exactly what new products and processes are going to emerge from long-range basic research—or precisely when they will appear. Much depends on the applied research and development of the next few years. Even more will depend on the actual costs of production and the wants and whims of the consumer. But here are a few of the possibilities of dramatically new consumer products—based on the research and development programs already underway.

• The new home of the 1960s may well be manufactured of collapsible panels so that a homeowner can change its shape to suit his whims, move it to another part of the country, maybe even trade it in at a "used house" lot. Lighting could come from electroluminescent panels occupying most of the ceiling and side walls of a room. Among many interesting features, homes may have all-plastic plumbing, ultrasonic dishwashers and spray-on carpeting. And there could be a small black box in the front hall—the symbol of tomorrow's electronic wonders— which automatically changes the swimming pool water, turns on the heat conductors under the driveway whenever it snows, and maybe even figures out the monthly bills for such luxurious living.

- The car of the future (consumers willing) may take its cue from the experimental "Firebird III" displayed in 1958 by General Motors. That would mean a gas-turbined, electronic-gadgeted, plastic-bubble model. It would boast finned flaps to aid in braking, a corrosion-proof exterior and parts made of "greasy" metals that lubricate themselves. And tomorrow's driver may well be an electronic gadget that straddles, electromagnetically, a cable buried in the middle of the traffic lane.

- Then there's the shopping center of tomorrow. Grass may grow on Main Street after all, but it will hardly be the symbol of the Great Depression. It will just mean that major downtown shopping areas have been transformed into pedestrian parks with vehicular traffic running underground. Noise-breaking circuits could keep major cities quiet. Consumers may be shopping for such standard items as irradiated foods, throw-away paper apparel, appliances with no moving parts. And instead of cash, customers might use magnetically inscribed cards in "cash registers" that flash the full transaction data to the bank, credit the store and debit their accounts.

These are just a few of the possibilities. The most dramatic "new product" of the next few decades may well turn out to be an impregnable anti-missile system of defense. Or it could be a cure for cancer, chemotherapy for mental illness, a cheap contraceptive pill to help overpopulated nations control their birth rates. And it might well be the achievements in outer space—such as lunar laboratories, scientific round trips to Mars and Venus, or civilian space travel.

Equally dramatic changes will be taking place throughout industry. Actually, this second Industrial Revolution is well underway as we move into the 1960s. Today's machine tool builders are not selling just machines, but complete production packages which include electronic controls for tools and automatic conveyors to carry work between tools. In the chemical process industries, automatic devices now "look" where men could not look before—inside metal furnaces and acid baths—so that production data are recorded while operations are still going on. These new developments, now taking place in spots, will become widespread in the years ahead.

Meanwhile, advanced research—in electronics, chemistry, metallurgy—is opening up even wider vistas for the industrial future. For example:

- There are new potential sources of energy and raw materials—nuclear energy, solar energy, maybe hydropower from the tides. In materials, there are the high-temperature plastics, ductile ceramics, and wonder-metal alloys. And there are the new processes such as chemical milling, spark and electrolytic erosion, explosive forming and powder metallurgy.

- In the chemical industry, new plastics, adhesives, fibers and foams are being developed and discovered at almost astronomical rates. According to Chairman Morse Dial of Union Carbide, "petrochemicals are growing at a rate of 10,000 newly synthesized products a year—and few are yet being commercialized." * And today's scientists are asking (and answering) fundamental questions that have never been answered—what is metal, how does catalysis in a chemical reaction really work, can living matter be synthesized in the laboratory?

- In the oil industry, nuclear energy could well turn out to be the most important development since the discovery of oil itself. There are prospects for moving oil through pipelines to refineries by push-button control, as radioactive materials in the crude oil turn pump stations off and on. And perhaps, in the future, underground atomic blasts will unlock vast reserves of oil from shale and tar sand.

- The office of tomorrow is certain to undergo a revolution. It will have a small number of electronic computers to replace large numbers of clerks. Executive staffs around the country

* Quoted in *Business Week*, Aug. 4, 1956.

will "get together" on two-way closed-circuit TV. And by 1970 the busy executive may have a date to jet over to London for lunch.

Taken as whole, the above examples of new developments in consumer living and industrial technology sound almost like an imaginative *tour de force*. They are hardly that. Such predictions are of technical possibilities—probabilities, in fact—as seen today by scientists, research directors and company executives.* Some of the developments are just around the corner. Others may take twenty years or longer. A few are the long shots that may never materialize. But all hint at the fantastic technological promise of the research and development programs now underway in U.S. industry.

ORIGINS OF THE RESEARCH BOOM

When did this surge of research activity start? Actually, technological innovation is not a new force in the American economy. Transistors, tranquilizers and stereophonic sound are postwar developments. But synthetic fibers, TV and plastics were all under development in the 1930s. And not too many years before that, there was the age of the automobile, of electric power, of railroads, of the steam engine itself. Each of these was a new product with substantial economic impact. Yet, something new has been added in recent years.

* In respect to source material the authors are particularly indebted to the scientific staffs of Bell Laboratories and Radio Corporation of America, for technical papers; the editors of *House and Home* and *Architectural Forum*, for their description of the home of the future; General Motors Corp., for data on the experimental Firebird III; Mr. E. B. Weiss, Director of Merchandising, Doyle-Dane-Bernbach Inc., for his roundup of "The Coming Electronic Communications Revolution"; Mr. W. T. Stuart, editor of *Electrical Construction and Maintenance*, for trends in electric appliances, shopping centers and computer banking; and the editors of other McGraw-Hill publications, for many of the individual developments mentioned in the text.

What is new is the *planned* application of scientific research to develop new products on a foreseeable schedule—a development that got under way during World War II. Wartime research projects proved convincingly that a concentrated application of science could produce practical results—such as radar, synthetic rubber or atomic bombs—within a measurable period. And it was during this period that the idea of harnessing scientific research, to achieve higher sales and profits, really caught on with American businessmen. The result is that the postwar years are not just the age of synthetics, electronics, automation, nuclear energy and space missiles all rolled into one. They are more properly called the age of *organized research*—by business, on a schedule, for a profit.*

Of course, the immediate postwar markets in the U.S. needed no new products and new technologies to make a boom. Expenditures on research did not spurt again until the Korean War, in 1950, brought substantial boosts in government contracts for research in aviation, electronics and related fields. Also at this time, there was a sharp pickup in research on atomic energy and its applications. The results of this 1950 upsurge have become apparent in the last few years. Improved military aircraft (like the B-58 bomber, supersonic fighters and the first guided missiles) and new atomic weapons are in the hands of the armed forces. The first nuclear power plants for civilian use are already in operation. And the commercial jet age was inaugurated in 1958.

When it comes to civilian products—for the consumer and for industry—the upsurge in research spending is even more recent. Of course, research has always been important in

* For a good discussion of this point, see *The Scientific-Industrial Revolution*, a pamphlet published in 1957 by Model, Roland & Stone, members of the New York Stock Exchange.

the chemical and electrical industries. But the new surge of spending in these and other lines of business started when the Korean War restrictions and the excess profits tax came to an end in 1953. The tax reforms of 1954 added a new incentive by making research outlays deductible as a current expense. (Formerly such outlays were ordinarily considered capital expenditures, deductible only over several years.) And by 1955, the research boom was in full swing. Tax changes were not the only reason, of course. Business was getting more competitive—and new products were needed to spark sales.

From 1953 to 1957 (according to the McGraw-Hill surveys), research expenditures more than doubled. Compared with $3.7 billion in 1953, outlays reached $8.2 billion in 1958, over $9 billion in 1959, and now show signs of approaching $11 billion by 1962. These figures are for research *performed* by private industry. In recent years (reflecting the emphasis on defense work), roughly half the work done in industrial laboratories has been *financed* by the Federal government. But in such cases, the personnel and facilities remain under private direction.

THE INDUSTRY OF INNOVATION

Which industries and companies do the research? Surprisingly enough, this is one of the often overlooked facts about the research boom. For, in terms of membership, the industry of innovation is a pretty select group. And this is so despite the fact that research and development (or R&D) can legitimately mean everything from changing the molecular structure of a hydrocarbon to changing the tailfin on next year's automobile.

For example:

1. Practically all of the research and development in U.S. industry is done by manufacturing companies. As a general rule,
   other industries—including construction, utilities, banking,
   transportation, service fields and retail and wholesale trade—
   do not do very much technical research.

2. Only four out of the twenty-four industries in manufacturing
   account for more than two-thirds of all industrial research.
   The aircraft manufacturing industry—including companies
   such as United Aircraft, Lockheed, Boeing—is spending some
   $3.3 billion on research in 1959. Next on the list come the
   electrical manufacturers ($1.6 billion) including General Elec-
   tric and Bell Laboratories, generally recognized as having
   the two best industrial laboratories in U.S. industry. Then
   there's the highly competitive machinery industry ($654 mil-
   lion), which has the largest number of companies doing research—well over 3,000 of them. Finally, there's the chemical
   industry ($638 million) which easily does the most *basic*
   research—probably more than aircraft and electrical industries
   combined.

3. Large companies do most of the research spending. This is
   simple economics—just as there are not many small companies
   refining oil, manufacturing steel or making automobiles. R&D
   usually involves a large research staff, heavy capital outlays,
   the special production and marketing costs (and risks) that go
   with a really new product or process. Not all the company research figures are available, but it's a safe guess that the 500
   largest research spenders account for over 90 percent of all
   research spending in the U.S.* A good example is the General Electric Company, which reported a spending of more
   than $260 million in 1957—more than some entire industries
   spend on R&D.

* In 1953, for example, the National Science Foundation found that 73
percent of the total expenditure for research and development in manufacturing was done by 2 percent of the manufacturing companies, all of
them with 5,000 or more employees.

4. Industrial research depends heavily on defense contracts. These are, in effect, a government subsidy for certain types of research. Such government support is typical of research in the primary defense industries (i.e., aircraft, electronics), less true of the defense-supporting industries (i.e., oil, rubber, chemicals).

On the surface, all these points look like severe limitations on the impact of today's industrial research. Research is largely confined to manufacturing, to a few industries in manufacturing, and to a relatively few large companies in those industries. Nearly half of all industrial research is defense work. Doesn't this mean that most lines of business, small business in particular, have been left out of the research boom?

This brings us to the single most important fact about industrial research and development. Research is done by relatively few companies, *but its impact is extremely widespread.* Thus, while manufacturing companies do practically all the research, some of the most dramatic revolutions in technology have been felt in other industries. The railroads did not develop the diesel engine themselves, but it was indeed a revolution. Electric utilities are continuing to show dynamic growth largely because the research programs of electrical manufacturers have developed new uses for power. Agriculture has been dramatically changed by the research of universities and chemical companies. The construction industry benefits from the many new materials and new machines developed by others. Computers have revolutionized banking—and so on.

This same criss-crossing of benefits applies to small business. Small companies cannot do much scientific research— since it is a highly specialized, risky and expensive business. But they can operate both effectively and profitably as suppliers and customers of the large corporations who do the research. Du Pont, for example, has about 30,000 suppliers; and 90 percent of its customers are small firms who convert, process and distribute the new products coming out of du Pont laboratories. These indirect benefits are particularly strong in retail and wholesale trade, where the bulk of small firms are concentrated. Thus, the apparel shop gets du Pont orlon; the auto dealer, the newest Chevrolet; the oil jobber, new products from Esso Research—although none of these small businessmen will ever have his own laboratory.

Moreover, small business, particularly in the "science-based" manufacturing industries, has a dynamic role to play in trying out new products. When a new field is opened up by research, there is usually a period of testing, experimentation, probing—a period in which the blue-chip corporation moves cautiously before making any large scale commitments of capital. As in the past, the pace of innovation would indeed be slower if established leaders did not have to cope with smaller, more adventurous firms that are willing to gamble on a potentially profitable new product. Henry Ford liked the Model T the way it was. General Foods bought out Birdseye after frozen foods were here to stay. Similar examples can be found in electrical manufacturing. According to Dr. Harold C. Passer of the Eastman Kodak Company,* both General Electric and Westinghouse turned down the opportunity to develop neon lighting and the photoflash bulb. In the latter case, the small Wabash Appliance Company took over the idea from the Dutch and was supplying three-fourths of the domestic market in 1940. More recently, small chemical and electronic companies have been building new markets in their own specialty fields. Even in autos, the small

* Harold C. Passer, *The Electrical Manufacturers,* Harvard University Press, 1953.

car was not pioneered by the Big Three. And some experts think that the first practical turbine engines will be offered to truck manufacturers by small foreign firms.*

In military research, which accounts for such a large percentage of all research, the effects spread out to firms of all sizes. The bulk of the original research contracts probably go to 100 or so large corporations. But, whereas the primary research is concentrated, the defense business which this generates is not. A single corporation is given responsibility for a "weapons system" (Lockheed for the Polaris, Bell Labs the early warning system against missiles), but there are over 40,000 prime defense contractors and hundreds of thousands of subcontractors. Most important, much of military research has civilian applications. We have already cited jet aircraft as one example. But the striking gains in high temperature research, new alloys, medical research, atomic power, weather control and forecasting are also outgrowths—in part, at least—of the Federal government's support of industrial research.

We mention all these interrelationships in the research field because without them it is impossible to grasp how big an impact research and development does have on the economy. R&D would be of limited consequence if it affected only the company that runs a research program. Instead, there is a whole chain of direct and indirect relationships involved, customer-supplier links between firms, industry-versus-industry competition. Looked at from a narrow viewpoint, one company's new product may be just a competitor's

* For convincing evidence that small firms, and scientists working independently, often play a key role in the initial stages of research and development, there is the recently published study by Professor J. Jewkes, David Sawers and Richard Stillerman of Oxford University: *Sources of Invention* (Macmillan). According to their findings, this was the case in over half of the 61 scientific achievements investigated—air-conditioning, jet engines, cellophane, ductile titanium, insulin, to name a few.

loss. Looked at in a larger perspective, the new products developed in the never-ending competition between all firms, and all related industries, represent a gain for the whole economy. It is to this larger payoff—in terms of general economic growth and stability—that we now turn.

HOW MUCH ECONOMIC GROWTH?

A company executive would say that research leads to business growth in three different but related ways: (1) by increasing sales through new products, (2) by requiring new producing capacity to make these new products, and (3) by cutting costs through more efficient means of production. An economist might say the same thing in a different way: Research increases over-all demand, raises the stock of capital in the economy, and leads to higher productivity. These are the key ingredients of economic growth. The question is how much growth is coming out of research and development—and when?

The strong stimulus of research to sales is already evident in company financial reports. A large share of sales in some of our leading corporations already consists of products which did not even exist at the end of World War II. In 1952, the du Pont Company estimated that half of the products it sold had been developed within the past twenty years. The General Foods Corporation reported that 16 percent of its sales in 1953 were postwar developments. In 1955, Corning Glass obtained 75 percent of its revenue from products developed since 1940. Now these companies are thinking of their future sales largely in terms of still newer "new products."

Surveys by the McGraw-Hill Department of Economics suggest that as much as half of the growth in manufacturing sales may be coming from new products over the next few years. In the spring survey of 1958, companies reported that, on the average, they expected some 12 percent of their 1961 sales to be in products that were not on the market in 1957. For the research-minded chemical, machinery and aircraft industries, the percentage ranged from 14 to 52 percent.

At the present time, however, the impact of research is still very gradual. Thus, while most companies reported plans to increase research expenditures sharply in the period 1958–1961, only 32 percent of the companies had started to make significant outlays for plant and equipment to manufacture new products.

This emphasizes the lagged impact of research on sales and investment. According to the Department of Economics' past surveys of research directors, the average time-lag from start of research to new product is about four to six years. However, in some industries, where innovation is primarily a matter of product improvement—packaged foods, apparel, autos and home furnishings—the payoff period for research may be shorter. For more complex products, such as completely new machinery or the dramatically new consumer durable goods, the time-lag is longer. But for industry as a whole, perhaps five years of research plus two years to develop a market is a good estimate of the time it takes for a new product to start paying off. Thus, it is at least seven years before research programs begin to affect product sales or capital investment for new plant facilities.*

* Capital investment particularly tends to lag because the expenditures required to begin output of a *new product* are usually quite small. Often existing facilities, or a part of them, can be converted to turn out trial quantities of the new product. And the really heavy expenditures required to build a complete new plant are not made until a year or two later. Similarly, expenditures to introduce a *new process* are not usually made until there is a relatively large production volume to justify these outlays. Especially in our heavy industries, new processes tend to be introduced (and, in fact, designed) as the low-cost way of adding new capacity. Therefore, capital

These lags in product development and new plant construction will determine the timing of economic developments growing out of the current research boom. Because of the lags, the results of the recent step-up in research activity will not be fully evident for several years to come. If we assume the usual seven years to develop products and markets, then—remembering that research started to expand rapidly in 1955–1957—it will be at least 1962–1963 before the new developments become a dominant factor in capital expenditures. But once this new flow of new products starts, it will accelerate sharply just as research has been accelerating.

The really basic changes in consumer goods should be in full swing by the mid-1960s—if not before. As we stated at the outset of this chapter, many of these are under development right now. Some of them can already be produced in test quantities. But it will take more research and development to get costs down, and more years after that for population and incomes to grow to the point where mass markets are created.

A wave of new consumer products in the mid-1960s, particularly new consumers' durable goods, would mean new "tooling up" for many plants. It might begin the greatest capital goods expansion in all history. For when industry expands in the 1960s, it will not be simply by adding more capacity of the same type. It will be with the new processes and new production equipment developed by research that is now underway. Thus, the auto industry hopes to have the truly automatic factory ready for mass production of the

---

outlays for both new products and new processes tend to be delayed beyond the time of strictly scientific development, until sales prospects justify the building of large-scale facilities. For a fuller discussion of this point, see Robert P. Ulin, "What Will Research Bring About?", *Harvard Business Review*, January–February 1958, p. 27.

turbine engine—with automatic machining, assembly and testing all controlled by computers. The steel industry is counting on continuous casting for the expansion of the mid-sixties. By then, the electric power industry hopes that a significant number of its plants can be atom-fueled. The building industry will be introducing complete prefabrication techniques. And many metal products may be produced by direct reduction of ores, powder metallurgy, and continuous casting techniques.

The combined impact of new products and new processes, to meet an expanding market, will thus be felt in the mid-sixties—eight to ten years after the sharpest acceleration in research spending. The time of greatest impact is that far away because of the lags for applied research work, pilot plant studies and market development. But to a large degree, this surge of economic growth has already been shaped by the research programs of the last few years.

RESEARCH AND ECONOMIC STABILITY

What now about economic stability? Granted that research establishes a great potential for economic growth over the long-run, what about the facts that markets are changed, jobs are revolutionized, plants are made obsolete? Will this disturbing process accentuate the ups and downs in business—the historical boom and bust cycle in American industry?

In a word, no—for several reasons.*

One of these reasons is the very magnitude of today's research effort. Isolated doses of research can cause instability (as Joseph A. Schumpeter pointed out in his theory of the

---

* For a fuller discussion of these reasons, see *Saturday Review*, Jan. 19, 1957, "Do We Have to Bust When We Boom?," by Dexter M. Keezer.

business cycle).* But this is the case when there are only a few innovations which tend to bunch and have an uneven impact on markets for capital, commodities and labor. When the process of innovation is as sweeping in scope and continuous as that provided by a yearly expenditure on research of more than $9 billion, the disturbances lose their isolated character and become merged in a steady surge of economic growth. In place of a series of shocks, there is a steady shove.

Similarly, large-scale research not only insures a steady flow of new products and processes, it also changes the very structure of industry. Under the impact of today's research, corporations are merging, diversifying, moving into new lines of business with the net effect that they are not tied to the irregular market for one particular product. Research can also smooth out the cycles in key industries—such as electric utilities, where midsummer air conditioning is offsetting the old winter seasonal peak loads; or in the steel industry, where the low-cost "hydrogen process" for refining iron ore, combined with smaller (electric) furnaces and continuous casting techniques, may extend the three-year bulge in capital spending that occurs with construction of giant furnaces and rolling mills. Moreover, research creates whole new indus-

---

* For example, in his *Business Cycles* Dr. Schumpeter wrote: "Industrial change is never harmonious advance with all elements of the system actually moving, or tending to move, in step. At any given time, some industries move on, others stay behind; and the discrepancies arising from this are an essential element in the situations that develop. Progress—in the industrial as well as in any other sector of social or cultural life—not only proceeds by jerks and rushes but also by one-sided rushes productive of consequences other than those which would ensue in the case of coordinated rushes. In every span of historic time it is easy to locate the ignition of the process and to associate it with certain industries and, within these industries, with certain firms, from which the disturbances then spread over the system." Joseph A. Schumpeter, *Business Cycles,* McGraw-Hill, New York, 1939, Vol. I, pp. 101–102.

tries and gives wider scope for the "rolling readjustment" where one industry's cycle cancels out that of another. As Professor Slichter has put it: "By adding to the number of industries, technological research tends to moderate the cyclical movements of the economy as a whole." *

Still another factor is that research and development is largely detached from the ups and downs in business activity. In 1958, for example, when capital investment declined sharply, research expenditures were increasing by more than 10 percent. Nor were there declines in the 1949 and 1954 recessions. This detachment is viewed by some as casting organized research and development in a positive role working for greater economic stability. For example, Professor Melvin de Chazeau of Cornell University finds that,

... through the new emphasis on research, the prospects of non-cyclical capital investments are vastly improved. The output of the research laboratory cannot be predetermined; and current insistence on a research staff that is adequate to protect research from diversions of staff members into customer service problems should ensure research developments removed from the influence of general market changes.

It is not easy for a firm to withhold from the market a product or process which it has perfected. The firm's leadership position, its goodwill with customers, its profits margins, and the morale of its own organization, all tend to require immediate exploitation of a perfected device even if markets are weak. The risk that rivals may approximate or better a company's own achievements can outweigh the risk of unsatisfactory current market returns. To the extent that this is true, the new competition in research and development will broaden the scope of non-cyclical programing and will contribute to economic stability.†

* In an address to the National Science Foundation, May 20, 1958.
† From an article, "Can We Avoid Depression in a Dynamic Economy?" by Melvin G. de Chazeau, *Harvard Business Review*, July–August 1954; p. 35.

Finally, and this is the most important way to state the case for increased stability, research is an antidote for the buildup of too much producing capacity. Excess capacity was the villain of the cycle, according to accepted theories of economics. First, a boom level of investment, leading to surplus capacity; then, too many goods and falling prices; finally, a dwindling rate of return on investment. The result was a steep and prolonged decline in capital investment and a serious depression.

Research doesn't take all the jiggles out of the business curve. But it does prevent them from becoming the disastrous plunges that can take place in a stagnating economy. For, even during a letdown, research insures that substantial investment may still be very profitable. This is investment for tooling up for new products and new markets a few years ahead. It is also the investment needed to cut costs and modernize old capacity.

In other words, under the impact of research, the very concept of capacity has changed. Even during good times, the research-minded company (and industry) will have some "idle" capacity. Part of it will be the result of the wider margin of capacity that comes with a diversified line of products. Part of it may be the result of a low operating rate of a new manufacturing process that is being introduced. And part of it may be the reserve capacity kept on hand to take advantage of the unexpected spurts in demand of a fast-growing, changing economy. But this isn't the "excess capacity" with the drastic consequences of an old-fashioned bust. It is the expanding potential for future economic growth.*

* On research expenditures and new concepts of capacity, see Robert P. Ulin, "Does Excess Capacity Mean Recession," *Challenge*, March 1958, pp. 49–53.

THE CONCLUSIONS

Now that we have stated the bright prospects arising from research, let us touch briefly on some of the problems that must be dealt with, if those prospects are to materialize.

First is an adequate supply of scientists and engineers. The experts assure us that while the supply of scientific manpower may be hard-pressed at times, this will not add up to a crippling shortage over the next few decades. Needless to say, there will always be a shortage of really top scientists and engineers. And, insofar as the demands for scientists have been met in recent years, this has been done in part by inducing university and college faculty members to leave the campus for greener (i.e., money-colored) pastures in industry. This obviously is no way to run a continuing research effort.

There is a possible shortage of basic research. Of industry's total research expenditures, probably no more than 5–10 percent currently represents inquiry into the fundamentals of scientific knowledge. As many scientists (and a good many of industry's own research directors) have pointed out, too many companies are looking for a quick return on R&D—the new product to boost sales, or the applied research to cut costs. They are not sufficiently concerned with the advances in the basic sciences on which all such technological innovation ultimately depends.

Finally, there are government and corporate policies which need to be updated in this age of innovation. For one, more attention could be paid to providing profit incentives (i.e., something more than just a cost-plus contract) in military research. Another possibility is further revision of our laws on depreciation—along lines suggested in Chapter 2—so as to increase the speed at which new processes developed by research are actually adopted. Also, there are corporate policies themselves. How much should be spent on research? What standard should be used in choosing between projects? How can the brilliant scientist get along with an Organization Man? Much needs to be discovered to get the right answers to these questions.

These problems—the need for good scientists, more basic research, better policies in the research field—are not likely to capsize the research effort. One reason is that recently the problems have been recognized and are getting attention. But they will remain important, if only because research itself is so important to the potential prosperity and growth of the United States.

We can now sum up that potential. The economy stands only a few short years from a dynamic consumer and industrial revolution based on the outgrowth of present research programs. The current massive figures on research spending indicate that industrial research is not only big business in the U.S. It is a growing business. And this growth will be reflected in future sales of both consumer goods and capital goods.

Most of these revolutionary products are still in the test-tube and pilot-plant stage. But as we move into the 1960s, increasing investments will be made in new processes and new machines. More and more sales will be coming from new products. And more and more plant and equipment will be needed to produce them. This is the key to economic growth on a stable and continuing basis in the decades ahead.

CHAPTER FOUR

The Changing Consumer Market

The burden of the preceding chapters has been that we have a bright prospect of maintaining a high and rising level of capital investment, and thus making a crucial contribution to steady growth and sustained prosperity *if* . . .

The *"if"* with which this and the following chapter are concerned is *"if"* we can also manage a strongly rising level of consumption.

Capital investment is not a self-contained and self-propelling element in our economy. In the longer run, and not very long at that, it depends for its justification and driving force upon consumption of the products for which the investment in producing facilities is made. If consumption shrinks, it ultimately paralyzes investment and in the process puts a deadly blight on the economy as a whole; for of the total volume of economic operations in our country, as measured by the Gross National Product, consumption accounts for about two-thirds.

Investment is, of course, the means of putting a great many people to work—and so providing the income for a higher level of consumption, which in turn leads to more investment. This is the sort of interaction that gives so much of current economic analysis a tail-chasing character and leads to frustration on the part of those who would like to separate the economy into neat compartments. But fortunately we need not pursue this frustrating course of analysis in order to arrive at some conclusions about the chances of maintaining prosperity. So far as consumption and investment are concerned, the practical answer follows the line of the popular song "Love and Marriage": They go together like a horse and carriage, and "You can't have one without the other."

Gross National Product, Major Sectors

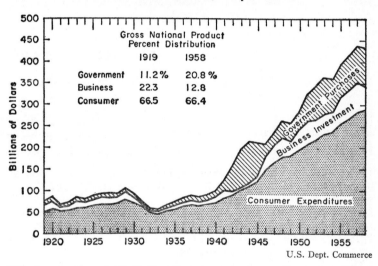

With the exception of World War II years, consumer spending on goods and services accounted for roughly two-thirds of the national product. In general, the consumer sector of the economy has been the most stable component of GNP.

Responding to this tune, consumption has moved along with investment, and indeed has set the pace for most of the postwar decade. Even when the explosive force of demands pent up during World War II had largely spent itself, as it had by 1954, consumer spending continued to increase. In 1955, manufacturing industry found itself short of capacity to meet a new upsurge in consumer spending. And it was this continuing pressure of demand that sparked a new industrial expansion in 1956 and 1957. In 1958, the same pattern developed, on a more moderate scale. Despite the recession in heavy industry, consumer expenditures again increased substantially, helping to bring the recession quickly to an end.

Will the demand for consumer goods continue to grow as it has in the past decade, and so provide a continuing stimulus for investment in producing facilities? To answer this question, we must examine the new forces at work in the consumer market during recent years.

WHAT MAKES A MARKET GROW?

It does not require much argument to show that the consumer market will grow by some minimum amount over the coming decades. A steady increase in the consumption of basic items, such as food and clothing, is assured by population growth.* And we might project a minimum increase in

---

* Since 1939, population has increased by 46 million—or more than 35 percent—to 177 million at mid-1959. In the five years 1954–1958, there were 20.9 million births, contrasted with only 11.8 million births in the five-year period 1933–1937. Moreover, the population is still increasing rapidly. Despite the 1957–1958 recession, births declined by only 1 percent in 1958, so that the population still has not levelled off, let alone declined, as many demographers in the 1930s and 1940s believed it would.

Only a decade ago the official Census Bureau estimate of the future *peak* population of the United States was 165 million. Actually, the 165 million mark was reached in 1955; and demographers now expect a population of nearly 200 million by 1965.

Moreover, the greatest surge will come after 1965. Today's families include more children than was typical two decades ago, an average of 1.4 per family today as compared with an average of 1.2 per family in 1940. As this wave of children which started in the 1940s reaches the age of forming families, we may expect a boom in new marriages and another, bigger baby boom.

Beginning in 1965, the number of marriages will increase rapidly, and by 1970, marriages will probably total close to 2,000,000 per year according to Paul H. Jacobson (*American Marriage and Divorce*, Rinehart and Company, p. 96, table 46, May 1959). Thus, the population of the 1970s will include a record number of relatively young families. These families pre-

expenditures for housing, automobiles and other durable items simply by toting up the future number of households in the U.S.

But a *dynamic* increase in consumer spending calls for something more. Such an increase depends less on the number of families in the market than on how well fixed these families are with money (i.e., spendable money that has not already been claimed by the tax collector, the landlord, or the grocer, but is available for extra purchases). Spending also depends heavily on how inclined people are to make those extra purchases, instead of making a trip to the savings bank. (On these questions of the amounts available for optional spending, and the inclination to spend, improved

---

sumably will include a record number of young children, and they will also form a market of unprecedented size for new homes, cars and other durable goods.

U.S. Population Growth

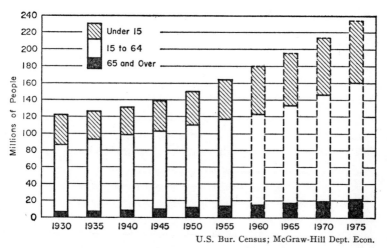

U.S. Bur. Census; McGraw-Hill Dept. Econ.

Total U.S. population is expected to pass the 200 million mark during 1967. Growth in population during the sixties will continue to be concentrated in our very young, young and senior members. The single biggest increase expected is in age 20–24.

consumer survey techniques now provide a considerable flow of information.)

Finally, and perhaps most importantly, a dynamic increase in consumer expenditure depends on skillful use of the arts of marketing to increase the inclination to spend. We shall have something to say about this point in our next chapter. In fact, as befits an economy of abundance, our discussion of marketing—or, in plain language, selling—will be longer and fuller than the present brief essay on the consumer market itself.

Our purpose in the present chapter is to describe the consumer market in terms of income structure, and in terms of social structure as it affects the inclination to spend. This market is different today from what it was ten years ago, or even five years ago. It is bigger, richer and more changeable. In contrast to coping with postwar shortages, consumers today are well able to leave a large part of what is produced on the shelves, if they wish to save more or work less.

The contrast with earlier periods in our history—say the Gay Nineties or Roaring Twenties—is even sharper, for today's consumer market is far broader than the markets of earlier times. It includes a much larger proportion of families on a high living standard, and even as consumers of what were once luxury goods. This "middle income" character of the new American market gives it far more stability than it had in previous decades, despite the occasional, short-term fluctuations that are inherent in any market that is well enough supplied to allow free choice.

In describing the consumer market, we shall refer frequently to these changes from earlier years. As we shall point out, continuing change (for the better) in incomes, social status and way of life of most American families is the main force working to increase consumer spending.

THE NEW AMERICAN MARKET

The market for consumer goods today is vastly larger than it was ten years ago. As a simple indication, consumers (i.e., individuals, as opposed to business corporations) had $317 billion of income after taxes to spend in 1958, compared with $227 billion in 1948. Their actual spending was $293 billion, compared with $215 billion in 1948. (These figures are all in terms of the 1958 price level.)

The consumer market now consists of 58 million spending units * (against 49 million in 1948). Moreover, the average

Disposable Income, Savings, Consumer Spending

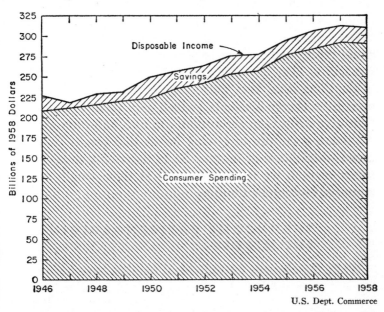

U.S. Dept. Commerce

Both disposable income and consumer spending showed very little decline in the 1957–1958 year-to-year comparison.

* A spending unit, as defined in the surveys of consumer income, savings and intentions to buy undertaken by the University of Michigan for the Federal Reserve Board, "consists of all related persons living together who pool their incomes. Husband and wife and children under 18 living at home are

income is higher. Median income for all spending units was $3,425 in 1948; it was $4,400 in 1958. (These figures are expressed in 1958 dollars.) And a surprising proportion of all spending units are close to this average figure or above it. In the 1958 Survey of Consumer Finances (conducted by the Survey Research Center of the University of Michigan for the Board of Governors of the Federal Reserve System) about half of all spending units reported income of $4,500 or more. This is well above the average household budget for basic necessities (including food, clothing, medical and personal care, and home operations) which, as reported in a study by *Life* magazine, comes to roughly $2,650 per year.*

Thus the American market today consists predominantly of families with sufficient income to indulge in what has been called "optional consumption." Families that once ate low-grade meats and canned food now have steak and frozen specialties. They buy new cars, instead of used cars. Instead of the dime store, they patronize the department store and even have charge accounts (which help them to buy more expensive items than are available in cash-and-carry stores). All this is a pattern of buying habits that results from the broad distribution of income. So in describing today's consumer market, we must first dwell at some length on the matter of income distribution.

THE INCOME PATTERN—BULGING IN THE MIDDLE

While the changes for individual families have been striking and even sudden, the progress toward broader incomes

always considered to be members of the same spending unit. Other related persons in the household are separate spending units if they earn more than $15 per week and do not pool their incomes." *Federal Reserve Bulletin,* July 1956, p. 690.

* *Life Study of Consumer Expenditures,* Time Inc., New York, 1957.

in the U.S. as a whole has been a steady and gradual development over the past twenty years. Consequently, most of us do not realize how completely the structure of national income has changed in the past two decades. Some years ago, Arthur F. Burns, then Director of Research of the National Bureau of Economic Research (and from 1953–1956 Chairman of the President's Council of Economic Advisers) wrote that "few Americans . . . are aware of the transformation in the distribution of our national income that has occurred within the past twenty years—a transformation that has been carried out peacefully and gradually, but which may already be counted as one of the great social revolutions of history." *

When we look more closely, we find that the revolution Dr. Burns described is both economic and social. In the past ten years especially, the rise in average wages has created an expanding middle class of skilled factory and office workers —plus a growing number of people in the professions and in "middle management" jobs. These are people who can afford to spend money in a substantial way, to achieve a standard of living that used to be reserved for owners of property.

Moreover, the revolution in incomes has affected ordinary workers, at least as much as technical and managerial staffs. Even where skills have not risen much, families have achieved higher incomes simply as the result of higher employment, averaging over 95 percent of the labor force since 1947, compared with 82 percent in the 1930s. And there have been sharper increases when, as in some recent years, wages and working conditions were so attractive that large numbers of married women were drawn into the labor force—along with teen-agers and oldsters taking part-time jobs. These opportunities have meant two (or more) jobs per family, in an increasing number of cases.

* "Looking Forward" *31st Annual Report, National Bureau of Economic Research, Inc.* (New York, National Bureau, 1951), pp. 3–4.

Steady work for at least one wage earner, and often two, plus substantially higher pay scales, have added up to "middle incomes" for the great bulk of our families who live on wages and salaries. At the same time, progressive taxation at the top, and welfare payments at the bottom, have reduced the number of families at the extremes of the income scale. According to the 1958 Survey of Consumer Finances, more than three-fifths of all spending units in the U.S. had incomes of between $2,000 and $7,500. One-half of all spending units, a proportion that obviously includes many working-class families, earned $3,000 to $7,500. The extremes of riches and poverty reached only a small proportion of American families, with 7 percent having incomes below $1,000 and another 8 percent earning $10,000 or over.

Just how revolutionary these figures are may be seen from a study by the Bureau of the Census which shows the proportion of all consumer income going to the top income brackets in 1929 and 1954. In 1929, the richest 5 percent of our population got 30 percent of total consumer income; in 1954, they had only 20 percent.* Since the number of very poor persons also decreased, there was only one place for the money to go—into the middle brackets that include most of today's American families.†

* See also Simon Kuznets and Elizabeth Jenks, *Shares of Upper Income Groups in Income and Savings*, National Bureau of Economic Research, New York, 1953.

† The trend of the 1950s toward middle incomes gives present consumer spending a stronger foundation than it had with the concentrated income structure of the 1920s. Then what appeared to be a booming level of consumer expenditures rested, in fact, on the unusually high incomes achieved by a small fraction of the population. Aside from the temporary riches garnered in the stock market boom of the twenties, most of the gains in income during that decade went to the owners of business, whose sources of income were acutely vulnerable to the ensuing decline in industrial production. Prosperity was not at all widely distributed, since neither farmers nor wage earners were making comparable gains in income.

PROBLEM AREAS

The remarkable broadening of incomes over the past two decades does not mean, of course, that we have eliminated poverty altogether. In recent years, a significant number of families earned less than $1,000. Aside from the disabled or otherwise unemployable, most of these low-income people are farmers (or farm laborers). In 1958, per capita farm income was just over $1,000, compared with the national average of $2,060. Since commercial farmers have incomes much closer to the national average, the really poor are mostly small subsistence farmers, principally in the Southeast.

We have other problem areas—for example, the coal mining districts of West Virginia, the old textile towns of New England, or the slums occupied by minority races in some of our large cities. (For a fuller discussion of problem areas in income distribution, see Appendix II.) But while it is important to see that they are eliminated as soon as possible, the existence of low-income areas does not alter the fact that consumer income generally is far more widely distributed than in the years before World War II. Nor can it be denied that this broader income base supports a rising trend in consumer spending.

As the income base grew narrower in the late 1920s, a high level of consumer expenditures came to rest more and more on excessive spending (supported by borrowing on both durable goods and stock market accounts) on the part of a minority of American families. And this, most economists now believe, was a basic reason for the eventual collapse of the boom in 1929.

In today's consumer market, the opposite is true. Its base has been steadily broadened. And this, as much as any single factor, explains the persistent strength of consumer expenditures and business generally during the 1940s and 1950s. With an income structure that is broadly based, there need not be an inevitable crash of the 1929 type at the end of each decade of prosperity.

In addition to the rise in incomes and the wider distribution of income, two social factors have been at work since 1947 to induce larger consumer expenditures. These are (1) the baby boom, which has by now turned into a teen-age boom, and (2) the increasing mobility of our population. Both of these are results of social patterns that started during World War II when earlier marriages became fashionable, and when families came to accept the idea of moving from one home to another as normal, and even as fun. In their inclination to marry early and have several children, and in their penchant for changing residence, modern families have acquired social habits that lead them (despite occasional, and generally ineffective, protests by the head of the household) toward habitually higher levels of spending.

ECONOMICS OF TEEN-AGERS

The baby boom of the 1940s is by now a matter of history (although the number of young children is still large enough to keep classrooms full and provide a booming market for specialties ranging from breakfast cereals to electric trains). But an even stronger pressure comes from the teen-age group that is now flooding our high schools and demanding even more from family budgets than when they were younger. In fact, teen-agers are probably the most potent force working on consumer spending today. Budget studies indicate that it costs a family about $500 a year *more* to support one of this group (age ten to nineteen) than it does to support a younger child.

In 1958, the 17 million teen-agers in our population spent an estimated $9.5 billion *of their own money* (two-thirds of this coming from parental allowances and one-third from part-time jobs) in addition to the much larger sums spent for their support by parents and by communities for education. Of the $9.5 billion, approximately 30 percent went for school lunches and school supplies, and 15 percent for books, magazines, records and movies. The remainder went chiefly for "dates," automobiles and gasoline in the case of boys, or clothing and cosmetics for girls.*

All of these items seem to be regarded by teen-agers as essential—and essential enough to work for in spare hours, if money is not obtainable from parents. With the teen-age population growing over twice as fast during the next decade as the population as a whole (an estimated 42 percent vs. 19 percent), the impetus of such teen-age needs to total consumer expenditures will obviously continue to be strong.

MOBILE AMERICA

The other social factor making for higher consumer expenditures is population mobility. A recent Census survey, for example, indicated that nine out of ten people one year of age or older have moved at least once in their lifetime. The survey also showed that one out of every fifteen persons in the nation moves into a different county *each year*—and one out of five persons changes residence each year. (In New York City alone, about three-fourths of a million change-of-address cards are filed annually with the post office.) In the process of changing residence, as anyone who has had the experience knows, a family usually finds itself spending more money.†

* "Profiles: A Caste, A Culture, A Market," *The New Yorker*, Nov. 22, 1958, Vol. XXXIV, No. 40, New York, p. 57.
† This statement applies particularly to those moving from rural areas to the city. During the last quarter of a century the urban population has been growing at the expense of the farm population. The farm population, beyond showing a decline in its share of the total population, actually registered a decline in absolute numbers. Today's farm population totals 21 million compared with 30.5 million back in 1930. Farmers have been

The most striking trend is the shift to the suburbs. While the population of central cities grew by about 14 percent from 1940 to 1950, the population of the suburbs around these cities increased about 36 percent, or about two and one-half times as fast as the population in the cities. The march to the suburbs is continuing; in fact, it has accelerated since 1950. Between 1950 and 1956 suburban areas grew about six times as rapidly as the central cities. And as people acquire suburban homes, frequently new homes, this creates many new demands for household goods, for automobiles to travel greater distances and for clothing to match the standards of suburban living.

Finally, a significant fraction of our population has moved all the way across the country. The Western region of the United States has been growing faster than any other section of the nation. It is not an accident that the Far West also has had the greatest housing boom and the highest ratio of car ownership. People moving there have needed new homes and cars. The center of the nation's population has moved approximately 150 miles to the west in the last fifty years.* (According to the Census of Population in 1950, the

---

leaving the farms to work in better-paying industries in the cities. And as city dwellers, their purchases of many kinds of goods—for example, stylish clothing and new home furnishings—have increased along with their incomes. A similar upgrading has taken place for factory workers moving from run-down industrial districts to "nicer" neighborhoods in the city or suburbs.

* The West is the only section of the four major divisions of the nation, Northeast, North Central, South and West, where the share of total population increased significantly between 1930 and 1958. In 1958, the West, made up of the Pacific and Mountain states, accounted for a little less than 15 percent of the nation's population. In 1930, this area accounted for less than one-tenth of the population. At the turn of the century, its share was only a little more than 5 percent—a very thin slice of the population pie. The Northeast and the North Central regions of the country lost three and two percentage points respectively from their 1930 shares of the total

new center was in Richland County, Illinois.) And it is still moving. By 1970, it will be many miles west of the Mississippi River.

This shift measures only *permanent* residence. The increasing speed and low cost of travel by automobile and airplane give the entire population increased mobility, at least during the vacation season. As a result, the city dweller's wardrobe may range from sports shirts to ski suits, even for a single vacation. And gasoline stations in Vermont and New Mexico are servicing cars from the more populous areas or local cars rented to people who would not drive at all if they stayed "at home." Of course this type of mobility (i.e., travel for pleasure) depends importantly on a high level of income. So do certain aspects of the teen-age boom, such as the surprising (to an older generation) amounts spent by today's teen-agers on entertainment, clothing and automobiles. So we return now to the key aspect of today's consumer market, the broad distribution of income.

INCOME AND MARKETS

The most striking effects of wider income distribution may be seen in our suburban shopping centers, or in the neighborhood supermarkets. The stores are bigger than a decade ago; the selection of merchandise is wider and richer; above all, the cash registers ring—and ring steadily. This demand for

---

population. The South's share of the nation's population increased less than one-half of one percent over the last quarter of a century.

In absolute terms, of course, population in all regions increased from 1930 to 1958. Only Arkansas, North Dakota and Oklahoma show a decline. The Northeast registered a gain in population of about one-fourth between 1930 and 1958. The North Central region increased its number of people by one-third. The South's population rose by two-fifths over the last twenty-eight years. But population in the West more than doubled from 1930 to 1958.

more and better goods exists because almost three-fourths of American families now earn over $3,000 a year. To put the matter simply, these families can afford the "good life."

They can, and do, have homes of their own. (Three out of five families own their own homes, according to reports of the Bureau of the Census. And most of the rest would like to, according to surveys by the University of Michigan). About 75 percent of all families own a car and aspire to own newer or bigger (or smaller) cars. They require five million cars per year just to maintain the number of relatively new (one to five years old) vehicles that are now on the road. They have better furniture and a more varied wardrobe than they used to have, spend more on education, recreation and medical care.

Above all, these families have a prodigious yen to buy "gadgets," the wonderful electric appliances that make life around the house easier (in the case of kitchen appliances) or more fun (with television, hi-fi and power tools). Spending on these items has run far ahead of early postwar forecasts, because they are items a family usually buys as soon as it becomes "middle income."

Moreover, "middle income" standards are steadily rising. *Fortune* magazine commented late in 1956, in reporting the appearance of a Sears Roebuck buyer at the Paris fashion showings: "The vast majority of American consumers are no longer content with minimum standards, but demand the abundance, quality, and style that used to differentiate the good life from ordinary living. They are demanding, because they can afford them, such things as 25–hp outboards, cashmere coats, second TV sets, second refrigerators, frozen shrimp Newburg, and high-style dresses." *

Some who have tried it might question the universal de-

_____

* "The Changing American Market: Still Changing," *Fortune,* October 1956, p. 127.

mand for frozen shrimp Newburg. But on a broader basis, the social urge to better living has real economic importance. Families have demonstrated—in 1954 and again in 1958— that they will reduce saving and borrow, if necessary, to maintain their newly-won standards. They will also, as the records of installment companies show, work longer hours or take extra jobs to earn the down-payments on a new car or TV set. (This appeal of installment credit as an "incentive" evidently has been noted by our Soviet adversaries, who recently instituted it.) * Simply maintaining present levels of housing, car ownership, clothing and home furnishings will require large consumer outlays in the years ahead since there will be more families, and more of them will be in the goods-hungry suburban areas. Raising the standards, as most families hope to do, will require a sharp rise in spending. Whether such an increase actually takes place will depend not on people's desire to spend, but on their ability to pay— on whether the upgrading of family income continues.

THE CONTINUING REVOLUTION

Throughout the early postwar years, forecasters assumed that when the ownership of cars and other consumer durables reached a certain point, markets would be saturated and consumer spending would decline. Such thinking persisted in many quarters even when consumer spending continued to increase in 1949 and early 1950, long after the postwar shortages had been eliminated and before the Korean hostilities had begun. However, since 1954, when consumer spending gave another demonstration of its amazing vitality, there has been increasing recognition of the fact that there are new "backlogs" of consumer demand accumulating every year the

* C. L. Sulzberger, "Capitalism as It Is Applied to Communism," *New York Times,* June 13, 1959, p. 20.

revolution in income distribution continues. The new middle-income families, owning their own homes for the first time, moving into areas where standards of clothing and home furnishings are higher, feel a pressing need to acquire these goods.

From 1950 to 1957 an average of two million families per year crossed into the $4,000-plus income bracket. During the next ten years, a minimum of 1.5 million families will reach this "middle-income" level each year. For these people, a new house (as opposed to a rented apartment) or a new car (instead of a used car) becomes a possibility for the first time.

To be sure, all this depends on a continuing increase in the number of middle-income families. Prospects for a further increase are bright. As we have already seen, the gains in real family income to date are the result of steadily higher wage and salary payments. And this trend will continue as the labor force continues to upgrade its skills, as more people move into the professions, and as worker productivity generally trends upward at the compound rate of 2.5 percent or more per year. These gains in productivity will permit higher wages, and our arrangements for collective bargaining pretty well insure that the full potential of higher productivity will be realized by the wage-earning group.

In fact, the increasing prevalence of long-term labor contracts, with annual wage increases provided for each of several years ahead, means that the rewards of productivity have been committed in advance—not to profits or income for proprietors (at least, not for the most part), but to a continuing gain in wage and salary income. And most of these same contracts carry provisions to compensate workers for any increase in the cost of living, so that the capacity of inflation—unless it reaches the dimensions of a real scare—

to reduce the spending power and inclination of working families is cut down. Not all workers are now covered by such favorable contracts, which to date are mostly in manufacturing industries, but over the years similar favorable terms are likely to be extended to wider and wider groups.

The fear that working agreements providing for systematic wage increases of the type indicated not only will result in inflation reaching the "dimensions of the real scare" but will ultimately wreck the economy via the inflationary route is considered in Chapter 8. Suffice to note here that this is not entirely a fanciful fear. But in terms of the capacity to consume an increasing output of goods and services, at least as measured by dollars (the subject matter of this chapter), it is clear that arrangements which systematically increase salaries and wages constitute an engine of expansion.

ARE MARKETS SATURATED?

As a result of expansive forces of the type indicated, we may expect that more than 1.5 million families each year will be reaching the $4,000-plus income range. By 1963, *more than half of all families in the U.S. will be earning over $5,000.* But what about those who are already "middle income"? Will their appetite for goods be satisfied? Once again the answer is that it will not be, if they keep moving up the income scale—and there is plenty of room to move up even within the middle-income range of $4,000 to $7,500.

According to the findings of interviews conducted by the University of Michigan's Survey Research Center, the acquisition of a basic stock of consumer durables does not lead a family to taper off its spending on such goods. Such might be the old theory of "marginal utility," but it is not the way families actually behave. According to the Michigan studies, it is the families with the highest *present* ownership of durable goods who are the most interested in the newer durables and who think the most about future purchases.

Those who, for one reason or another, have lost hope of increasing their income generally come to accept a fixed standard of living. But when families hope to earn more in the years ahead (as most of those interviewed did hope), each purchase of a new car or electric appliance seems to stimulate interest in still newer "gadgets." They may not need a second refrigerator, but they will buy a dishwasher or an air conditioner or a power lawn mower.*

Similarly, new home owners are the ones most interested in a bigger home or in moving to "a nicer neighborhood." The ones who are really reluctant to move are those who are stuck in the slums—because they have never experienced the joy of something better and so are not inclined to think much about such improvements.†

These new facts about consumer psychology strongly reinforce the basic data on population and incomes. All three factors point to an expanding consumer market and a steady upgrading of purchases within the market. It is impossible to predict accurately what goods will be most favored. Certainly there will be shifts in the types of goods desired by the average family. Some marketing experts have suggested there will be a notable change to more services and leisure products, and less spending proportionately on necessities or semi-

---

* According to *Electrical Merchandising,* nine out of ten homes still do not have ironers, dishwashers, food disposal units, or the new "built-in" electric ranges. Similarly, nine out of ten do not have a dehumidifier or food blender, although nine in ten do have electric clothes washers. *Electrical Merchandising,* McGraw-Hill Publishing Company, Inc., New York, January 1959, p. 59.
† These findings of the Survey Research Center on the effects of present durable goods (or home) ownership on future purchases are summarized in a paper by Dr. George Katona, presented at the Conference on the Economic Outlook, University of Michigan, Nov. 15, 1956, pp. 14–15.

luxuries in favor of what today seem real luxuries. But over-all consumer spending may well show more growth in the next ten years than it did in the past decade—reaching $445 billion (in 1958 dollars) by 1968, about $150 billion more than in 1958.

In a consumer economy of this size, it has been estimated there would be demand for 8.5 million new automobiles per year, 4 million automatic clothes washers, 10 million television sets, 5 million air conditioners. These figures range from 15 percent to 300 percent higher than the comparable figures for sales in 1955, the peak year for consumer durable goods. Such an increase will be well within the capacity of our productive facilities. But it indicates that the prospects for consumption are such as to keep our productive resources employed at profitable rates of operation.

PROMISE AND PERFORMANCE

These are estimates of what American families *could* buy —what they *will* buy depends on how they are sold. As a people we have become so rich that we have a broad option to consume or not to consume if we are so inclined. Studies by the McGraw-Hill Department of Economics indicate that "optional consumption" covers as much as one-third of every-thing that is consumed. This means that as a nation of con-sumers we could probably get along on only two-thirds of what we are currently spending for consumption of goods and services.

Hence we face the problem of whetting consumer appe-tites. How can the American family be tempted each year to buy more and better goods and services than it bought the year before? To devise such temptations is a key part of the art of marketing, with which we deal in the next chapter.

CHAPTER FIVE

The Fateful Art of Marketing

"Selling is not only a job; it is a symbol of a free society."

At first glance this statement, made by Harry Walker Hepner in a book on marketing,* may seem a bit pretentious. On closer examination, however, it holds up quite well. In fact, broadly defined, as it properly can be, to include the whole range of marketing operations from product design through pricing and advertising right on through to doorbell pushing and the final sale, selling or marketing not only is a symbol of a free society but is in ever-increasing measure a working necessity in our particular free society.

It is obviously much more compatible with freedom to be required to sell things to people having a range of choice than it is to dictate what they shall and shall not have, as is the Communist custom. Also, perpetuation of freedom in the large degree in which we enjoy it has come to depend in ever-increasing degree on selling.

Thanks largely to the driving force imparted to our economy by its free institutions, we have as a nation become so rich that we are under no compulsion of immediate necessity to consume a large share of what is produced. So far as our immediate comfort and convenience is concerned, we can take it or leave it. As we suggested at the conclusion of the preceding chapter, it is indeed possible to make a plausible case that at least one-third of everything that is currently

* *Modern Marketing*, McGraw-Hill, New York, 1955, p. 3.

produced falls into this range of what is commonly called optional consumption. American consumers, in contrast to those living in an economy operating at a bare subsistence and survival level, have a broad option to take it or leave it. But if they were to leave it, a depression which would make that of the thirties seem almost mild would not be far behind.

Seen in this perspective, marketing takes on the character of an absolutely basic economic operation. There is a widespread inclination in the United States to regard the manufacturing of steel or the digging of coal or the building of houses as basic, and the marketing of them as something much more superficial. Understandably enough, many economists share this inclination because down through the ages in most places the dominant economic problem has been production—the problem of producing enough to meet elemental wants, a problem that most of the world has yet to solve. But this inclination, to which some salesmen also contribute by a shortage of self-respect, is out of touch with current realities. In an economy of abundance such as that which has been created in the United States, successful selling is a key ingredient of successful performance.

In a delightful discussion of "The Economist as a Modern Missionary," * W. Beckerman, writing in Paris, puts it in a somewhat different way by remarking that "In an economy such as the United States of America, where leisure is barely moral, the problem of creating sufficient wants (i.e., competing ends) to absorb productive capacity may become chronic in the not too distant future." Of the economist in this situation Mr. Beckerman remarks, "How much happier he can be in a backward economy where scarcity of resources relative to all the wants *he* can envisage (if not the indigenous population) is paramount."

Hence, in gauging the prospects for sustained prosperity

* *The Economic Journal*, March 1956, pp. 108, 112.

over the next decade, it is necessary to form a judgment as to whether the marketing end of the operation will be up to the successful performance of its crucially important role. Directed to this end, this chapter reaches the conclusion that, while it is anything but an open and shut question, there are developments which encourage the hope that it will.

In all of its ramifications the business or art of marketing involves, in one way or another, virtually the entire range of economic activity. For example, the general connotation of the term "sale" as used in marketing is that prices have been reduced. And a pursuit of the subject of pricing quickly gets into costs and hence deep into the processes of industrial production.

Here we are not essaying a deep searching analysis of marketing and all its facets. Rather we are dealing with a number of newer developments which have, or may have, an important bearing on the ability of marketing to fulfill the enlarged role in sight for it in the years ahead.

In dealing with these developments we make no pretense to being accredited experts in modern marketing. We are more like tourists, being guided by experts in whom we have confidence, but tourists who must somehow find their way in the right direction because of the critical bearing of the terrain on the successful operation of our economy.* The aspects of marketing with which we shall be particularly concerned include:

* In all frankness, it might also be added that we are rather uncomfortable tourists, too. For of the chapters in this book this one created more qualms among more of the authors of the book than all the other chapters combined. But even if we did not succeed in handling it with any high degree of self-satisfaction, the great importance of the subject matter in an economy of abundance such as that we have developed in the United States decisively counselled us not to ignore it. In our efforts we are particularly indebted to Carl Rieser, now associate editor of *Fortune,* for material he brought together while he was marketing editor of *Business Week.*

The striking growth of distribution
New lines of research on consumer wants and motivation
A new promise, partially fulfilled, in advertising
Efforts to gear manufacturing more closely to the market
Mass methods of retail selling
The sales role of consumer credit
The lagging art of civic salesmanship

Geoffrey Crowther, formerly chief editor of the (London) *Economist,* contends that spending operates independently in response to its own mysterious laws. He says:

The flow of spending shows a distressing tendency from time to time just to fall of its own accord. The public, for reasons which are difficult to understand and impossible to predict, from time to time just gets tired of buying. It may be that everybody has filled up their closets, has bought as much as they need of everything, and that nothing new has come along to excite their attention. Nobody quite knows why, but there are times when out of a blue sky the public suddenly decides that it doesn't want to buy any more. This doesn't usually show up so much or so quickly in terms of consumer goods, the things that you can buy at the neighborhood store, as in the purchase of raw materials by the industries of the world. Raw material prices are notoriously unstable, and there are times when for no reason that anybody can predict beforehand the bottom seems to drop out of the demand for raw materials. That is one of the things that can go wrong.*

If Mr. Crowther is right about it, the steady maintenance of a high level of consumption may be in part a function of prayer. However, there is some reason to believe that arrangements of the sort discussed in this chapter have a bearing on our capacity to sustain the high level of consumption essential to fulfillment of the promise of steadily sustained prosperity.

* "The Wealth and Poverty of Nations," Part III of a lecture by Dr. Geoffrey Crowther, Nov. 20, 1956, Claremont, California, pp. 13–14.

GROWTH OF DISTRIBUTION INDUSTRIES

The key to the importance of marketing can be grasped clearly from the following figures on changes in employment by industrial groups over the last eighty years. There has been a marked increase in the relative importance of distribution and other service employment, and it seems fairly evident that this shift will continue. Perhaps as productivity in manufacturing becomes greater, there will even be an acceleration of this shift, which broadly speaking reduces the relative number of those engaged in commodity production and increases that proportion engaged in distributive and other service functions.

The increase since 1870 in the relative importance of employment in distribution and other services is pointed up in a book by Harold Barger of Columbia University.[*] In his study, Barger cites these as the percentages of people employed in nonfarm industries:

	1870	1900	1930	1940	1950
Commodity production	70.0%	62.7%	47.6%	44.4%	40.4%
Construction	5.9	5.8	6.4	7.0	6.4
Commodity distribution	6.1	8.6	12.9	14.4	16.4
Other service	18.0	22.9	33.1	34.2	36.8
	100.0%	100.0%	100.0%	100.0%	100.0%

There is, of course, a difficulty in analyzing these figures. It is impossible to sort out people by occupation and function, except broadly. Manufacturers employ many salesmen. Also, it is evident that a number of people in "other service" industries are performing either directly or indirectly functions

[*] *Distribution's Place In The American Economy Since 1869,* National Bureau of Economic Research, New York, 1955, p. 6.

that are related to marketing, or owe their jobs to a function growing out of the needs of distribution. For instance, a number of jobs in banks, or in other financial institutions, have grown directly out of the financing of consumer goods.

In any case, the growth of mass-distribution and the increasing specialization of function are part and parcel of the same broad movement. What these figures show is the growth of a vastly complex society and economy in the U.S. They also show an increasingly productive society, in which relatively fewer and fewer people are needed to turn out an increasing stream of goods and to grow ever larger crops. But more and more people are needed to market them.

Actually, the factors behind the relative growth of employment in distribution are extremely complicated and not easy to assess. There are at least four major factors involved:

Shorter hours for workers in distribution constitute an important factor. The people who work in these trades had depressingly long hours back in the last century. In 1889, they averaged, in wholesale and retail trades, sixty-six hours a week as against fifty-two in manufacturing. Now the two are approximately even in hours worked, which means that the drastically shortened workweek in distribution required a great increase in number of workers.

Distribution has broadened its scope. More and more goods passed into formal distribution channels as transportation widened the horizons and markets of both manufacturers and farmers who once sold their output in their local markets. Air cargo lines are perhaps going to make the U.S.—from coast to coast—one large local market.

An increasingly large number of functions have been taken on by distribution. The example that immediately comes to mind is packaging. Once packaging ceased to be merely brown paper, a whole new world came into being—and so did more jobs. Now there are service and other functions that accompany a vast outpouring of complicated goods requiring special handling, selling techniques, and repairs.

Productivity in distribution has not kept up with that in manufacturing or farming. During the last century the increase in productivity in distribution has been relatively small. The disparity between productivity gains in distribution and in manufacturing has been great enough to have caused some of the need for additional distribution workers.

The last factor would seem to imply that historically there has been a sharply rising cost of distribution as compared with the cost of production. Actually the cost of distribution rose steadily from the mid-nineteenth century to about 1929. After 1929, it appears to have levelled out. Since that time, distribution and production costs have stayed at about the same ratio. What has happened is that we are doing a much bigger job in distribution—selling more, and more complex, goods to a wider, more varied consumer market.

GEARING MANUFACTURING TO THE MARKET

In addition to more people engaged in distribution, we now have many more people in manufacturing companies whose primary job is to help distributors sell and service manufactured products. Involvement in marketing and distribution has created some profound changes within the manufacturing company's organizational structure.

The classic pattern of industrial organization, of course, was along production and manufacturing lines. Companies grew normally by grouping together those manufacturing facilities that naturally went together. Steel companies, for example, have blast furnaces, open hearths and rolling mills as part of their basic facilities. Expansion and diversification logically grew out of the manufacturing process. The organization of the company's management also flowed out of this pattern. Production was usually the key. It influenced the selling organization as well.

A major change in thinking is now making itself felt. Today, the orientation of manufacturing companies is increasingly toward the market and away from production. In fact, this change has gone so far in some cases that the General Electric Company, as one striking example, now conceives itself to be essentially a marketing rather than a production organization. This thinking flows back through the structure of the company, to the point that marketing needs reach back and dictate the arrangement and grouping of production facilities.

In rough outline, here is how the process works:

The market research department of a manufacturing company is constantly seeking ideas for new products. By interviewing distributors and customers, or by more elaborate techniques, the market research department obtains a wide variety of ideas about products people would like to have. Not long ago, most of these ideas would have been quickly ruled out by the production department as impractical in terms of costs, or perhaps with the idea that it was not feasible to fabricate the products. Today, however, the dream-products represent objectives for product development by the research and engineering teams whose job it is to find ways of producing the new things economically. Out of the combined work of market researchers and production researchers come the final designs for new products that can be made *and sold*.

But at this point, the work of the manufacturer's research organization is just beginning. In order to move a new product in volume once it reaches the consumer market, today's manufacturer takes several steps to aid distribution. These include testing consumer reactions (before a final design for the product is adopted), attractive packaging (for quick recognition and consumer convenience), extensive advertising (so that customers will know the product's advantages and look for it in the store), and education of dealers in the best ways to merchandise the product and to take advantage of the manufacturer's efforts in packaging and advertising.

The several steps taken by the manufacturing company— consumer research, packaging, advertising and dealer education—add up to what has come to be called *pre-selling* the product. (It is an unattractive term reminiscent of pre-digesting a food, but it is descriptive.) In other words, a substantial selling job is done before the retailer takes over. The aim is to increase the effectiveness of the final selling effort by the retailer and make it possible for him to move more goods. As it is attained with increasing effectiveness, it has potentialities for making a key contribution to new sales records. We have neither space nor knowledge to deal definitively with all the advances, or at any rate changes, that are being made in the broad field of marketing as carried on by manufacturing companies. Two developments, however, deserve treatment in some detail because they have such bearing on more effective marketing. These are *consumer research* and improved *national advertising*.

CONSUMER RESEARCH

The gearing of product fabrication more closely to consumer preferences has quite naturally been accompanied by greatly increased emphasis on marketing research.

In its ever-increasing entanglement with the marketing process, industry must reckon with the challenging characteristics of the consumer market. They include the great magnitude of the mass market in the U.S., both geographically and in terms of sheer numbers; the vast outpouring

of goods and products, many of them new and relatively un-
tried; people's ability to withhold their money and defer expenditures for many goods. All these make it wise for firms
to keep a finger on the consumer's pulse, or whatever part
of his being shapes his impulses to buy.

Today, there is increasing emphasis on psychological and
sociological research. While conventional marketing research
continues in large volume, more stress is being put on research into what, in the patois of the operation, makes the
consumer tick—what his underlying attitudes are, what he
wants, what he feels, what he will do next. It is this area of
research that has provided the liveliest new developments in
the field of marketing research during the past decade.

Many of those with credentials in such matters insist that
what passes today for "motivation research" involves no new
techniques. However, it is obvious that though the techniques—from projective tests to depth interviews—may not
be new, they are being put to some new uses.

In one way or another, a considerable amount of research
is being done that is slowly filling in our knowledge of people
as consumers. Here is a partial list of some recent investigations:

- Bell Telephone Laboratories used psychological research to
  find a name for its new long-distance dialing system, the one
  that makes it possible for subscribers to pick up a phone and
  dial anywhere in the country without going through an operator. (The winner: Direct Distance Dialing.)

- Wroe Alderson, a distinguished Philadelphia market researcher,
  is seeking to find women's basic shopping habits through psychological tests. (One question: How many stores will a woman
  go to before she decides to quit?)

- The Chicago Tribune did research to find out people's underlying attitudes towards cigarettes, beer, and cars. (It seemed

they like beer at home, but are unimpressed by advertising that connects it with "men of distinction" or society parties.)

- The Ford Motor Company tested attitudes to find out whether the safety theme in selling cars would backfire. (Answer: No.)

- Philip Morris spent thousands on opinion and habit research before redesigning its latest package for cigarettes. (By putting its Marlboro brand in a *cardboard* package, Philip Morris found out more or less accidentally that this is a kind of package that really sells cigarettes. So Philip Morris cigarettes are now in a box, too.)

An interesting example of how business and academic research get intertwined is provided by the Survey Research Center at the University of Michigan, which has made some of the most important contributions in the consumer research field of the past decade. The Board of Governors of the Federal Reserve System sponsored for a decade one of the two or three surveys of consumer intentions to buy which the University of Michigan researchers carry out each year. In addition, the Federal Reserve is now sponsoring consumer buying intention surveys conducted every three months by the United States Census Bureau. That this august and exalted body of money managers should be sponsoring a doorbell-ringing process of probing a cross section of consumers, in an effort to divine their attitudes and intentions, is a further reflection of the broad sweep of the newer techniques of consumer research.

Interest in studies of consumer buying plans attained new intensity in 1958. Continuing surveys of consumer buying plans were initiated by two of the leading research organizations in the U.S., the National Bureau of Economic Research and the National Industrial Conference Board. The National Bureau conducts its surveys by mail among subscribers to a consumer magazine, *Consumer Reports,* while the Conference Board interviews consumers by means of telephone calls.

In addition to investigating consumer buying intentions the Survey Research Center's surveys also aim to check on how incomes, prices and general business conditions affect consumer attitudes toward spending on durable goods and housing. With a bold adaptation of traditional statistical techniques, some of the results of these surveys are embodied in indices of the consumer's state of mind—in degrees of optimism and pessimism—about his own economic prospects and those of business generally.

Economists are still arguing over whether the Michigan studies do indeed forecast the level of consumer buying and saving. The basic question: Is this level predicated on consumer attitudes or rather on the level of income, which goes back to economic conditions anterior to anyone's attitude? However, the surveys have won at least one blue ribbon—for correctly indicating that auto purchases would soar during 1955, when almost everyone else figured on a normal year. The prediction came true; 7.2 million cars were bought by consumers that year. The Survey Research Center surveys called the turn on the 1958 auto market, too.

Much consumer research is still directed to determining an immediate advertising "pitch." For example, many cigarette companies, faced with the cancer scare a couple of years back, quickly shifted from health (there had been a doctor or health claim in practically every ad) to happiness or "pleasure" as the goal that should dictate the buying of their product. In fact, most cigarette companies today are selling a "pleasure" brand as well as a "filter" cigarette.

To be sure, these shifts were partly the result of a sterner attitude toward cigarette advertising claims by the Federal Trade Commission. But the shift toward advertising "pleasure" was also in large part a product of motivation research and specifically of the work of the motivation researcher, Dr. Ernest Dichter, who had been preaching the pleasure doctrine for several years. His advice, based on much depth and

other phychological probing was: Connect by subtle suggestion—or at least by as subtle suggestion as the cigarette
industry finds possible—the idea of cigarettes with the idea
of a moment of relaxation, reward for having accomplished
something, or pleasurable moments in the past.

But more and more consumer research is taking on another function, one that may become increasingly important
as time goes on. Namely, this is to find out the kind of goods
people *really want.* One way of doing this is for stores to use
electronic computers to report at the end of the working
day what consumers actually purchased during that day, and
how much inventory is on hand to meet the next day's demand. Large scale purchases of any item can quickly be
translated into reorders. Thus the female consumer's fancies
in hemlines and shoe styles can be quickly converted into
additional sales. Early in 1959, the director of research of
Sears Roebuck underlined this possibility when he said,
"There has been a growing feeling with some of us that
electronic equipment could serve the merchandising end
of our business as well as or better than the accounting end." *

Perhaps this new trend in consumer research will do
nothing more than tell manufacturers what they should have
known all along through reasonably acute observations of
their own. But if it does that, it will at least not be playing
a negative role in improving the marketing process.

ADVERTISING AS AN ECONOMIC STABILIZER

In recent years the total expenditures for advertising in
the United States ($10.1 billion in 1958) have accounted for
almost 2.5 percent of the nation's total volume of business.

* R. M. Seyfarth, Director of Research, Sears Roebuck Company, in a paper
delivered before the National Retail Merchants Association, Jan. 15, 1959.

But in most discussions of the performance of the American economy by economists, particularly academic economists, advertising plays little or no part.

One of the explanations for this strange void is to be found in what might be termed a professional or cultural lag. For most of the time span of human existence in most

Growth in Advertising

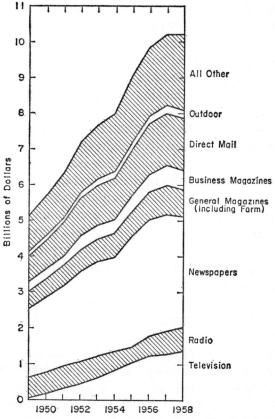

Printers' Ink; McGraw-Hill Dept. Econ.

Total advertising dollar volume approximately doubled between 1949 and 1958. Every advertising medium, including radio, has increased its revenues since 1949.

places on this planet, the pressing economic problem has been that of producing enough to satisfy elemental human wants. Hence economists, understandably enough, tended to acquire something of a fixation on problems of production which makes it difficult for them to shift to the economics of marketing and selling, even though in the American economy abundance has made this a top priority field of inquiry.

The void is also accounted for in part by the fact that when economists have looked at the performance of advertising they have not liked what they have seen—for two principal reasons. One of the reasons, stated very broadly and loosely, is that advertising has seemed to many of them to be simply a device for switching customers from one product to another, without making any consequential contribution to consumption as a whole. The other reason is that where they have, at least for the sake of the argument, made the concession that advertising might help produce sales, they have observed that advertising has usually been cut during recessions when sales have declined and been increased during booms when sales have been expanding. This has led to the conclusion that insofar as it contributes to increasing sales, advertising does it in a completely perverse way, shrinking when more sales are needed and expanding when sales are going well anyway—thus becoming a positive contributor to economic instability.

Over the years there has been much in the record of advertising to support the contention that it has been a force for economic instability, contracting when it should be expanding and *vice versa*. As the chart indicates, the volume of advertising followed the volume of sales into the depths of the Great Depression of the early thirties and followed the same general course again in the lapse from recovery in the late thirties. Since the end of World War II, however, advertising has shown very definite symptoms of becoming a stabilizing economic force. It has given increasing evidence of being a positive force to expand consumption.

In both the recessions of 1948–1949 and 1953–1954, as the chart also shows, the dollar volume of advertising did not go down as sales dipped. In both cases advertising expenditures rose and thus made a contribution to keeping these recessions quite mild. On the basis of this constructive performance, advertising was hailed as having come of age in fulfilling the role of pressing for sales when sales were needed rather than going into retreat. During the recession of 1957–1958, however, it developed that the arrival of advertising at economic maturity had been assumed a bit prematurely. The volume of advertising fell into the old pattern of going down with sales, but it did not fall anywhere near as far or as long as it had during some earlier recessions. In fact, between 1957

Corporate Sales and Advertising Expenditures

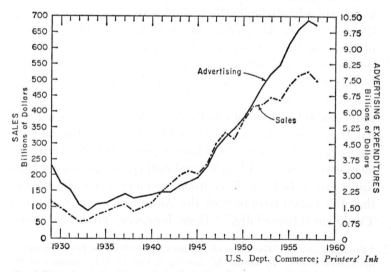

U.S. Dept. Commerce; *Printers' Ink*

The dollar volume of advertising expenditures did not follow the downward curve of business in 1949 and 1954. Even in 1958, when advertising did reflect the recession, it declined at a rate of only one-third the drop in business.

and 1958 there was a drop year to year of only 1.5 percent in the volume of advertising, in contrast to a drop of 4.5 percent in sales in trade and manufacturing.

This record provides the basis for hope that advertising will come consistently to provide both a much more expansive and stabilizing force than it has historically, by being much more steadily sustained in the face of sales adversity. This hope is also backed up by analysis of the revolution in income distribution to which Chapter 4 was devoted. It is argued that the controlling business reason why advertising expenditures tended to collapse during earlier depressions and recessions was that there was really no point in trying to persuade consumers to buy more because, by and large, their purchasing power was quite thoroughly shattered. Now, however, income is so widely and deeply distributed that such reasoning becomes largely irrelevant and out of date.

In its upward sweep since the end of World War II, the volume of advertising in the United States has far outstripped the increase in the volume of business generally. The significance of this development lies not only in its reflection of the increased intensity of effort to make sales to an ever more bountifully stocked consuming public, but also in the broader and richer base it has provided for the services of the press, radio and television both in the fields of communication and entertainment. "Advertising provides the general press with about two-thirds of its total income, and virtually all of the income of those providing TV and radio programs comes from this source. Indeed, it is upon revenue from advertising that the entire structure of the American press, radio and TV depends financially." * Here, however, our primary con-

---

* From a paper on "The Place of Business Publications in the Economy of the United States," by Dexter M. Keezer, at the Twelfth Congress of the International Federation of the Periodical Press, Copenhagen, Denmark, May 1956.

cern with advertising is its performance as a marketing instrumentality.

THE IMPACT OF TELEVISION

The most striking enlargement of the role of advertising in the marketing process in recent years has, of course, come through the development of television. In one of those spectacular technological surges that have characterized the economic development of the United States, no less than 44 million homes were equipped with TV sets in the brief period of thirteen years, between 1946 and 1958. And today it is the unusual home that does not house one of the total of about 50 million TV sets in use. The census of housing for 1960 will no doubt show that a TV set is more universal a piece of household equipment in the United States than a bathtub.

In its dimension as a marketing instrumentality, TV has opened up the possibility of reaching the national consumer market more completely than ever, for the obvious reason that products can actually be *seen*—and in action if that serves the selling purpose—as well as described to potential customers in their homes. This has given manufacturers of consumers' goods a broad new avenue through which to try to "pre-sell" their wares.

The usefulness of TV in selling to industrial consumers is much more limited because the products involved are generally highly specialized and the potential customers for them so limited in number that it is wasteful to try to reach them through a mass medium such as TV.

One consequence of the massiveness of the TV approach to the national market is that its services are very expensive to engage. For example, in 1959 it cost about $60,000 to engage the facilities (time charges only) of a television broadcasting network for a half-hour evening show. This is

exclusive of the cost of the entertainment, which for some of
the big TV shows runs as much as $150,000 per hour.

The high cost of TV is commonly cited as a key reason
for the fact that in 1957 and 1958 its great surge as an advertising medium showed signs of playing out. Another reason
assigned is that the amount of time available for TV entertainment is all out of proportion (on the high side) to the
quality of the entertainment which TV producers have found
it possible to provide. Also, of course, there is the fact that
the original novelty of the technical marvel of TV has substantially worn off, and along with it some of the zest for both
its selling efforts and its entertainment, upon which it depends primarily to bring the customers in.

There is no reason to doubt, however, that TV has made
and will continue to make a major contribution to mass marketing in the United States. As the chart on page 103 indicates, the expansion of TV advertising has not been a sub-
stitute for other kinds of advertising. It has been primarily
an addition to advertising media which were in business
before it burst upon the scene.

As the result of this expanded advertising effort all along
the line, goods move faster off the shelves, and the job of
the retail merchant is simplified. He does not need to devote
as much time or floor space to demonstrating products or to
displays to catch attention. If the system has worked according to design, the customer has already seen what he wants
to buy—in a national advertisement. And the merchant can
concentrate his efforts on having the right stock of goods at
the right price.

MASS METHODS OF MERCHANDISING

Above all, the retailer can now concentrate on volume—
not on making individual sales, but on moving goods in

volume, at a lower distribution cost per unit. This is not the traditional way of running a small shop. However, it is the way that large chains have always hoped to operate, and do operate in large degree today with the help of the manufacturers' "pre-selling" efforts.

The most obvious case of mass merchandising is the supermarket, where food and similar products (such as beer or soap) are purchased largely on the basis of brand advertising, with no help from clerks except at the check-out counter. Some big drugstores, some large gasoline stations and an increasing number of "5 & 10s" have gone on this basis. But the really striking trend is the adoption of "supermarket merchandising" by stores selling higher-priced goods—autos, appliances and clothing.

The basic idea is simply that a merchant backed by manufacturers' national advertising can satisfy the customer very well if he just offers the advertised goods at low cost—in plain showrooms, with very little service, at low profit margins but in tremendous volume. The idea of selling more units at less profit per unit, but at a greater over-all return, has worked out successfully for more and more retailers. The Robert Hall clothing chain has had notable success, operating with a mark-up of about 30 percent compared with the usual 45 percent of its competitors. And the "discount houses"—low-price, self-service stores for household goods—have taken such a large share of the home appliance and furniture business that department stores are now following the trend to "supermarket" merchandising.

In the aggregate these mass methods of merchandising constitute a revolution in marketing that is much more than a pale companion-piece of the revolution in production. For the first time, we are getting higher productivity—per worker, and per foot of floor space—in retailing as well as in manufacturing. We are reducing the number of people needed to

distribute the basic items made by our mass-production industries.* To put the matter differently, improvements in retailing methods give promise of moving goods off the shelves
as fast as improved manufacturing methods speed up the
production of them. However, the number of workers in distribution trades may well continue to increase, because we
can afford more and more of the luxury goods and services
that require personal attention.

MORE TO COME

As in the case of production methods, the revolution in
distribution methods is still in an early stage. Supermarket-
ing and discounting are relatively new practices. Much is still
to be learned before consumer research or national advertising can be as effective as their proponents hope. But no
one doubts they will become far more effective than they are
today. Consequently, retail executives look forward to the
time when inventory will turn over far more rapidly because
it is better selected and better advertised, and when volume
per foot of floor space is far higher than now.

In the case of the food market, where mass merchandising
started, near-automation is already on the horizon. Some of
the large supermarts have installed vending machines, from
which shoppers can make their purchases in off-hours. As
more and more items become standardized, this practice
seems sure to increase. It is to be hoped and expected that
retailing will continue to provide more outlets for creative

* A notable exception to this statement occurs in the transportation industries, which are outstanding for their archaic equipment and rife with
inefficient practices. "Featherbedding" work rules in trucking, railroading
and longshoring constitute one obstacle to what otherwise might be impressive cost reductions in these fields. In food distribution, for example,
increased costs of trucking have offset many of the economies made by
supermarkets in their own operations. Some of these costs have been
charged to outright racketeering.

sales effort than those offered by the vending machine. The demand for less-standardized items will provide those outlets. But mechanized merchandising, the ultimate development of mass merchandising, will take us a step further in the basic task of distribution—to move larger quantities of goods faster.

THE SALES ROLE OF CONSUMER CREDIT *

The role of consumer credit in retail selling is essentially the same as that of supermarket methods—to help move the goods faster. If a man waits until he can save the money to buy a car, he may defer his purchase a year or more. If he uses consumer credit, it still takes more than a year (perhaps more than two years) to pay for the car. But it moves out of the dealer's showroom as soon as the decision to buy has been made.

In the case of department stores, the more liberal use of credit has served to extend the "purchase horizon" for such things as appliances, furniture and expensive clothing. Few people can afford to buy a refrigerator, a new bedroom set or a $130 overcoat out of one week's paycheck. Charge accounts give them a month or two—in some cases three months—to pay. And the new "revolving credit" plans, which permit the customer to have continuing credit with the store, up to a fixed dollar amount, mean that he can pay for a typical purchase over as long as six months.

Let us assume that a newly married couple can save $50

* It is also possible, and in some cases desirable, to treat consumer credit as an aspect of credit policy generally, or as one item in the general picture of consumer income and savings. We have elected to deal with it here from the more limited viewpoint of the retailer—as a sales stimulant—not because we are unmindful of the other aspects, but because the most important impact of consumer credit in particular, as opposed to general credit policy, is on the volume of retail sales.

a month to buy furniture and the set they want costs $300. The store can sell this set at once on a $300 revolving credit plan and collect the price over six months. In addition, before the six months is over, the purchasers will be sufficiently below their credit limit ($300) to buy some new spring clothes under the same credit plan. If they were saving up to make a lump payment for furniture, they might eventually buy both the furniture and the clothes. But the goods would not move as fast. What the credit plans really do for the department store or the auto dealer is to speed up the buying decision and move the goods at the time when the desire to buy is strong—a desire that might cool in the months it would take to save up.

A new development in this field is the entry of giant-sized New York City banks into the charge account business. For many years now banks in other cities have offered various types of charge account plans with success. But it was not until the end of 1958 that the Chase Manhattan Bank started its charge account plan for retail dealers and consumers. Within six months it had registered 5,000 retailers (locations) and about 300,000 individual charge account card holders. The acceptance of the plan is growing rapidly, with dealers soliciting their customers to join and customers asking their dealers to become members of the plan.

The First National City Bank in following the Ready-Credit Plan of the First National Bank of Boston extends a line of credit ($120 to $3,000) to approved personal loan applicants. Qualified people are then able to draw checks against their line of credit. Other large banks offer credit plans that are essentially similar to one of the types described above.

There are some who view the continual temptation of the consumer with consumer credit as a vicious practice. They contend that it does away with such old-fashioned virtues as thrift and prudence, and leads families to contract larger debts than they can sensibly hope to repay. Of course, on the other side of this same argument there is the more cheerful view that meeting consumer credit commitments is a form of saving of which the commitments act as monitor and that therefore consumer credit is an incentive to thrift. There is no doubt, however, that arrangements for consumer credit can be stretched beyond sensible limits—and frequently have been. But representatives of both the stores and the credit companies report that, where reasonable terms are required, one effect of increased consumer credit has been to make people keep better track of their obligations and budget more carefully. More people are borrowing, but fewer borrowers are defaulting, than in prewar years.

At times when consumer credit has shown an especially rapid expansion, as it did in 1955 and again in early 1959, it has caused a special case of shivers to those who feel that a high level of consumer indebtedness will lead us eventually to economic disaster. However, such violent spurts in the use of installment credit have usually been short-lived. The longer-term trend shows only a modest increase, with total consumer credit rising from 11 percent of consumer disposable income in 1940 to an estimated 14 percent at mid-1959. This gradual rise from prewar levels appears simply to reflect the increased number of families who are eligible for credit, with today's more even distribution of income.*

Actually, the expansion in consumer debt over this period has been at about the same rate as the increase in life insurance, savings deposits and other forms of thrift. Thus, although people are borrowing more against their incomes,

* For a comprehensive report on the role of consumer credit in a growing economy see the five-volume report *Consumer Instalment Credit*, Board of Governors of the Federal Reserve System, United States Government Printing Office, Washington, 1957.

they are saving more also. In fact, the proportion of income saved has been slightly higher since 1950 than it was in the years before World War II. This relatively high savings rate suggests that, with the great increase in scope and variety of credit facilities, it may be possible to accelerate consumer expenditures by more intensive use of credit over the next decade.

There is good reason to believe that, as time passes, people will indeed save relatively less for *future* purchases and buy relatively more from their *present* incomes. By using consumer credit, they can "buy now, pay later." And more people are doing so, as old taboos against the use of credit are broken down. This would not need to involve a wave of foolish borrowing by people who cannot afford to do so. It has been estimated that only about one-third of the people whose incomes and savings make them excellent credit risks are now making use of such credit facilities. As more of these people speed up their purchases by the use of time-payment plans, there is created the potential for a great expansion in consumer spending. This product, like any other, requires marketing. But the vigorous advertising campaigns of banks and finance companies are making credit more popular. So are the "revolving credit" plans of well-known department stores. And credit is being extended to fields like travel and entertainment where it was never used until recently.

The upshot of all this is that within ten years, perhaps half again as many families as now will be taking advantage of consumer credit, not from "loan sharks" but from the banks and stores (as well as the established auto finance companies) with which they regularly do business. The impact is hard to estimate. Even if consumer credit adds only 1 or 2 percent to consumers' spendable income, that will be $4 billion to $8 billion per year at the 1965 level.

CIVIC SALESMANSHIP—A LAGGING ART

Newer methods of marketing, designed to see to it that the rich American consuming public does not exercise its broad option not to consume if it sees fit, are largely the creation of private enterprise. This, it is argued by some, leads to an ill-balanced economic society in which badly needed civic services, such as those for education and metropolitan housekeeping, languish while products and services pushed by "Madison Avenue" (the symbolic and in substantial measure the physical center of the advertising business in the United States) pile up higher and higher.

There is clearly some factual foundation for this line of reflection. Even in a society which insists on providing a large part of its formal education free of charge, it is a striking commentary, made by President Nathan Pusey of Harvard University, that whereas average student debt for college education is about $20, average family debt for durable goods (including housing) is about $3,000.*

In a somewhat similar line of contrast it has been observed:

. . . we have over 7 million individually-owned pleasure boats and are spending over a billion dollars a year on them; but many of the streams and rivers on which they are operated double as open sewers.

In New York City we have sent scores of magnificent buildings up into the sky in the last decade, but the sky into which we have sent them is so smoggy and soot-laden that it is almost possible to mine a week's fallout. And not far from the bases of these handsome structures are the wretched gang-breeding slums which expand apace as the more prosperous city dwellers take off for the

* "The Need for Public Support," an address delivered at the forty-first Annual Meeting of the American Council on Education, Chicago, Oct. 10, 1958.

suburbs. Much the same sort of smog and sink holes characterize many other of our large cities.

It has been estimated that on any given day there are 50 million tons of manmade dirt in the air above the United States. The cost of this mess in damaged crops, defaced buildings, ruined clothes and delayed traffic by land and air is $2 billion a year. The damage to health and happiness has, so far as I know, not been calculated. But 12 cents a year per capita is about what most cities pay to eliminate this manmade blight.*

In his best-selling book, *The Affluent Society*,† Professor John Kenneth Galbraith of Harvard University argues that economic wisdom dictates that we in the United States stop putting so much emphasis on increasing production (we are rich enough already) and concentrate on using what we have in such a way that needed civic services are not slighted. This is, of course, one way to approach the problem presented. But to give up greater production and economic growth as an objective because we have not learned how to use all of the results wisely would seem to partake of throwing the baby out with the bath. A far more salubrious solution would seem to be to develop more inventiveness in creating a demand for more and better civic services (fine schools, clean streets, clean streams, clean air, etc.) as essentials of a society we can well afford.

In the meantime, while we suffer from a shortage of what might be termed effective civic salesmanship, our society will remain more skimpy than it should be in providing some important social amenities. But it does not follow from this unfortunate fact that our central thesis in this volume—that we have the prospect of quite steadily sustained pros-

* From a lecture presenting "Some Observations on the Economics of Abundance," by Dexter M. Keezer, at Occidental College, Los Angeles, California, May 1958.
† Houghton Mifflin Company, Boston, 1958.

perity in the decade ahead—is thereby tarnished. It simply means that we do not have as high a quality of community economic and civic life as we can afford.

CONCLUSION

The upshot of the discussion in this chapter is that there is substantial foundation for the expectation that in the years ahead the marketing sector of the American economy will successfully perform its crucial role in providing relatively sustained prosperity. In terms of the share of our total work force engaged in marketing, we are increasing our marketing facilities more rapidly than our manufacturing facilities. And the effectiveness of these facilities, in wholesale and retail trade, is being increased, particularly by beginning the marketing process with manufacturing and carrying it right through to the ultimate consumer.

Manufacturing firms are making a key contribution to more efficient marketing by improved consumer research and product design, by greatly enlarged national advertising programs, by effective packaging and other aids to dealer display. At the retail level, mass merchandising techniques promise to lower costs and hold down prices to the consumer —as well as make it possible to offer a greater volume of goods for sale with the same personnel and facilities. Finally, more widespread use of consumer credit is making it easier to purchase the "big ticket" items, such as cars and home furnishings—by making "little ones out of big ones," in terms of the monthly cash payments.

None of this means that marketing has become or has the promise of becoming a simple, mechanical process. There is, and will continue to be, much art in marketing at all stages. And there will continue to be need of inventive and imaginative development of the art as, in the phrasing of Dean

Charles C. Abbott of the Graduate School of Business Administration of the University of Virginia, "*the* business problem shifts from being one of production to being one of marketing, distributing and selling." * But it is a lively and developing art, and one giving promise of not letting the economy down too badly in this crucial sector.

* In a speech before the Richmond Chapter of the Virginia Manufacturers Association, Dec. 11, 1958.

The Role of Government

In all of its ramifications, government—Federal, state and local—has the potential of decisively affecting the nation's prosperity, for better or for worse. As a purchaser of goods and services, government now accounts for about one-fifth of the nation's output. How it handles this tremendous procurement job has a vital bearing on how well the economy as a whole performs. And so does the way in which government collects the taxes to pay its bills, or most of them.

By a myriad of laws and regulations, in addition to those directly concerned with getting and spending money, government shapes the course and level of business. The laws and regulations follow airplanes into the upper ether, they follow miners deep into the earth, and there is very little activity on the earth's surface which is not touched by them. To provide even a summary of the ways by which government, through laws and regulations, affects in a consequential way our prosperity and the chances of sustaining it would call for a much bigger volume than this is designed to be.

However, to form a balanced judgment about the prospects

119

for consistently maintaining prosperity over the next decade it is necessary to deal, at least in broad strokes, with the government's part in shaping these prospects. Will it manage the spending of its large part of the national income so as to promote the degree of *both* growth and stability essential to the maintenance of a high level of prosperity? Will it handle its tax collections in the same way? Will the Federal government discharge the constitutional duty, assigned to Congress, to "coin money and regulate the value thereof" so as to avoid disastrous destruction of the value of money through inflation? Will the Federal government's enforcement of the antitrust laws adequately protect the indispensable competitive foundations of our economy? And will the political forces be such that rocking the economic boat or trying to keep it steady will be the more alluring political performance?

It is with such questions that these remarks and the three chapters to follow will deal. The next chapter will deal with the role of government as a spender and tax collector in shaping our prosperity and the prospects of continuing it. The chapter to follow will explore, primarily with reference to Federal antitrust law enforcement, the prospect of having our economy sufficiently lubricated and animated by competition to provide one of the most essential foundations of continuing prosperity. Then, to wind up the consideration of the place of government in shaping the future course of our prosperity, we shall examine the possibility of avoiding a debilitating plague of price inflation. Here we shall be particularly concerned with wage increases which outstrip the capacity of employers to pay them without increasing prices.

In dealing with the government's part in shaping the course of economic developments over the next decade we are making one key assumption in the field of politics. It is that there will not be a violent swing to the left or right by the party in control of the Federal government, but that the controlling policies in the field of political economy will remain clustered along the middle of the road.

As matters stand, both major political parties are firmly committed to the dual objective of maintaining a high level of employment, production and purchasing power and of sustaining what has been established by the experience of recent years as the going rate of economic growth. And both parties are also committed to attaining these objectives through a free competitive economy which, viewed in the light of our history and traditions, is the conservative way of doing it.*

* The basic national policy, adopted by overwhelming bipartisan majorities in both Houses of Congress, is stated formally in the Employment Act of 1946:

"The Congress hereby declared that *it is the continuing policy and responsibility of the Federal Government to use all practicable means* consistent with its needs and obligations and other essential considerations of national policy, with the assistance and cooperation of industry, agriculture, labor, and State and local governments, to coordinate and utilize all its plans, functions, and resources for the purpose of creating and maintaining, in a manner calculated to foster and promote free competitive enterprise and the general welfare, conditions under which there will be afforded useful employment opportunities, including self-employment, for those able, willing, and seeking to work, and *to promote maximum employment, production, and purchasing power*." (italics supplied)

The House of Representatives, in its final action on the Employment Act of 1946, approved the conference report by a vote of 320–84, Republicans voting 114–67 for adoption of the report, Democrats 204–17. The Senate approved the report by a voice vote. In 1945, it had voted 71–10 (six Republicans and four Democrats voting against) for passage of the Senate bill "to establish a Government policy to promote full employment." In the conference, the House managers succeeded in softening the objective from "full" to "maximum" employment.

The Presidential conventions of both parties have reinforced this commitment. In 1948, for instance, the Republican platform declared that government "should take all needed steps . . . to promote a stable economy so that men and women need not fear the loss of their jobs or the threat of economic hardships through no fault of their own." And in 1956, the plat-

If either party were to make a successful drive to carry the country to the extreme right or left in economic policy, our calculations of economic prospects over the years ahead would, of course, be drastically modified. This does not by any means imply we are assuming that regardless of which major party is in power in Washington, or decisive parts of it, the policies shaping economic performance will be just the same.

Both in general attitude and on specific economic issues we expect there will continue to be very consequential differences between the major parties and between shifting coalitions of more or less conservative, or radical, fragments of them. For example, as a very, very broad proposition we expect the Republicans to look for economic prosperity (which is probably the most important ingredient of political success) by doing those things and providing those incentives which make business firms and their employees thrive. In seeking the same end, we expect the Democrats to continue to concentrate both their oratory and some key political efforts on building up the "purchasing power" of the masses and thus having it nourish and invigorate the business community.

From these general political attitudes of the major parties, or at least major parts of the parties, flow important disagreements on specific issues. For example, given the possibility of tax reduction, the Democrats tend to favor the individual

form adopted by the Republican convention proclaimed that "the purpose of the Republican Party is to establish and maintain a peaceful world and build at home a dynamic prosperity in which every citizen fairly shares."

The Democratic Party pledged itself in 1956, if elected, to strive to attain a number of "full prosperity objectives for all American families." These specific goals included a national product of $500 billion "in real terms"; "an increase of 20 percent or better in the average standard of living"; and an increase in the annual income of all Americans, "with special emphasis on those with incomes below $2,000."

taxpayer, while the Republicans have more interest in relieving the burdens of business firms and, through them, the burdens of their employees. In passing, we might remark that purely from a vote-getting point of view this general posture of the Democrats seems much more profitable.

However, with all their conflicts on specific economic issues and in general policy, the fact remains that the major political parties are operating well toward the middle of the road. We realize that in assuming that they will continue to do this over the next decade or so, we are in a sense simply reaffirming our optimistic estimate of the economic outlook over this period. Our expectation is that the economy will turn in a rather consistently good performance in the years ahead. If it were to turn out otherwise and we were to be plagued by a severe recession or depression, we would expect to see those seeking to exercise political leadership swinging toward much more radical positions on economic policy than have prevailed in the postwar period.

But both on the basis of what we see in prospect in the economic realm and what has happened, we believe that our assumption that our major political parties will be traveling not far from the middle of the road is reasonably valid. We have not yet fully succeeded in fulfilling the promise to make every man a king, on which the late Huey Long made such a meteoric political ascent. But, as brought out in Chapter 4 we have gone a long, long way toward getting all Americans into the "middle class." This, we believe, reinforces the validity of the assumption that there will be relatively little political nourishment in political extremism over the stretch of years ahead.

THE ROLE OF GOVERNMENT

CHAPTER SIX

Government's Expanding Role

The role of government in our economic life is far larger today than is agreeable to many people, and vastly larger than before World War II. Government revenues absorbed 12 percent of personal income and over half of all corporate income in 1958. Government purchases took more than 20 percent of the national output of goods and services. The administration of these revenues and expenditures cannot help but affect both private investment and private consumption.*

The present chapter deals with the influence of these government decisions on collecting and spending a large share of the national income. The effect of government regulatory policies, in such varied fields as resources, business competition and pricing, money and credit, are dealt with in subsequent chapters.

In discussing the influence of government action on our prospects for growth and stability, we shall first take up the matter of defense expenditure, which is the preponderant sphere of government action, and show how large-scale defense on a permanent basis has changed the role of government in the economy. We then turn to the general subject

---

* The Federal, state and local governments employ 10 million people, and control $200 billion of tangible assets. For a further statement of how importantly this affects the total economy, see Solomon Fabricant, *Government in Economic Life*, 35th Annual Report of the National Bureau of Economic Research, New York, pp. 1–15.

of Federal budget policy, and the part that may be played by specific changes in tax or spending programs. We conclude with a discussion of the "automatic stabilizers" provided by such programs as unemployment insurance, and a summary of the total contribution of government toward growth and stability.

THE ARSENAL ECONOMY

When President Franklin D. Roosevelt described the United States as the "arsenal of democracy," he was speaking of our emergency role in World War II. Few people thought then that the U.S. had taken on the problems of an arsenal state for many years to come. But indeed it has. Except for what proved a temporary demobilization in 1946–1947, the U.S. has been continuously involved with the problems of war and defense for the past eighteen years. The cost of defense and taxes to pay for it have made the Federal government a major factor in our economic life.

One of the first policy decisions of the Eisenhower administration was to put the defense program on a long-term basis, instead of proposing new programs as each foreign crisis occurs. Since 1953, we have had some reduction in defense spending. But the slimmed-down program is on a permanent footing. Smaller in scale than the World War II program, and less feverish than the Korean rearmament, it is nevertheless a very large program, aimed at defending the United States from aggression by the largest military power in the rest of the world.

National security expenditures are estimated at over $46 billion in calendar 1958,* of which $42 billion was for the

* After this chapter was completed, total national security expenditures included in the gross national product was replaced by national defense expenditures—representing a somewhat smaller coverage than national security. The new defense expenditures component corresponds closely with the "major national security" category of the U.S. budget.

Department of Defense and the Atomic Energy Commission (the remainder consisting of foreign military aid and expenditures on civilian defense and mobilization). These two agencies employ 77 percent of all Federal employees. They purchase as much "hardware" (i.e., durable goods, such as missiles, aircraft, ordnance, machine tools and atomic reactors) as all the manufacturing firms in the United States are spending for new plants and equipment this year.* Defense business is regarded as a continuing business not just by aircraft companies, but by such firms as General Motors, General Electric and Westinghouse, which have permanent divisions with permanent staffs to handle defense work. The Eisenhower administration has stated that its long-range

National Security Expenditures

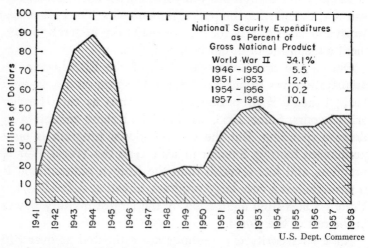

National Security Expenditures
as Percent of
Gross National Product

World War II	34.1%
1946 – 1950	5.5
1951 – 1953	12.4
1954 – 1956	10.2
1957 – 1958	10.1

U.S. Dept. Commerce

Over the years since 1941, the curve of national security expenditures resembles a picture of a roller coaster. In the period since 1954, however, the ups and downs have been flattened out considerably.

* Total expenditures of the Department of Defense are larger than the national product of Canada, Japan, China or India and more than the total expenditures of all our state and local governments.

policy is to maintain the present level of preparedness as far into the future as we now can see.

Moreover, this defense may have to be maintained indefinitely in a world where the rapid pace of scientific development is sure to produce new weapons that greatly increase the potential of an aggressive power—and so demand an equally great effort in time, money and scientific manpower on behalf of defense. The cheapness (at first glance) of an atomic attack on the Soviet Union—the "once and for all" method of dealing with the threat—has appealed to some amateur strategists. But the United States is committed, by world opinion and our own moral standards, to a posture of defense, not aggression or "preventive war." And the cost of this defense, continuing over many years, comes high.

Obviously, if we did not devote as much of our manpower, particularly scientific and technical manpower, to the defense program, we might make greater progress in other fields. (Although it should be noted, in passing, that feedback controls, electronic computers, TV, synthetic rubber and a host of other features of postwar America owe much to military developments in World War II.) Furthermore, if we did not have to pay for a defense program, it might not be necessary to maintain Federal taxes at rates that take more than half of all corporate and of many personal incomes. Capital would be released for other fields of development. The argument may, therefore, be advanced that the defense program is a millstone around the neck of the U.S. economy and prevents it from growing at the maximum rate.

To be sure, defense is not the only reason for government expenditures or for Federal taxes. But it is the preponderant part of the Federal government's role in the U.S. economy. In the budget for fiscal year 1960 (July 1, 1959–June 30, 1960) defense spending accounts for nearly two-thirds of total budget expenditures, and many Congressmen and military leaders have criticized this as inadequate. Most of the remaining government expenditures, except for interest on the Federal debt, are for projects to support the private economy in its productive efforts (i.e., schools, highways, power dams, statistical and technical services) or else they consist of income payments to veterans, farmers and others who can spend the money for consumer goods. But the defense program is a specialized matter. Any aid it gives to private productive activity is purely incidental. Its primary purpose is to keep the results of this activity from disappearing in a few days of atomic warfare. To have this protection, we must give up a certain amount of progress. We are as beholden to the Strategic Air Force as the farmers and craftsmen of the Middle Ages were to their feudal lords, who possessed the ultimate weapons of that day.

How much are we giving up? How much will the growth of the U.S. economy, and particularly the part represented by a rising standard of living (consumer expenditures), be held back by the diversion of resources to defense?

As we see it, the diversion need not prevent a satisfactory rate of growth for the economy because:

1. efficiency in the science of war, and the procurement of weapons of war, will hold down the dollar amounts that must be devoted to the defense program

2. the yearly increase in productivity of our economy is sufficient to absorb some increase in defense expenditures with a fairly wide margin left for increased living standards

3. a better program of developing scientific manpower—which is the greatest bottleneck in both the defense program and civilian production—can alleviate the principal strain which the defense program now imposes.

Efficiency in the arts of war is a subject with such appalling human implications that it may seem cold to discuss it in terms of costs and taxes. It is, nevertheless, a fact that our defense establishment is getting more efficient in terms of destructive power. One missile of the latest type, equipped with atomic explosives, can deliver more destruction than a score of World War II bombers carrying conventional explosives. Ships with atomic engines can remain at sea indefinitely, eliminating fleets of tankers. Relatively small bodies of troops carried by helicopter can accomplish scouting missions that used to require large task forces. Even the foot-weary infantry man has had his firepower increased many times since World War II by the use of new recoilless hand artillery pieces.

To be sure, the potential enemy has this sort of weapons, too. But since a potential war may be fought to a finish by relatively small numbers of men, carrying weapons of enormous destructive power, the long-run cost of a defense establishment is the cost of complexity in weapons and a high degree of training for scientific and military personnel, not the cost of masses of men and equipment. This means that if we are sufficiently ingenious in the design of weapons (with cost, as well as performance, a factor to be considered) and sufficiently alert in training large numbers of technicians, we can hold the cost of defense within bearable limits.

We shall return to the problem of technical manpower (which is also the key to development of complex weapons) in a few paragraphs. But let us assume for the moment that defense spending can be held relatively constant over the next five years. Perhaps an increase of $2–3 billion in the annual budget must be allowed to take advantage of major technological "breakthroughs," and there will be some additional cost increase. But it is not unreasonable to assume that total defense spending can be maintained within a range of $5 billion above the fiscal 1959 figure.* This will scarcely be enough drag on economic growth to be concerned about.

Assuming 3.5 percent growth in national product each year after 1959, our total gross national product by 1963 should exceed $540 billion (in 1958 prices). Defense spending of $51 billion—$5 billion higher than in 1958—will be only 9.5 percent of GNP, compared with 10.6 percent in 1958 and 14 percent in 1953, the year of peak defense spending under the Korean War program. Moreover, defense spending under this schedule would diminish in importance, compared with the potential tax revenues of the Federal government. At present tax rates, a 3.5 percent annual increase in gross national product will raise Federal revenues at least $12 billion by 1963. Thus, the defense program could be raised considerably more than we are estimating here and still leave ample room for both tax reductions needed to spur private activity and greater spending on productive government services.

The main problem, as referred to above, is the problem of containing the cost of technical "breakthroughs." While any advance in military science is desirable from a military point of view, what is desired from the economic viewpoint is the sort of advance that will give us more defensive power cheaply, or at least not very much more expensively. This, of course, presents a difficult problem, and it emphasizes the need for having the defense program in the hands not just

* Higher figures have, of course, been proposed. For example, the "Rockefeller Report" on problems of U.S. defense estimated that an adequate program would require successive annual increases of $3 billion per year for several years, which would mean a total addition of more than $10 billion to the defense program in the period we are discussing ("International Security—The Military Aspect," Special Studies Report II of the Rockefeller Brothers Fund, N.Y., 1958, p. 58). However, such estimates, when prepared by military experts who are understandably concerned to have the best and latest equipment for every contingency, invariably tend to the high side.

of military men, but of adequately trained civilians as well.*

The main job of these civilians will be to marshal our scientific and technical resources to meet the military problem. (The need for more scientific personnel to carry on research and development in industry has been referred to in Chapter 3.) Ways in which industry and government are moving to increase the supply of such personnel, and broaden their effectiveness, include:

1. Improved high-school instruction in science and mathematics to stimulate interest in such careers. In the past two years 43 percent of all our secondary schools have revised their curricula in mathematics and 37 percent in science courses.†
   The National Defense Education Act provides $280 million over a four-year period to strengthen further the instruction programs in these subjects and in foreign languages.

2. Better salaries for scientists and engineers and for teachers of science, mathematics and engineering.

3. Fellowship aid to help teachers continue their own training. The National Defense Education Act authorizes a total of 5,500 of these fellowships.

4. A movement by employers to hold down on intense recruiting among teachers of science and engineering, which a few years ago threatened to undermine the training of future scientists and engineers.

5. Better utilization of existing technical manpower and wider employment of women, older men and members of racial minorities in technical fields. The President's Committee of Scientists and Engineers, before its dissolution at the end of 1958, made a notable contribution through numerous local conferences on utilization.

* For an analysis of this problem by an experienced civilian administrator, see David Novick, *A New Approach to the Military Budget,* Rand Corporation, June 1956.
† "Mathematics and Science," *Research Bulletin,* Vol. 36, No. 3, p. 67, National Education Association, Washington, October 1958.

Some progress is already being made in these directions, and undoubtedly there will be more progress in the next few years as better instruction programs spread and utilization of professional manpower improves.* Therefore, we can expect an increase in the number and quality of available technical manpower, which would greatly reduce the time now required for development and testing of military equipment, as well as eliminating many production problems, with substantial over-all cost savings to the government. An adequate supply of technical personnel, and a sufficiently tough attitude toward costs by civilian administrators in the Defense Department should enable us to attain the economy desired in both design and application of weapons.

Thus, the defense program need not hold back the rest of the economy. While it will remain something we should at all times be glad to see ended by more peaceful developments, defense is a problem that we can handle without slowing down the rate of general economic progress.

DEFENSE AND STABILITY

It is considerably more difficult to find any assurance that the defense program will not continue to get in the way of economic stability. As indicated at the outset of this volume, the greatest fluctuations for any component of the Gross National Product have been those in defense spending, whether we consider the entire period 1946–1958, or the shorter pe-

---

* For more detailed discussion of the shortage of technical manpower and ways to overcome it, see *The Shortage of Scientists and Engineers,* a booklet reprint of five editorial messages prepared by the McGraw-Hill Department of Economics and published in McGraw-Hill magazines in 1956; Dexter M. Keezer and William H. Chartener, "The Shortage of Engineers—An Opportunity as Well as a Problem," in *Problems and Practices in Engineering Management,* Special Report No. 24, American Management Association, New York, 1957, pp. 23–31.

riod 1951–1958 which includes only the rise and fall in expenditures since Korea. The range of these fluctuations is shown in the table below:

	National Security Expenditures (Defense, Atomic Energy and Foreign Military Aid)	
	$ Billion	Percent
1945–1946: decrease	—56	—73
1947–1948: increase	+ 3	+20
1950–1953: increase	+33	+83
1953–1956: decrease	—10	—19
1956–1958: increase	+ 4	+ 9

The importance of these fluctuations is easy to appreciate, for—as stated earlier in this chapter—defense expenditures for durable goods alone are comparable in size with those for all producers' durable equipment, or consumer expenditures for automobiles. Moreover, an important part of new private investment in plant and equipment (roughly 25 percent at the height of the Korean War, and at least 10 percent in 1958) is in defense or defense-supporting facilities. Similarly, an important part of changes in inventory formation is accounted for by the changing requirements of military production, both on military work-in-process and on stocks of raw materials and semi-fabricated items. Including the declines in spending for defense plants and inventories, the 1954 recession was caused almost entirely by cutbacks in the defense program. The same might be said for the brief recession in 1946. And lower defense expenditures contributed to the declines in business during 1949 (although that was predominantly an inventory recession).

Perhaps more important in 1949 was the unwillingness of government economists to prescribe measures that might have anticipated business weakness in late 1948, because in

1948 it was expected that we might face a large and inflationary increase in defense spending, if hostilities resulted from the Berlin blockade.* A similar expectation of large defense increases to come influenced government policy in 1957–1958. In fact, sudden increases in the defense program were an inflationary factor in 1947, 1951 and 1953; and indeed, we may not have seen the last of such experiences.

One might feel somewhat better about the economic instability engendered by changes in the defense program if it could be shown that these were related to military necessity. But it can be truthfully asserted that the changes have not been well-timed from a military—that is, a strategic—viewpoint either. According to Thomas K. Finletter, former Secretary of the Air Force, "This [amount of money appropriated for defense] varies with the external stimuli, with the way the country feels about the menace of war at the moment." † In other words, it is not related to any long-term plan for either defense or economic stability. Mr. Finletter goes on to say what it is related to, namely a dollar ceiling which represents the amount of money the administration thinks it can get from Congress in the particular year. "This dollar ceiling in peacetime is very real. It does not come through legislation or openly avowed policy. It comes from the political inability or unwillingness, when there is not the stimulus of war or of a crisis, of any administration in power to ask for (in the case of the Executive Branch) or to enact (in the case of Congress) a level of defense appropriations which would seriously increase taxes or affect the balance of the budget." ‡ This makes the necessary

* Benjamin Caplan, "The 1948–49 Recession" in *Policies to Combat Depression* (A National Bureau Conference), Princeton University Press, 1956.
† Thomas K. Finletter, *Power and Policy*, New York, 1954, p. 198.
‡ *Ibid.*, p. 252.

increase in defense spending sharper when a crisis does occur, and the cuts are also sharper when the crisis is over, because nothing has been tied in with long-term needs.

These remarks relate primarily to the period 1948–1953, when Mr. Finletter was actively concerned with military policy. Since 1954 (except for a brief hiatus during 1957) * the defense program has been more stable, and the administration has repeatedly stated that cuts in 1953–1954 were made for the purpose of getting the program down to a level that might be sustained for years. But it remains to be seen whether this stability will, in fact, continue, or whether public outcry at another Russian development in guided missiles will start us on another roller coaster.

The problem, it must be emphasized, is not how to stabilize *minimum* defense expenditures. Barring a totally unexpected degree of improvement in international relations, we are close to the minimum now in terms of men and equipment. The increasing complexity of weapons, with its greater cost, will offset any reduction that can be made in the size of future forces. The problem is how to control the *maximum*—how to prevent "crash" programs that lead to temporarily greater spending on some section of the armed forces, only to have this spending cut back later when interest wanes. The problem also is how to choose between various types of new weapons—all deadly, all expensive—which, if all were adopted, would quickly raise the cost of the defense program to unsustainable levels.

We have already indicated two ways in which the govern-

* New orders for defense products were cut back sharply in the summer and fall of 1957, then increased sharply in early 1958 reflecting the shift from aircraft to missiles, and in part a decision to hold down the level of the total defense program during this period. However, final expenditures on national security remained within a range of $44 to $45 billion throughout 1957–1958.

ment is moving to control this tendency of defense expenditures to explode upward: (1) by planning a basic level of expenditures that can be sustained for the long-term and (2) by improving our scientific and technical staffs to the point where we do vastly better in the selection, development and production of complex weapons, thus limiting the additional costs which these new weapons will inevitably impose.

In addition, we may hope for a better public understanding of the need for a stable program of defense outlays. Until such understanding is more in evidence, both Congress and the administration will be subject to demands for sudden changes.

If, as we indicated early in this chapter, the defense program can be held within $5 billion of present spending during the next five years, this program will become a positive factor for stability. The increase will be too small to exert inflationary pressure, and the size of the program which is maintained will be a stabilizer against recessions that start elsewhere in the economy. Since defense expenditures account for over 85 percent of all Federal purchases of goods and services, stability in this sector means essentially stable government expenditures. Gerhard Colm, chief economist of the National Planning Association, has estimated that stable government spending may forestall 20 to 25 percent of the decline in the gross national product that would otherwise occur in a recession. This seems to be, in fact, a conservative estimate, since in addition to Federal spending, the expenditures of state and local governments are also rising steadily.

The government's total contribution to economic stability includes more than the effects of a continuing defense program. The total budget of the Federal government is an instrument of economic policy, as well as a means of balancing income and expenditure.* The government can act power-fully to counteract a recession by reducing taxes, by spend-ing more on its own civilian programs and by increasing grants-in-aid for state and local construction. If necessary, it can spend considerably more than it takes in, resorting to bank credit for the extra funds, and so increase the total supply of money circulating in the economy. As we have stressed above, the section of the Federal budget that is affected by these optional measures is not large enough for the measures to be effective unless the defense program, which takes up most of the budget, is held stable. But granted this condition, the remaining Federal decisions on taxes and spending are an important influence on the course of the economy.

THE NEW ATTITUDE TOWARD THE BUDGET

The idea that the government can adjust its taxing and spending policies in such a way that they have a positive influence on the economy and help keep it on an even keel is something new since the early 1930s. Then (in the thirties) most professional economists and the leaders of both major political parties agreed that the best policy for government to follow in a depression was to balance the Federal budget —through increased taxes and lower expenditures. The Re-publicans and the Democrats tried to outdo each other in their zeal to carry out this policy.

President Hoover, for example, declared in a message to Congress on May 5, 1932: "Nothing is more necessary at this time than balancing the budget." He asked for higher taxes, and a month later he signed a bill that increased—by stag-

* See Arthur Smithies, *The Budgetary Process in the U.S.*, McGraw-Hill, New York, 1955, and the review by Gerhard Colm, *Review of Economics and Statistics*, February 1956, p. 105.

gering amounts for those days—estate taxes, personal and corporation income taxes, gift taxes, excise taxes and postal rates. The Democrats answered, essentially, that what we needed was more of the same. In endorsing a Democratic platform pledge of more economy in government, Franklin Roosevelt promised "a saving of not less than 25 percent in the cost of Federal government" and "a Federal budget annually balanced." * The Roosevelt administration, after its election in 1932, tried—if briefly—to keep its pledge by boosting tax rates and trying to offset emergency government spending by cuts in other areas, including veterans' pensions.

The practical effect of the effort to balance the budget, most economists would now agree, was to aggravate the general economic decline. Government spending was held down. And since tax revenues were falling as unemployment grew and income dropped, tax rates had to be raised to produce higher yields. The effect was, in short, to drain off a larger share of consumer income, thereby reducing the spending power of consumers and business, without filling in the gap by increasing government demand for goods and services. Only a large increase in spending on emergency welfare programs by the Roosevelt administration, after its brief flirtation with budget-cutting, kept this policy from having a more depressing impact.

Since the early 1930s the professional opinion of economists has swung far the other way. The idea to which an overwhelming majority of economists now subscribe is that, in time of serious recession or depression, the government should try to offset rather than compound the depressing forces in the economy. This means reducing taxes, to leave more spending power in the hands of business and consum-

* Address on July 30, 1932, cited in *The Memoirs of Herbert Hoover: The Great Depression*, 1929–1941, New York, 1952, Vol. III, p. 271.

ers. It means maintaining, even increasing, government spending to sustain demand for goods and services. It means, in short, unbalancing the budget.

Much of this change in professional opinion is the result of the influence of the British economist John Maynard Keynes, whose *General Theory of Employment, Interest and Money* * is one of the most important books of this century. Relatively few economists now admit to being thoroughgoing Keynesians; many of his premises have proved unsound, and some of his policy recommendations are now lightly regarded. What Keynes did was provide economists with a new theoretical framework for considering the economy and its interrelated parts as an entity—the theoretical counterpart of the development, on the statistical side, of our national accounts (discussed in Appendix III). And he succeeded in convincing not only a great many professional economists, but also important governmental policy makers in Britain and in the United States, that government can profoundly affect the general level of economic activity.

There are still economists and governmental leaders who have a high regard for the sanctity of the Federal budget, even in time of recession. President Eisenhower's first Secretary of the Treasury, George Humphrey, was of this persuasion. He declared that he would rather resign than use government deficits to fight a depression.† Secretary Humphrey resigned (on May 29, 1957) for other reasons before the recession of 1957–1958 would have put his determination to a test. But his abiding influence on the Eisenhower administration in fiscal matters has been credited with having been a powerful force in shaping the President's decision not to

* Published in the U.S. by Harcourt Brace, New York, 1936.
† Press conference, Jan. 16, 1957, as reported in *The New York Times,* Jan. 17, p. 20.

try a general cut in Federal taxes as one of the devices to reverse the recession of 1957–1958.

However, in taking this course the President did not thereby avoid deficit financing as a means of coping with economic recession. On the contrary, Federal expenditures for which no compensating revenues were provided were increased for the avowed purpose of stimulating business activities in some key areas. The result was that the Federal government ended its fiscal year 1957–1958 with a deficit of $3 billion, and its fiscal year 1958–1959 with a deficit of $12.5 billion.

The fact that business did recover from the recession of 1957–1958 without benefit of a general Federal tax reduction is hailed by some as a triumph of both fiscal courage and orthodoxy. Others, including the President's former economic adviser, Arthur F. Burns, have questioned the wisdom of the course followed. Dr. Burns has argued that the expenditure programs adopted, in lieu of a tax cut, became effective only after recovery had already begun and that as a result "we have only recently entered the expanding phase of actual expenditures, and although the private economy is advancing, a sharply rising scale of Federal spending is still ahead of us. This is precisely the condition that responsible advocates of a general tax cut sought to prevent." * A broadly-based tax cut, according to Dr. Burns, would have caused prompter stimulation of private spending when it was most needed, and would not have committed the government to longer-range expenditures in future years of possible inflation.

The argument as to what would have been the best course to follow in 1958 is sure to carry on for many years with no clear-cut decision. We cannot live the same time span twice. What was done, however, validates the general proposition

* Speech to the Joint Council on Economic Education, Washington, D.C., Nov. 20, 1958.

that, where a generation ago deficit financing by the Federal government was regarded as completely irresponsible, it is now a widely—and among economists—a generally accepted method of combatting business recession.

STABILIZERS—AUTOMATIC AND NONAUTOMATIC

Budgetary measures to counteract a recession (and conversely to curb inflation) are of two kinds—automatic and nonautomatic.

Automatic stabilizers, or "built-in stabilizers" as they are sometimes called, consist of provisions in existing laws that bring about changes in the rate of tax collections or in government spending through automatic response to changes in business conditions. Under the progressive income tax, for example, tax liabilities automatically decline with incomes; "pay-as-you-go" payroll deductions make this response almost immediately for a large share of personal income tax payments. Other taxes based on a percentage of wages, such as those for social security, rise and fall with employment. Excise taxes go up and down with sales. On the spending side, a decline in employment automatically brings an increase in claims for unemployment compensation and—from older people—for old age insurance benefits. If a slump affects farmers, then price support payments increase.

Nonautomatic stabilizers include specific reductions in tax *rates* and specific increases in government spending programs that may be voted by Congress to deal with a particular situation. Examples of this type of stabilizers would be expanded public works programs or direct income payments such as a veterans' bonus.* The administration also has some discretion as to when to spend or not to spend cer-

* Both automatic and nonautomatic stabilizers are discussed by Fabricant, *op. cit.,* pp. 9–10.

tain appropriations that can aid in stabilizing the economy.

Both automatic and nonautomatic stabilizers helped to moderate the recessions of 1953–1954 and 1957–1958. In the earlier recession, wage and salary disbursements and other labor income ran $1.6 billion lower in 1954 than in 1953, but unemployment benefits rose over $1 billion. Congress enacted wholesale revisions in the tax laws that resulted in a revenue loss to the government from personal income taxes of some $3 billion. The result was that disposable personal income (personal income after taxes) was over $4 billion higher in 1954 than in 1953. Since tax reduction played such an important part, the 1954 recovery must be viewed primarily as a result of nonautomatic stabilizers.

In 1958 there was no tax reduction, but the automatic stabilizers played an even more important role. Not only did tax liabilities fall sharply, but social security payments (which had been raised by action of the previous Congress) increased, as did unemployment benefits and price support payments to farmers. Altogether, these various "transfer payments" rose by an annual rate of $5 billion from the third quarter of 1957 to the third quarter of 1958, offsetting most of the loss in wage and salary income. The principal nonautomatic stabilizers voted by Congress were an increase in pay for government employees (amounting to nearly $2 billion, including retroactive pay) and larger expenditures on defense, highways and publicly-financed housing. Although most of these nonautomatic actions did not become effective until after the turn in business, they did accelerate the speed of recovery.

Mainly reflecting the effectiveness of automatic stabilizers in this particular situation, personal income and consumption were relatively well maintained in 1958. As compared with a 3.8 percent drop in the gross national product, income after taxes and consumer expenditures dropped by less than one percent (from quarterly peak to quarterly trough). This strength in consumer spending was, in turn, the principal element in reversing the downturn in business inventories and starting business generally on the way to recovery.

Both the recessions of 1953–1954 and 1957–1958 were, of course, comparatively mild. In the event of more serious trouble, we cannot be so confident that the stabilizers would work as well. It depends largely on the timing of corrective action and the mass reaction of business and consumers to what the government does.

The timing of tax reductions, or changes in monetary policies, or in government spending may well be wrong. Particularly, it may be too late. In the first place, the administration in power always has a strong tendency to argue things are fine, especially in election years. This may hold it back from making recommendations or from taking action until the economy is on a pretty swift slide. Beyond this, there can be snags in getting a program through Congress, unless things have become desperate. It takes time, even after Congressional action, to put new tax rates into effect and let the results filter through business and consumers. In the case of spending programs, it may take a year or more to set up a construction program or some such device to pump money into the economy—unless, as a Southern governor proposed a few years ago, an arrangement were made whereby everybody just got a check from the government for one reason or another.*

If only because such a great length of time is required for

* For a discussion of the various difficulties in achieving a timely change in taxes, or in government expenditures requiring Congressional action, see Herbert Stein "An Appraisal of Fiscal Policy Performance During Recession," Papers presented at the Sixth Annual Conference on the Economic Outlook, University of Michigan, Ann Arbor, Michigan, Nov. 3–4, 1958, pp. 82–85.

Congress to debate and enact nonautomatic measures, the automatic stabilizers have a primary role in government policy to combat recession. For example, Benjamin Caplan, formerly of the staff of the Council of Economic Advisers, has written as follows:

It is a fundamental question as to how rapidly a government can change its position.... The whole machinery of government grinds too slowly for changes to be made quickly. Even in emergencies where basic changes in policy can be taken quickly, the implementation is frequently agonizingly slow.

Another basic difficulty lies in the confusion of short-run with long-run problems. I think it is fair to say that, on the whole, we have not really been able to develop any satisfactory short-run policies other than our built-in stabilizers.*

To be sure, really massive government action will always require special legislation. But such action is necessary only to deal with a prolonged recession, which will not materialize if the automatic devices work as planned, or the sudden shock of a drastic change in the defense program, which cannot be anticipated in the present scheme of automatic stabilizers.

In fact, precipitate government action could give people the idea that things were falling apart. This could easily result in pulled-in belts, curtailed spending programs, hesitancy to make consumer or mortgage loans—that would largely offset whatever the government did.

Secretary Humphrey argued a heavily unbalanced Federal budget might scare people enough to produce just this result:

Now when you're in a declining volume of business, when you're in what we refer to as a depression, the real cause of that is lack of confidence in the people; the people become fearful. They do

* Caplan, *op. cit.*, p. 52.

not buy; they curtail their own expenditures. The thing that will end that is to restore confidence . . . I think that in most cases you would find that confidence would be more shaken by a deliberate big deficit spending than you would by having the government do more constructive things and restore confidence so that the people themselves would begin to spend.*

It is conceivable that ill-advised Federal programs could have this effect. But nearly all economists agree that it is also important to maintain widespread public confidence that the government will, when really necessary, take steps to bolster employment and incomes, and take stronger and more effective steps than were taken in 1929–1932. In this sense, large-scale economic action by the Federal government may be compared with the coastal defense guns which were an important part of pre-World War II armaments. Its success will be evidenced if it never has to be used. Public knowledge that the government stands ready to act on a large scale if necessary will help preserve confidence. It will mitigate the severity of recessions by encouraging people to go ahead with planning for the upturn and to use their savings if necessary to maintain spending during a temporary fall in incomes.

IMPROVING OUR STABILIZERS

Moreover, we can expect that the present array of *automatic* stabilizers will be strengthened so as to provide a really substantial offset to any recession that may take place. In particular, there is great scope for extending the benefits from unemployment insurance, which now average only about one-third of regular income for covered workers. (The duration of these benefits, but not the amount, was temporarily increased during the 1958 recession.) Professor

* Appearance on "Meet the Press," Jan. 27, 1957.

Sumner Slichter of Harvard has suggested that the average could be raised to two-thirds without reducing the incentive to work. And in fact, the new program of "supplemental unemployment compensation" inaugurated in 1955 by the Ford Motor Company provides total income for an unemployed worker that is equal to two-thirds of his regular take-home pay.* This suggests a target toward which government and industry together may work during the next five years. Further extension of unemployment insurance to workers not now covered, and probable reductions in the age at which old-age insurance benefits are available, will also have stabilizing effects.

The other great field for improving the degree of "built-in stability" is in Federal tax policy. For example, the statement on tax policy of the Committee for Economic Development suggests that tax rates should be set to balance the budget at nearly-full employment, with a lower tax take (and a deficit) resulting when employment drops and a surplus for debt retirement when the economy operates beyond its normal capacity. In this way the fiscal operations of the budget (its effect on the money supply) would be counter-cyclical.† Other authorities have suggested that both tax and spending policies should recognize the rate at which national income is growing, and tax revenues are increasing, over the longer term. They recommend that increases in both defense and nondefense spending programs be geared to long-run revenue prospects and planned for several years ahead. In any case, the growth of national income means that periodic tax reductions are possible as long as government spending—particularly defense spending—does not grow too rapidly

* Supplemental benefits of this type, paid by auto, steel and other companies, are estimated to have reached a total of $100 million, or more, in 1958.
† Committee for Economic Development, *Taxes and the Budget: A Program for Prosperity in a Free Economy*, November 1947.

(see p. 132 above). This will aid both growth and stability if the tax reductions come at the right time.

It is always difficult to decide when the time is "right" and even more difficult to translate such a decision by the administration promptly into legislation by the Congress. But with reasonable luck in timing, periodic cuts in tax rates, which are entirely likely, will powerfully reinforce the automatic flexibility in tax revenues which now takes place with falling incomes.

SUMMARY

The government's contribution to economic stability may be summed up as follows: (1) a large volume of stable to slightly rising expenditures by the Federal, state and local governments; (2) a readiness to make specific tax cuts or spending increases when necessary—the main effect of which is to preserve public confidence in the early stages of a recession; (3) automatic increases in income payments and automatic reductions in tax collections, compounded periodically by reducing tax rates, to maintain incomes at somewhere near full-employment levels.

What does all this add up to? The record to date is impressive. In 1954 and again in 1958—with smaller Federal programs than envisaged here for the future—the reduction in personal taxes and increases in Federal payments to the unemployed, farmers and others, more than offset the reduction in disposable personal income caused by lower employment and earnings.*

In a more serious recession, it has been estimated that the operation of these automatic stabilizers would still offset as

* Personal income after taxes actually was $253 billion in 1953 and $257 billion in 1954. It was $308 billion in 1957 and $317 billion in 1958. Even at the bottom quarter of the 1958 recession disposable income had declined only $1 billion from the peak annual rate of 1957, and all of this decline was recovered in the succeeding quarter.

much as 30 to 40 percent of the decline in gross national product that would otherwise occur, and that including the stabilizing effect of continuing Federal expenditures, the offset might reach 50 percent. *

Let us consider what this figure means. As an example, the initial forces of decline would have to be nearly twice as great as in 1937 to give us a recession of that magnitude (i.e., a 6 percent drop in the gross national product, compared with the postwar declines of under 1 percent. This is a startling difference from earlier concepts of the instability of the American economy. But it is a difference that has developed along with the increasing role of the Federal government in maintaining a permanent defense establishment and adding to the stability of private incomes. In both these roles the government faces problems. But as discussed here, they are problems that are well within our capacity to cope with. In fact, as the technical problems of defense production are better handled—and as the total Federal budget reflects more long-range planning—government may exert a greater influence for both growth and stability than it has done even in these remarkable postwar years.

* Comments by Gerhard Colm on David W. Lusher "The Stabilizing Effectiveness of Budget Flexibility," *Policies to Combat Depression*, Princeton University Press, 1956, pp. 104–105.

CHAPTER SEVEN

Will There Be Enough and Rugged Enough Competition?

For its driving force the American economy relies in decisive degree on business competition. Where a Communist regime counts on obedience to orders from a high command to get things done, a key part of the American way of getting them done is to maintain the conditions which prompt individuals and companies to do them voluntarily. None of these conditions is more important than the maintenance of fair competition.

In recognition of these facts, government in the United States, and more particularly the Federal government, has pioneered in the development of a body of law designed to remove obstructions to fair competition and prevent private monopoly. The development of this body of "antitrust" law, which has had few emulators abroad, may well constitute the most distinctive and important American contribution to economic statecraft. It not only offers a basic inducement to do things that need doing, but also is counted upon to provide assurance that there will be no unjust exploitation in the process.

However, over the years since 1890 when the first and still most basic of the Federal antitrust laws, the Sherman Act, was passed, broad legislative escape hatches from prosecution for antitrust law violation have been created. Among them are those for labor unions, farm cooperatives and, in varying degrees, those for so-called natural monopolies where government regulation is substituted for competition as a basic guarantee of performance in the public interest. Also, in the process of applying the laws in specific cases, the courts have made interpretations which make sweeping departures from the traditional concept of "pure competition" as developed in the professional economic literature on the subject.

As a result of such developments, there are those who contend that the antitrust laws no longer effectively thwart private monopoly which, in their view, is becoming the order of the day. For example, George Romney, president of the American Motors Corporation recently said, "I believe that our principal economic problem arises from the fact that the principle of competition is vitally threatened—vitally threatened by industrial concentration." He had reference both to concentration of ownership and of management when he observed that, of the 1,500 automobile companies which have operated in the United States, only five are left, and that there is "a union structure premised on monopoly." *

1957 Division of Sales, Profits, Assets in Mfg.

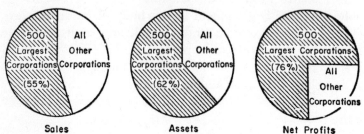

Fed. Trade Commiss.; Securities & Exch. Commiss.; Fortune Magazine

The 500 largest industrial corporations account for a very large slice of the industrial pie. Their shares in three important gauges of industry size range from more than half to more than three-fourths.

* An address by Mr. Romney to the Annual Meeting of the American Petroleum Institute in Chicago, Nov. 10, 1958, printed in the *Commercial and Financial Chronicle*, Dec. 11, 1958.

Those who support the contention that business competition is a dangerously waning force in the United States commonly cite the fact that the management of American industry has been concentrated to a degree where the 500 largest corporations (less than one-tenth of 1 percent of the total number of corporations) account for well over half of all corporate sales, assets, and net profits. They also often refer to the continuing wave of corporate mergers, which, according to the Federal Trade Commission, totalled some 6,526 in the 1951–1958 period.

What are the facts and prospects in the case? Is American industry on the whole vigorously competitive and does it promise to remain so? Or is competition giving way to concentrated control which increasingly moves in the direction of more or less complete private monopoly? In this chapter we shall take a look at these questions, which are basic to the prospects for expanding prosperity. In doing so we shall not concern ourselves with the detailed legal niceties of antitrust law interpretation and enforcement, important as they are, but look broadly at such questions as:

1. Whether the nation's industrial giants have outgrown the compulsion of competition insofar as their relations with their customers and each other are concerned

2. Whether small business has a chance to carry on successfully in an economy where the industrial giants bulk so large

3. Whether the wave of corporate mergers in recent years has increased corporate concentration and weakened the competitive structure of the economy.

COMPETITION AMONG THE TITANS

In dealing with competition in American business, an essential first step toward useful observations is to try to clear away the confusion created by the fact that economists and businessmen still tend to attach quite different meanings to the term "competition." By and large, businessmen use the word in its most commonly accepted meaning, that of rivalry—or, as more specifically applied to business, rivalry in securing customers or markets. In confusing contrast, economists commonly use the term competition, at least in what is characterized as its perfect state, to indicate that situation where the number of competitors is so numerous that no one of them can affect the market, but all of them are governed by forces stemming from the market itself.

If the economists' definition of competition is used, it is easy to demonstrate that giant industrial firms (and many small firms, too, for that matter) are anything but perfectly competitive. Most firms commonly stick for months on end, and sometimes even years on end, to the prices they have established for their products, instead of moving them up and down in the market. They also base these administered prices, so called, on costs loaded with expenditures for advertising and product development which are definitely designed, in large part, to have a direct influence on the market. Thus, they give a continuing demonstration of their capacity to influence the market, at least over the short turn, rather than being pawns pushed around by the forces emanating from the market, as fulfillment of the economists' concept of perfect competition would require.

When, however, the concept of competition is changed to that of rivalry for customers, the conclusion about the competitive posture of our giant business establishments changes along with it. Typically these establishments not only vie for customers very strenuously with the other companies in their industries, but the vigor of the struggle tends to increase rather than decrease, if and when a few very large establishments come to handle most of the business in their industrial field. And, in addition to the rivalry for customers within their own industries or product groupings, most of these giant establishments are in increasingly formidable degree subject to invigorating rivalry provided by other industries and alternative products.

The automobile industry will serve well as a case in point on the vigor of competition between industrial giants, for virtually all Americans are somewhat familiar with its performance. Since 1921 the number of companies assembling passenger cars in the United States has declined from 88 to 5.* Of these surviving companies, three assembled over 94 percent of the 40.1 million passenger cars put together in the period 1952–1958. And in 1958 one of them, General Motors, assembled over 51 percent of the total.

But as the ranks of the automobile assembling companies have been thinned, there has been no proportionate thinning of the vigor of their rivalry for customers. On the contrary, by engineering innovation and improvement, by styling changes worked out and launched in a secrecy maintained rather better than many wartime security arrangements, by intensive and persuasive selling techniques, the major automobile producing companies carry on a titanic struggle to beat each other in the market. Indeed, this struggle at times attains an intensity which tends to carry over into personal relations between the representatives of the contending companies.

What has changed greatly is the character and range of the competitive struggle involved. In the effort to win customers, there is much more emphasis on quality improvement and style appeal and much less emphasis on cutting the selling price than at times in the past. This is due in part, of course, to the fact that the wage arrangements in the automobile industry put a more or less continuous leverage

* R. C. Epstein—*The Automobile Industry,* Shaw, p. 176.

under costs and hence prices, and thus narrowly limit if not altogether eliminate the possibility of product price cutting. But it is also due to the fact that the American consuming public has reached a degree of affluence and is so abundantly stocked with automobiles, of which no less than 57 million were in operation in 1958, that something better or newer or more attractive stylewise has a far better chance of fetching the customers than something which is simply cheaper.

Of course, the interlocking of price and quality is such that what amounts to a price reduction may be provided by an improvement in quality without a proportionate increase in price. Indeed, a plausible case can be made that dollar for dollar of purchase price, the 1959 model automobiles give the consumer more for his money than the 1949 models. It still remains true, however, that the American market is so bountifully provided with both automobiles and purchasing power that the emphasis in the competitive struggle for customers has tended to shift to quality and style appeal, and away from straight price considerations.

This fact of relatively plentiful supply in a market whose customers are, as a whole, very well heeled financially applies quite generally to the markets in the United States. Flowing from this fact, of course, is the greatly increased emphasis on the importance of developing new and better products, or at least products that are new. Responding to this emphasis, the rivalry for customers, not only in the automobile industry but in other fields, generally takes the form of rivalry through more and better industrial research and development.

In this rivalry in industrial research and development, as was noted in Chapter 3, it is the large industrial corporations which are taking the lead. For example, the National Science Foundation has found that of the total expenditure for research and development in manufacturing in 1953 over 70 percent was accounted for by 2 percent of the manufacturing companies, all of them with 5,000 employees or more.*

By their massive enterprise in industrial research and development, however, the industrial giants tend to increase the intensity of competition with each other. The research and development increases their capacity to improve their products and methods and thus, as Professor Sumner Slichter of Harvard University has remarked, "every enterprise is threatened to a greater extent than ever before with the possibility that its rivals may bring out products which consumers prefer to its own product."

"The new competition," Professor Slichter goes on to observe, "may even come from another industry, because one of the principal effects of technological progress is to supply industry with an ever growing variety of materials, processes and products. Thus, there is far more inter-product and inter-service competition than there was even twenty or thirty years ago. The only protection against competition from new and better products and methods is to improve one's own product and one's methods faster than one's rivals improve their products and methods. Thus, the competition created by technological change tends to become keener and keener." † And both in creating and being subject to competition, the lead is taken by very large industrial firms.

When the competition in an industry has been so rugged as to reduce the field to a handful with perhaps only two giant survivors, it is altogether possible that, without some let-up in the competitive struggle, only one company will survive as the undisputed "champ." The possibility of such a development appears to be one of the grounds on which

* National Science Foundation Study, *Science and Engineering in American Industry*, 1955, p. 15.
† From an address, "Some Basic Trends in the American Economy," to the New York Society of Security Analysts, Nov. 8, 1956.

the Antitrust Division of the Federal Department of Justice
has instituted a grand jury inquiry into the degree of control
the General Motors Corporation exercises in the automotive
industry. Whether the investigation will eventuate in a government suit to reduce the bulk and competitive power of
General Motors remains to be determined. If it does it is a
safe speculation that it will be years before the final verdict,
following conventionally long drawn out trials and appeals,
is entered.

Seeing the survival of one or two overpowering manufacturers as the shape of things developing in the automobile
industry, George Romney, whose concern about industrial
concentration was mentioned earlier, would "provide for the
creation of new companies out of the most efficient company
or companies, when the number of competitors reaches a
minimum level. If the competitive system is going to be the
means of economic death to eliminate the inefficient," he
remarks, "then we must have a means of replacement or
economic birth." * Desirable as it might prove to be at a future juncture, "no means of replacement or economic birth"
is needed now to safeguard rugged competition between
the giants in American manufacturing industry, including
the giants in the automobile industry.

DAVID AND GOLIATH

But what of the smaller firms? How do they fare as compared with the industrial giants in the general struggle for
customers and survival? Or, to put the question in the cus-
tomary political formulation, what about small business?

On this question, the two principal lines of evidence to
which one might appeal in seeking a general answer seem
to suggest conflicting conclusions. One of these lines of

* *Op. cit.*

evidence is provided by the total number of business enterprises, of all sizes, over the years. The other is the profit-making record of business firms in various size brackets.

If the total number of business enterprises in operation, large and small (a total of over 4.6 million) is taken as the

Growing Number of Businesses

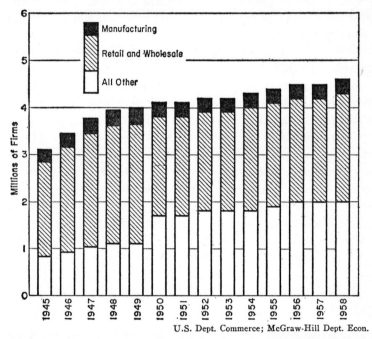

U.S. Dept. Commerce; McGraw-Hill Dept. Econ.

There are more than 4.6 million business firms in the U.S. The total has changed only slightly since 1955. Nevertheless, the trend in number of businesses is still up.

gauge of the health of the small as well as the large business, there is not much the matter with it. This number of business firms represents an increase of about 50 percent between 1945 and the end of 1958. Also, this increase has been attained by a quite steady rate of growth. So, as has been remarked, "the big get bigger"—but the small get more numerous. And, viewed in this dimension, the record suggests that small business is enjoying good health and vitality.

However, viewed in terms of the attainment of the prime objective of business enterprise, profits, it would appear from figures compiled by agencies of the Federal government that small or relatively small business is in a less thriving condition. To test this proposition we used data compiled by the Federal Trade Commission and the Securities and Exchange Commission on the profit performance of manufacturing companies with varying amounts of assets. Companies with less than $5 million in assets were counted as small business enterprises, based on the latest concept used by the Small Business Administration, and those with assets of over $100 million as engaged in big business.

There are, of course, many different concepts of small business, both official and unofficial, with the appropriateness of the concept tending to vary from one field of business to another. A shoe repair shop or a beauty parlor with forty-nine employees would clearly be a titan in its field of operations, while a manufacturing company with this number of employees would just as clearly be small business in its field.* At this juncture in our nation's economic development, however, the dimensions, in terms of assets, for large and small manufacturing business which we used seems reasonably valid.

* Some of the official definitions of small business have been as follows: The United States Department of Commerce defined as small business manufacturing plants with 100 employees or less, wholesale establishments with less than $200,000 annual net sales and retail and service establishments with annual net sales or receipts of less than $50,000. The Commerce Department revised its definition of manufacturing business to vary according to the specific industry so that the number of employees determining a small business now varies from less than fifty workers in some industries to 2,000 employees in others. The Select Committee on Small Business of the United States Senate counted manufacturing companies with assets of less than $250,000 as falling in the small business category.

Using the basis of comparison indicated, the chart on this page shows that in most of the period since the end of World War II, the small companies in their relative performance have fared badly. In the immediate post–World War II period when there was a tremendous rush to overcome the famine of goods created by wartime rationing, the profit-making performance of the small companies was as good as that of the very large companies. Since 1947, however, according to the figures charted, the small manufacturing companies have made a sorry showing compared with the very large companies.

There is foundation for the view that the profit figures for the small companies very considerably understate their actual profit performance. In his excellent study on the "Adequacy of Financing for Small Business since World War II," Irving Schweiger of the University of Chicago * provides documentation for the proposition that "unincorporated busi-

Mfg. Profits (after taxes) per Dollar of Sales

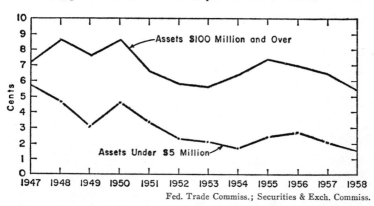

Fed. Trade Commiss.; Securities & Exch. Commiss.

In 1947 profits of small corporations accounted for 5.7 cents per dollar of sales. Big corporations made only 1.5 cents more per dollar of sales. In 1958 profits of small corporations dwindled to only 1.6 cents per dollar of sales, while big corporations made a profit of almost 4 cents more out of every dollar of sales.

* *Journal of Finance,* Vol. XIII, September 1958, No. 3; pp. 323–347.

nesses, especially small ones, show a tendency substantially to underreport income and overstate deductions." Part of the documentation is taken from a report of the U.S. Small Business Administration * which, after an analysis of *Statistics of Income* data showing relative changes in earnings of large and small corporations from 1947 to 1955, remarked that "comparisons of rates of return on net worth, before or after taxes of large and small corporations are likely to be misleading since, in small corporations owned and managed by the same persons, the dividing line between dividends and compensation of officers is less clearly drawn. Payments to officers may reflect, in part, return upon investment."

After the most searching study of the financing of small business with which we are familiar, it is Professor Schweiger's general conclusion that "the strength and general soundness of small business in the generally prosperous postwar

Mfg. Profits (after taxes) per Dollar of Stockholders' Equity

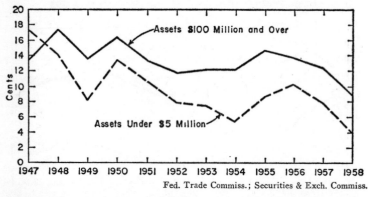

Fed. Trade Commiss.; Securities & Exch. Commiss.

Profits of small corporations amounted to 17.4 cents per dollar of stockholders' equity in 1947. This was 4 cents more per dollar of stockholders' equity than the big companies made. In 1958, however, big corporations made 8.8 cents per dollar of stockholders' equity, while this profit ratio dropped to only 4 cents in the case of small corporations.

* U.S. Small Business Administration, 7th Semi-Annual Report, p. 18.

years have been seriously underestimated ... It is indeed astonishing that there has been so little recognition of the vigor and flexibility of small business and the tremendous volume of capital which it has utilized in the postwar period." *

Among the many weaknesses of the available statistics about the relative profit performance of large and small companies is the failure of statistics arrayed simply in terms of size to reflect variations from industry to industry, where small business may be more or less concentrated. For example, the textile industry is an industry where profits are relatively hard to come by and where there is a large concentration of small companies. But this special concentration of both small units and profit-making difficulties in this industry does not show up in general compilations of profit-making records in terms of size.

It seems clear enough that when all of the appropriate adjustments are taken into account, small manufacturing companies as well as small businesses generally have done much better in making profits during the postwar period than the sketchy figures available would suggest. But in some key particulars they have obviously operated at a disadvantage in comparison with giants in the same industries. Among the disadvantages commonly arrayed are those that:

1. The mass markets of the United States have outgrown the financial capacity of the small manufacturing companies to exploit them effectively. It used to be said that if a man made a better mouse trap the world would beat a path to his door. Nowadays a very large advertising and selling outlay is required to get word around the mass markets of the United States that the mouse trap has been built and is available. Small manufacturing companies typically lack the resources for such a mass selling effort.

* *Op. cit.*, p. 347.

2. The small companies are handicapped relatively in making the large outlays for research and development which have become a prerequisite for leadership in the profit-making race. For example, it took a coordinated effort by several parts of one giant firm and about $27 million in research outlays before the first commercial pound of nylon was produced. Dacron polyester fiber was an $80 million project.

3. In many industries, notably manufacturing industries, the cost of modern capital equipment exceeds the financial resources of all except very sizeable companies. For example, it takes at least $50 million to build an up-to-date automobile assembly plant, and at least $200 million for the jigs, dies and other new tooling required to bring out a new model passenger automobile.

4. The present corporate income tax, which takes 52 percent of all corporations' profits above $25,000 per year, continuously prevents all but the very smallest corporations (which now pay 30 percent of profits up to $25,000) from using retained profits to build up their financial resources. And, during the critical period of postwar growth during the Korean crisis, a Federal excess profits tax, which was in effect from July 1950 through December 1953, cramped the capital-accumulating capacity of small companies even more badly.*

* Under the excess profits tax, small firms trying to expand were hit even harder than large corporations—for the tax was computed as follows: Five-sixth's of a firm's average earnings for its three best years during 1946–1949 was considered "normal income" and taxed at the 52 percent rate. Anything over this amount was considered "excess profit" and taxed at 82 percent (with an over-all limit on total taxes of 70 percent). Obviously, comparatively new small businesses that were struggling to get started during 1946–1949 were saddled with a low base figure in computing what part of their earnings was to fall under the excess profits tax. No matter what size the firm was, it was heavily penalized for expanding its income during the period 1950–1953. According to the National Association of Manufacturers, about 78 percent of the companies paying the excess profits tax were those with fewer than 500 employees. Particularly for these firms, it was really an anti-growth tax, since there was neither incentive to grow nor the chance to accumulate enough money to finance expansion plans.

Strengthened by the emotional and political appeal of helping those who are small, there is always an active movement in the United States Congress to have the Federal government overcome the disabilities of "small business." In 1953, the Small Business Administration was set up on the administrative side of the government to minister to the financial needs of small and medium-sized concerns. Specifically, this agency is empowered to make loans to small businesses, often in partnership with private lenders, for periods that are usually longer than regular commercial loans and on more favorable terms than the small borrower could arrange by himself. It also provides free counsel on managerial problems, technical processes and new products which would be too expensive for the small firm to hire professionally. Also, in recent years the Small Business Administration has tried to see that more of U.S. defense contracts are channeled to smaller firms.

In the summer of 1958 another move on behalf of small business was provided by the eighty-fifth Congress. An act was passed making the Small Business Administration a permanent agency and increasing its capacity to make loans directly to small concerns.

For the purpose of increasing the flow of outside capital to small businesses, Congress authorized the Small Business Administration to approve and to help finance a new set of financial institutions to be known as Small Business Investment Companies. Congress also passed a series of tax reform measures designed to provide stronger incentives for direct investment by individuals in family-owned corporations and in unincorporated businesses.

Combined with the tax relief measures, the establishment of the Small Business Investment Companies may be the most important development of many years in business finance. The main purpose of the Small Business Investment

Companies is to provide long-term loans to small firms that need these outside funds to grow. Generally, small companies have been unable to obtain long-term credit from commercial banks or other financial institutions, particularly in periods of tight money—periods defined merrily but not without a touch of realism as times when it is as hard to get into debt as it is to get out of it.

In the past many small concerns have been able to finance new equipment only with short-term credit at high interest rates. In a period of tight money this puts small firms in a difficult position because banks may refuse to issue or renew loans to them. In addition, dependence on short-term credit impairs their ability to survive when business is bad and earnings are low, since it is difficult at such times to liquidate tools or buildings. If a high proportion of their capital is in long-term loans, however, small firms might be able to ride out the storm.

Because the Small Business Investment Act is such a significant step on the part of Congress to help small businesses, it is important to spell out in detail the main provisions of this new legislation. These provisions along with the arguments for and against the program are covered in Appendix IV.

But even if this new legislation fails in its purpose, does this mean that small business is doomed? Not at all. There are many lines of business, and very important lines, in which small business has peculiar advantages. As a broad general proposition this tends to be true of many of the service industries, such as retail and wholesale trade, transportation and real estate, which, as the chart indicates, now use more labor than the industries producing goods. And it also remains true of many lines of manufacturing. This accounts, in large part, for the fact that in 1956 the General Motors Corporation, the nation's largest manufacturing concern, with almost 600,000 employees, paid over $6 billion to 26,000 suppliers, over 64 percent of which employed fewer than 100 people in their operations.*

The du Pont Company offers another striking example that the relationships between large and small companies do not, as one writer put it, present a case of "David fighting Goliath in the business world." According to a study by du Pont, over 90 percent of its sales are not to the ultimate consumer but to 75,000 smaller concerns which further process, convert, distribute and finally sell their products. For supplies of services and raw materials du Pont counts heavily on about 30,000 small companies. Even in du Pont's massive outlays for new plant and equipment, which have been running over $130 million a year, over half these expenditures

Shifting Employment Patterns

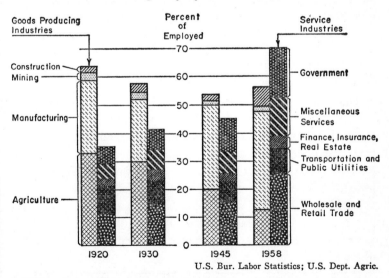

U.S. Bur. Labor Statistics; U.S. Dept. Agric.

In 1920 workers producing goods outnumbered service workers two to one. Employment in service industries has now pulled ahead by a wide margin.

* Statement by Harlow H. Curtice, President of General Motors Corporation, as reported in the *New York Times*, Jan. 10, 1957.

wind up as subcontract business for firms with fewer than 500 employees.*

What our discussion of the problems of small business adds up to thus far is this: In a good many lines of industry, small business cannot do as well profitwise as big business; and while there have been and no doubt will continue to be legislative efforts to redress the balance in favor of small business, the chances that they will be completely successful are not bright. But this will still leave large fields to small business, which can produce many goods and services much more effectively than big business.

Where it outstrips small business in the pursuit of profit, big business does not thereby escape the compulsions of competition. In its pursuit of customers, it still has the rivalry not only of other large companies in its field, or fields, but with the increased scope and tempo of research and development it is continuously exposed to dangerous competition from companies in other industrial and business sectors.

THE NEW WAVE OF MERGERS

The third question raised at the outset of this chapter— whether the wave of corporate mergers in the 1950s has increased corporate concentration and weakened the competitive structure of the economy—has been answered in large part by what has already been written in this chapter. As long as several concerns are left in the field or fields involved, the fact that they are made bigger by merger does not make for less competition. It may, in fact, make for more by increasing the competitive strength of the larger units.

It may be and is argued that ours would be a happier so-

* *The Story of Business: Large and Small,* E. I. du Pont de Nemours & Co., 1956.

ciety and a safer society for political democracy if we remained a community of small independent craftsmen and husbandmen rather than, in increasing numbers, the employees of large and impersonal business enterprises. Regardless of what there may be in this line of argument— and some think there is not much *—it does not alter the fact that, in terms of rivalry in the market, an economy increasingly characterized by very large business units remains a highly competitive economy.

However, so much has been said and written about the effects of mergers in stifling competition that it is in order to indicate briefly the nature of the merger movement in recent years and its consequences for business competition.

Since the end of World War II, there has been a lively industrial merger movement. From 1949 through 1958, there were 3,559 mergers in manufacturing and mining large enough to be included in financial journals. While in 1939 there were only eighty-seven such mergers, in 1949 there were 126, and in 1958 a total of 457.† The 1958 figure on mergers, however, is smaller than that for 1956 or 1957.

* For example, in a paper "Dinosaurs and Personal Freedom," Dean Harlan Cleveland of the Maxwell School of Citizenship of Syracuse University, remarks: "My impression is that 'large scale' organization generally implies loose organization. Precisely because big organizations make most of the vital decisions affecting our destiny, more people are participating in those decisions than ever before. The number of decisions which *are* important to our individual lives is multiplying so rapidly that it takes a growing proportion of the nation's available leadership to get them made at all. The result of bigness is actually a diffusion of the decision-making and decision-influencing process far beyond the wildest dreams of those worshippers at the shrine of Louis Brandeis who wanted to keep power diffused by keeping the units of society small."

† These and subsequent figures are from the tabulation on mergers in manufacturing and mining compiled by the Federal Trade Commission from the records of Moody's Investor Service and Standard and Poor Corporation. This series is not strictly comparable with the over-all merger series kept by the Federal Trade Commission, but is very important from a trend stand-

Recent trends indicate a definite shift to consolidations between the larger companies. In 1958 about three-fourths of the industrial mergers involved companies with assets of more than $10 million. In the last few years at least five companies have pushed their way into the circle of the 100 largest corporations in the U.S. via the merger route.

Such figures, however, become less imposing when related to past merger waves in the U.S. In the period 1899–1901, more than 2,000 firms were merged, while in 1927–1929 some 3,100 companies were brought together. But in the three years, 1956–1958, fewer than 1,500 industrial mergers were reported. And this was despite the fact that there were about 60 percent more firms and corporations than there were thirty years ago.

Measured by the size of assets involved, recent mergers are also too small to have had a significant impact on any particular market or industry. This point was stressed by Dr. M. A. Adelman of MIT's Department of Economics.* He points out that the formation of the U.S. Steel Corporation in 1901, typical of the giant mergers of that period, consolidated the six biggest iron and steel companies. In effect, the parent company (Carnegie), which was already the largest corporation in America, tripled its assets in the merger. A similar tripling of assets today would require the Standard Oil Company (N.J.) to acquire assets of over $14 billion. According to Dr. Adelman, this is far more than the total assets involved in all mergers since the end of World War II. His

---

point because the statistical series has been kept continuously since 1919. In fact, it is used by the Federal Trade Commission in making long-term studies of merger trends and includes all the important mergers in the industrial sector of the economy.

* Address by Dr. M. A. Adelman, associate professor of Economics and Social Science, Massachusetts Institute of Technology, to the American Management Association, New York, Oct. 31, 1956.

estimate, based on data published by the Federal Trade Commission, is that from the beginning of 1951 through 1954 assets involved in all industrial mergers did not amount to much more than $5 billion—about 2 percent of the total worth of the industries concerned.

The purpose behind the merger movements has also changed over the years. In the early 1900s—the era in which most of the great trusts in steel, tobacco, smelting, petroleum and shipping industries were formed—the mergers took place with the frank purpose of imposing control over the industries involved. In the 1920s there was a shift toward merging for other reasons, many of them connected with selling securities in the booming stock and bond markets. Often the assets of the second, third and fourth ranking companies in a field were pooled to improve or protect competitive positions within the rapidly growing industries. Post–World War II mergers, however, seem to be different from either of these two previous waves.

Mergers of firms producing similar product lines (called "horizontal" combination) still take place, but the merging companies are not usually both leaders within an industry. Typically, an industry leader buys out a relatively small company, or the merger is between "independents" who are trying to cut costs, lengthen their lines, improve their market facilities so as to be able to compete with the giants in their field. The mergers of independents in the auto industry in 1953 is the most striking example.

Similarly, there continue to be a fair number of "vertical" mergers, or integration of companies at different stages of fabrication with the intent of obtaining a secure source of raw materials or control over market outlets. The large-scale textile mergers which occurred a few years ago had as one motive the linking up of separate stages of spinning, weaving and processing. Likewise, numerous mergers in the food field have been aimed at setting up ties between processing, retailing and wholesaling activities.*

But what is most striking about mergers of the 1950s is the large number which do not fall into either of these two categories. Rather, they are mergers aimed primarily at diversification, in which a firm switches from single to multiple products, often in an entirely new line of business. It is a good guess that roughly 40 percent of recent mergers fall into this class,† and it is hard to make out a case that they curtail competition or have a sizable impact on established market patterns.‡

Many reasons have been given to explain why firms should want to diversify their interests. Often a company with an uneven pattern of sales tries to link itself with a firm whose line of business is more stable, as a sort of cushion against temporary setbacks. Or it may be that the different lines of business have a logical relationship via similar production techniques and marketing conditions. But more important is the fact that companies in declining industries try to shift their spare capital into new growth industries.

* However, recent court interpretations of Section 7 of the Clayton Act (as amended in 1950) seem to place a substantial legal barrier in the way of either horizontal or vertical mergers, from this point on, unless (1) the companies involved are both relatively small in relation to the total business of their industry or (2) one of the companies (presumably a small one) lacks the financial or management resources to continue on its own. At this writing, the Supreme Court has not yet ruled on a case brought under the new Section 7, but the Federal Trade Commission and the lower courts have been ruling as just indicated and Supreme Court rulings under the older law (e.g., in the du Pont–General Motors case) have been in the same direction. Paul W. Cook, Jr., "Thinking Ahead: Trends in Merger Activity," *Harvard Business Review*, March–April, 1959, pp. 15–18 and 164–166.

† Estimate by Ralph L. Nelson in "Do Mergers Kill Competition?" *Challenge*, New York University, December 1956.

‡ So far, the Clayton Act has not been interpreted to challenge this type of merger. Cook, *op. cit.*, p. 16.

This new type of merger may work a significant change in the evolution of American business. It may mean that business corporations, once established, see themselves as having a durability extending beyond their commitment to any particular line or lines of business. Such firms, often endowed with a real *esprit de corps* among employers and stockholders, will not willingly shut up shop even if there is nothing further for them to do in their original field or fields. With a pool of management, techniques, equipment and capital—which is too valuable to scrap or not to use to full capacity—the company will seek new worlds to conquer. But the important point is that such a merger has nothing explicitly to do with increasing or decreasing competition *per se*.

Of course, the wave of mergers of the 1950s—evaluated by any single standard such as numbers, concentration of assets, or even the predominancy of any one type—can never tell the full story of a particular merger or group of mergers in any related, or unrelated, field. There is always the much more fundamental question of who buys out whom, in what industry or market, and how this either increases or decreases the existing state of competition. This fact was brought home with extraordinary clarity by an officer associated with Federal antitrust enforcement. Commenting on the difference between two of the more important merger cases of the 1953–1958 period, he remarked: "It didn't look to us as though those independent automobile companies had a chance of surviving against the competition of the big three unless they were merged, so we smiled on the mergers as actually promoting competition. But, as matters stand, all of the steel manufacturing companies can compete quite effectively with Big Steel or any of the others, so we think the merger of Bethlehem and Youngstown is unnecessary and so oppose it." The final decision barring the merger between Youngstown and Bethlehem was made in December 1958.

Prosecution under the Federal antitrust laws has been anything but lax in recent years. It has been estimated that from mid–1953 to 1958 the Department of Justice completed action on more antitrust cases and initiated more new suits than it had in the previous 63–year history of the Sherman Act. In 1958 alone, the Department of Justice initiated fifty-seven new suits—almost twice as many as seven years ago. And in early 1959, the President recommended several changes in the antitrust laws that would make it possible for the Federal government to take quicker action against proposed and actual mergers which are not in the best interests of the U.S. economy.* But even as matters stand, the fact remains that the wave of mergers of the 1950s has not undermined the foundations of competitive business enterprise in the U.S. In fact, it may well be argued that many of the mergers have actually strengthened competition through a process of industrial diversification which arrays many not only new, but powerful, competitors against each other in an intense struggle to keep in the front ranks.

MORE AND MORE COMPETITION

The upshot of this chapter is that if the American economy does not turn in a distinguished record of growth and stability over the next decade, it will not be because a softening of competition has permitted business enterprise to start taking it relatively easy. In its rivalry for customers, Ameri-

* Most of these are quite technical points, such as increasing the Attorney General's power to get documents without grand jury proceedings, making Federal Trade Commission "cease-and-desist" orders final unless appealed to the courts, advance notice of intended mergers, use of preliminary injunctions and extension of antitrust coverage to banking. *President's Report to Congress,* January 1959, p. 53.

can business remains not only vigorously competitive but, as Professor Slichter remarked, "the economy is becoming more and more competitive." *

Difficult problems are involved and probably will continue to be involved in working out socially and politically acceptable *lebensraum* for small business and big business. Even more difficult, and perhaps insoluble, are the political problems involved in bringing labor and farm cooperative organizations back into the orbit of competition from which they have escaped by gaining exemption from the Federal antitrust laws.

But even if, in the nature of the legislative exemption involved, they must be lopsidedly applied, the antitrust laws remain a bulwark of the business system. By safeguarding fair competition they help to give profit making a social justification which it loses when monopoly takes over. Hence, in spite of its legislatively enforced failure to dispense even-handed treatment to all elements in the economy, continuation of vigorous antitrust law enforcement provides insurance that the capacity of the economy to sustain steadily a high level of prosperity will not be blighted by a withering of business competition.

* From the address to the New York Society of Security Analysts, *op. cit.*

CHAPTER EIGHT

Prospects of Avoiding Disastrous Price Inflation *

Even among those who are otherwise sanguine about the prospects for the American economy, there has developed in recent years a widespread fear that the *coup de main* will be given to steadily sustained prosperity by the rampant force of price inflation. In what was, in other respects, a glowing description of the economy, President Eisenhower stated in his Economic Report to Congress for 1959 that:

A persistent upward movement of prices would do great harm to our economy ... If price increases were to accelerate, the continuing upward movement would sooner or later undermine the confidence on which our economic system depends and would eventually release drastic corrective forces.†

Other authorities have been equally insistent that rising prices are a menace, perhaps the chief menace, to the growth and stability of the U.S. economy. Secretary of the Treasury Robert B. Anderson, testifying recently before the Joint Economic Committee, contended: "Growth requires capital formation, through saving and investment ... We cannot indefinitely expect people to continue their saving if they expect prices to go on rising indefinitely." The same view was

* Some of the substances of this chapter appeared in *Lloyds Bank Review* (London) for October 1957.
† *Economic Report of the President,* Jan. 20, 1959, p. 48.

presented by the nation's chief monetary official, William McChesney Martin, Jr., chairman of the Federal Reserve Board: "An atmosphere of price and financial stability in general is necessary both to the incentive to save and to rapid technological advance," both key factors in economic growth.*

In this chapter we explore this fear of inflation and come to the conclusion that, while it is no idle fear, there is a good chance that it will not be fulfilled in any devastating degree. In the course of this exploration we deal with the traditional problem of monetary inflation and with the capacity of the Federal Reserve System to handle it. In so doing, we shall note the special difficulties posed for the monetary authorities by recurrent Federal budget deficits, as well as the inflationary push that may be given the economy by higher Federal spending for goods and services. Finally, we shall deal at some length with the special, and somewhat newer, variety of inflation that seems to arise primarily from the strong push of organized labor on wage costs and hence on the industrial price structure.

At the outset, let us make clear that any of the varieties of inflation † with which the United States may have to cope over the next decade is likely to be less severe than the runaway type of inflation that has had its origin (in the U.S. and in other nations) in war and in the resort of war-harassed governments to the printing press as a means of financing. Most of the severe nineteenth-century inflations were of this type, as was the spectacular German inflation of

---

* *January 1959 Economic Report of the President,* Hearings before the Joint Economic Committee, 86th Congress, 1st Session, pp. 401 and 467.

† The term "inflation," or, interchangeably, "price inflation," is used here in the popular sense of the term to mean a general increase in prices. The term inflation is frequently used in technical literature to designate in a collective way the forces making for a general increase in prices rather than the increase itself.

the 1920s. The inflation resulting from World War II was considerably more complicated, but it also had its roots in wartime finance, albeit of a more sophisticated variety.

Basically what happened from 1941 to 1945 was that, in the course of financing World War II, our government created a large supply of money and credit that became available—once the special demands of war had ceased—to finance private purchases of scarce goods. This was the origin of the first great postwar wave of inflation from 1945 through 1948 which, as indicated by the chart, resulted in an increase of about 34 percent in consumer prices. The same factors were largely responsible for the surge of inflation that accompanied the Korean War and which, in a single year (1950–1951), resulted in a price increase of 8 percent. Combined, these two waves of inflation account for about three-fourths of the total increase in consumer prices since the end of World War II.

Two Postwar Waves of Inflation

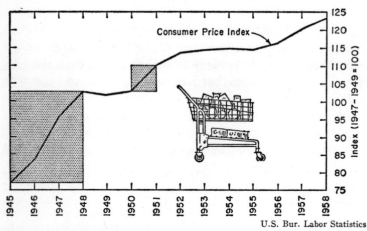

U.S. Bur. Labor Statistics

Almost 75 percent of the total increase in consumer prices since 1945 occurred in two periods—the immediate postwar years 1945–1948 and the early part of the Korean War 1950–1951.

This sort of inflation—on the order of 7 to 8 percent per year—is (on the record at least) a phenomenon of war or its aftermath. It would be difficult to produce in peacetime even with the strong ingredients of inflation that are brewed up by labor union pressure on the wage level. In both 1946–1948 and 1950–1951, increases in the general level of wages went along with increases in the general level of prices. But this was not a simple case of cause and effect. Wage increases, especially in the years 1946–1948, were among the events that caused the wartime hoards of money and credit to begin circulating rapidly through the economy. However, given the scarcity of goods relative to the supply of money, inflation would not have been long delayed in any case; and there is little ground for making union labor the culprit in this situation.

Possibly it overstates the case slightly to say, as Professor Lloyd Reynolds of Yale University has said, that money wage rates (and presumably prices) would probably have gone up as much as they did between 1945 and 1955 if there had been no unions at all.* But the influence of the unions in contributing to the first round of postwar price increases was strictly incidental to a general situation in which consumers and business firms alike were bidding up the prices of scarce goods without much concern as to labor or other costs. It is only in the later and milder phases of the post–World War II inflation—since 1953, and particularly since 1956—that labor costs seem to have been such a primary determinant of prices that unions can reasonably be brought to the bar and charged with being the culprits.

Both to see why this is so and to gauge the prospect that the labor unions will in the years ahead constitute themselves

* Lloyd Reynolds, "The General Level of Wages," *New Concepts in Wage Determination*, edited by G. W. Taylor and F. C. Pierson, McGraw-Hill, New York, 1957, p. 256.

an engine of price inflation, it is necessary to take a more detailed look at inflation since the end of World War II. The first great postwar wave of inflation, which by 1948 had brought the purchasing value of the prewar consumer dollar down to 58 cents, had two major causes:

1. The compounding of war-created shortages into a postwar rush to spend a tremendous pile of money, or something readily convertible into money such as war bonds, for goods that had been rationed.

2. The lack of effective monetary and credit controls, most of which had been dismantled as a part of the program for financing the participation of the U.S. in World War II, and the unwillingness of the Federal authorities to restore these controls in the early postwar period.

The acute shortages prevailing and the lack of monetary controls gave this earlier inflation a special character.

EARLY POSTWAR INFLATION

During the war years the opportunities of both individuals and companies to spend their incomes were restricted by wartime rationing. As a result, at the end of the war individuals held liquid assets (i.e., money or its equivalent) in the sum of about $155 billion, an increase of $105 billion or 210 percent during the war years. Also, business firms had piled up money to spend for new producing facilities, which they had been largely prevented from building during the war. By the end of 1945, this accumulation reached $73.0 billion—276 percent more than it had been at the outbreak of hostilities.[*]

With the abandonment, or breakdown, of direct price and

[*] L. V. Chandler, *Inflation in the United States 1940–1948*, Harper & Brothers, New York, p. 79.

rationing controls, both individuals and companies rushed into the market after 1945, utilizing their wartime savings to make long-postponed purchases. In the classical inflationary manner—too many dollars chasing too few goods—this rush to buy quite naturally bid up prices.

The rush was facilitated by easy access to credit for both consumer and business purchases. If the Federal Reserve authorities had kept a tight rein on credit expansion, by making banking reserves relatively scarce and permitting interest rates to rise, they could have restricted the inflationary effects of the scramble of already well-heeled individuals and companies for goods. For in its capacity to bid up prices, a dollar of credit goes just as far as a dollar of cash.

But the controls available to the Federal Reserve authorities to keep a tight rein on credit had been relaxed during the war, as a part of the process of borrowing $157 billion through marketable securities, to finance the war effort. The controls were not restored in 1945 by the Truman administration, because it was feared that their use to make credit scarce would (1) drive up interest rates on new borrowing, (2) cause a sharp decline in the price of outstanding, low-interest bonds, including government bonds and (3) precipitate a general financial collapse among banks, insurance companies and other financial institutions with heavy investments in government bonds. The decision not to reimpose credit controls was also influenced by the fear that putting them in place again, and using them to make credit scarce, would greatly increase the cost of carrying the huge war debt.*

This, very briefly, is what had happened to the machinery for credit control: Those in charge of borrowing the billions

---

* Interest charges on the public debt have risen, indeed, from $3.6 billion in the fiscal year ending June 30, 1945 (when the debt itself was $259 billion) to an estimated $8 billion in the fiscal year ending June 30, 1960 (on an estimated debt of $285 billion).

of dollars required to fight the war felt that they had to rely
on the nation's commercial banks to put up a large part of the
money. In order to encourage the banks to buy bonds, the
Treasury persuaded the Federal Reserve authorities to provide what amounted to a guarantee that the bonds would
not go below a fixed price, or par—by making such purchases
as might be necessary from time to time to hold them at par.

The commercial banks in the Federal Reserve System,
which do about 85 percent of the commercial banking of the
country, had acquired $80 billion in government bonds by
the end of the war. If the Federal Reserve authorities had
been able to prevent the banks from cashing in their bonds
to get lending reserves, this restraint would have tempered
the inflationary surge, because fresh credit would not have
been added to the piles of cash people were already spending. But at that point, a "tight money" policy would unquestionably have resulted in driving the price of government bonds, carrying a low fixed rate of interest, below par.
When these bonds matured, they would then have had to be
replaced with bonds carrying higher rates of interest, thus
eventually leading to a much higher cost of carrying the
Federal debt. It was also feared that tighter credit would
put a brake on general business activity at a time when some
considerably trusted government forecasters were predicting
that the transition from a war to peacetime economy would
result in our having about 8 million unemployed.

As a result of calculations of this kind, the wartime policy
of having the Federal Reserve authorities make sufficient
purchases of government bonds to maintain them at par was
continued. By making the purchases of bonds necessary to
carry out this policy, the Federal Reserve authorities continued to keep their member banks more than abundantly
stocked with banking reserves. When the Federal Reserve
System purchased government bonds—and between March

1946 and June 1948 it purchased no less than $9 billion to keep the price at par or above—it issued checks payable in the funds of the Reserve banks. The proceeds of these checks, in the nature of our Federal Reserve banking system, constitute reserves for the expansion of credit by the member banks. Indeed, under the setup prevailing, all the government bonds held in the community, whether by financial institutions or individuals, were potentially excess banking reserves.

The net effect of these arrangements was to make credit both very abundant and very cheap at a time when the billions of dollars backed up during the war were pouring into the markets of the country in a long-deferred rush for goods. The magnitude of this rush, built up by four years of wartime rationing, was so great that, regardless of the credit arrangements prevailing, it would unquestionably have resulted in a substantial increase in the general price level. That was a more or less inevitable cost of the war. But the inflationary surge was unquestionably aggravated by having the machinery for credit restraint out of commission at the time.

KOREA—AND AFTER

The machinery for effective monetary and credit control was still out of commission, in the way that has been indicated, when a new rush for goods and services was touched off by the outbreak of the Korean War in June 1950. This resulted in a second postwar surge of price inflation. For some time prior to the outbreak of this war, there had not seemed to be any particular urgency in making arrangements to cope with the dangers of price inflation. Indeed, in 1948 and 1949 there had been a substantial business recession, attended by a slight drop in the level of consumer and wholesale prices. This development led to widespread conviction that the postwar buying rush had run its course, and that preventing deflation and recession rather than containing price inflation might be the dominant problem henceforth.

However, the recession had run its course and prices were moving up again by mid-1950. Then, when the Korean War broke, memories of wartime rationing were fresh enough to start a stampede into the markets to get hold of things which, it was feared, might soon be rationed again. Since most people and companies were still well supplied with money and credit remained both cheap and readily available, in the absence of effective restraints by the Federal Reserve, this new rush to buy resulted in strong upward pressure on prices. Both consumer and wholesale prices rose about 10 percent within eighteen months.

Although the full record of the development remains to be revealed, and probably will for a long time to come, there seems little doubt that the new surge of price inflation touched off by the Korean War was most influential in convincing the Federal Reserve authorities—and perhaps more important, the President and the Treasury officials whose cooperation was essential—that the time had come to reassert effective control over money and credit conditions. At any rate, in March 1951 a so-called "accord" was reached between the Treasury Department and the Federal Reserve authorities by which the Reserve authorities no longer had an obligation to keep the price of government bonds pegged at par or above, and by which, in effect, their prewar powers over the supply and price of money and credit were fully restored.

The Federal Reserve authorities used their recovered powers over money and credit to temper the last phases of the surge of price inflation touched off by the outbreak of the Korean War, and also set to work to do what was necessary in their field for the longer run, to prevent a recurrence of violent inflation with each expansion of the economy. The first step in this direction was to restore some flexibility to interest rates, so that new demands for credit would mean a higher cost. This was accomplished by unpegging the price of government bonds, so that yields on these bonds, and hence on credit instruments generally, could rise.

As had been predicted, prices of government bonds went below par when these actions were taken in 1951, although at first only moderately. The 2½ percent December 15, 1967–1972 securities, which had been selling above par before the "accord," fell about four points by May 9. Subsequently, other Federal Reserve powers were used to make credit generally harder to get, especially for speculative purposes. By 1953, the 2½s of 1967–1972 fell below 90, and interest rates generally had tightened to the point where there were loud outcries from affected business and political interests. But President Truman, and after 1952 President Eisenhower, stood firmly behind the "accord" restoring the independent powers of the Federal Reserve System over money and credit, and these have been firmly exercised up to the present writing. Since 1951, banks have not been allowed to acquire lending reserves at will, and the use of credit to bid up prices has been greatly reduced.

This is not to say that controls over the use of credit have been so complete as to eliminate price pressures. Especially in years when the Federal government incurs a large budget deficit and must therefore borrow heavily from the banking system, there is bound to be a substantial increase in the money supply. The point made here is that since the Treasury–Federal Reserve accord of 1951 such increases have been much better controlled and their effects on prices greatly mitigated. In the calendar years 1951 through 1953, the accumulated deficit resulting from the Korean War was over

$18 billion. However, the general level of prices advanced only 3 percent during this entire period. And the economy continued to enjoy relative price stability during 1954–1955.*

Unfortunately, the recession of 1954 led both to new deficit financing by the Federal government (over $6 billion total during 1954 and 1955) and to a premature relaxation of the controls over credit. As an anti-recession measure, the Federal Reserve Board restored the liquidity of the banking system, made loans cheaper and easier to get and in general followed an "easy money" policy. The effects of its actions

---

* The general price stability of this period, however, obscured—and might be regarded as the result of—divergent cross-currents in particular prices. The Bureau of Labor Statistics wholesale price index, for instance, increased only a little over 1 percent between January 1953 and December 1955. But wholesale prices of farm products (a component of the BLS index) *dropped* 16 percent in this period, while industrial wholesale prices *rose* 6 percent.

Price Movements, 1951–1959

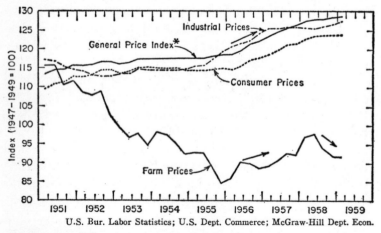

U.S. Bur. Labor Statistics; U.S. Dept. Commerce; McGraw-Hill Dept. Econ.

* G.N.P. price deflator

Stability in the general price level does not necessarily mean that all individual prices are stable. Throughout 1955 and early 1956 the general price level was quite stable. But this stability was based on three different types of price movement: consumer prices stable, farm prices declining sharply, industrial prices rising moderately.

were magnified by a simultaneous, and uncoordinated, easing in the terms for government-guaranteed mortgage loans effected by the Federal housing agencies and by a very rapid easing in the unregulated terms for consumer credit. The full impact of these combined actions was not clear until fairly well into 1955, so that it was late in that year before the Federal Reserve authorities again moved decisively toward tight money.

By that time, a substantial part of the financial reserves freed by the easy money policy of 1954 was pouring into the spending stream, and at a more rapid rate than it was possible to increase the supply of goods. Before the monetary authorities could turn down the flow, there had been created a sufficient increase in the circulating money supply to support renewed price advances in 1956. Once again, however, the increases in prices that actually occurred were smaller—in fact, smaller by one-half—than those of the 1945–1951 period.

WHAT HAVE WE LEARNED?

The experiences with deficit financing during 1951–1953 and again during the 1954 recession should remind us that, even on something less than a wartime scale, an unbalanced Federal budget complicates the task of the Federal Reserve System in trying to limit bank reserves. Since banks are the main underwriters of Federal debt, the Federal Reserve cannot very well follow a policy that makes it altogether impossible for them to buy the bonds. And in a business recovery, the banks can and will sell government bonds to acquire lending reserves.

However, the recent experience also makes clear that—once free of its obligation to maintain a pegged price for government bonds—the Federal Reserve can, by increasing the risks of purchase, limit the *amount* of such bonds that the banks purchase with an eye to future resale, as well as the *amount* that is actually converted to lending reserves at any one time. The Federal Reserve can, therefore, greatly mitigate the violence of inflationary cycles that have their origin in deficit financing. In fact, with somewhat better coordination of housing and consumer credit policies than was the case in 1954–1955, the restored powers of the Federal Reserve authorities over bank credit appear adequate to hold monetary fluctuations to a moderate scope.

Thus, if the preceding history of inflationary developments and eventually successful attempts to control them in the period 1945–1955 has served its purpose, it should be clear that the most menacing forms of inflation are now some distance behind us.

The U.S. has made progress, very substantial progress, in dealing with the two problems that lay at the root of the early postwar inflations. The first of these was shortages of goods, a problem dealt with most effectively by the production of 56 million new automobiles, 63 million television sets and comparable quantities of other items, ranging from motorboats to baby carriages, over the past decade. The second problem, lack of effective monetary controls, has been dealt with by the restoration of Federal Reserve powers, as described above.

Short of renewed warfare on a major scale, there is little likelihood that these circumstances, which we noted earlier led to inflation in the range of 7 to 8 percent a year, will be repeated anytime soon. In fact, we are making continuing progress both in warding off the danger of future shortages and in sharpening the instruments of monetary control. Of key importance is the increase of 31 percent in manufacturing capacity since 1953, which has created a substantial cushion of reserve producing capacity in most of our major industries.

Over the past two years, manufacturing operations have ranged between 70 and 85 percent of capacity and even if this ratio were to move upward slightly, there would be greater reserve to accommodate a sudden rush of demand created by war or other crisis than was the case in 1945 or 1950.

In the monetary field, the power of the Federal Reserve authorities has been strengthened by an increasing degree of cooperation from the Treasury, which since 1953 has been paying the "going rate" on its bonds and accepting higher interest rates as a cost of fighting inflation. There is room for greater cooperation, however, from some of the independent monetary agencies such as the Federal National Mortgage Association, whose policies in furnishing money to the mortgage market sometimes run counter to the general monetary policies set by the Federal Reserve. Congress shares with these lending agencies the responsibility for seeing to it that they and the Federal Reserve authorities do not work at cross purposes. Another great loophole remains in the field of consumer credit, much of which is dispensed by unregulated sales finance companies.

NEW—STYLE INFLATION: 1956—1958

With these improvements in the monetary mechanism and little likelihood of shortages that would stimulate scare buying over the years immediately ahead, the future danger to economic stability need not be measured in terms of violent inflation. But there remains the question of whether "creeping inflation," say on the order of 3 percent a year, (1) will be our lot, and if so, (2) whether it will be a menace to tolerably sustained prosperity. This was the approximate pace of inflation during 1956–1958, a period when large wage settlements, obtained in the face of restrictive monetary policy, exerted the main push on prices—a new phenomenon which has been dubbed "cost push" inflation.*

If our sole defense against "cost push" inflation were monetary policy it seems clear that it would be inadequate. In the nature of the American political economy what can be done through the general control over the supply of money and credit to contain the boosting of costs, and hence prices, through wage agreements has important limitations. If, for example, the Reserve authorities were to restrict the total supply of money and credit so that there would not be enough available to validate price increases prompted by wage increases, the pressure thus exerted could hardly escape having some adverse effects on other prices occupying essentially the role of innocent bystanders. Thus, so long as the Federal Reserve authorities cannot pinpoint their measures so as to spare innocent bystanders, they are under special compulsion to apply monetary and credit restraints with great care. Likewise, the Federal Reserve can exert a credit and monetary squeeze tight enough to be plausibly charged with having contributed directly to unemployment only upon pain of courting a prompt and violent reaction in Congress.

It may be, and indeed is, argued that the incidental suffering of the innocents which attends the broad exercise of monetary and credit controls is a cost we must pay if prices are to play their key role in allocating resources effectively within the limits imposed by a generally stable price level. If, however, the innocents are politically powerful, as they

* This phenomenon is discussed effectively and in considerable detail in the new book *Can Inflation Be Controlled?* by Harold G. Moulton, president-emeritus of the Brookings Institution, Washington, Anderson Kramer Associates, 1958.

well may be, their complaints will be heard in influential political circles from which, in the last analysis, the Federal Reserve cannot be completely detached.

In its customarily guarded way, the President's Council of Economic Advisers took account of these realities in the opening section of the President's Economic Report of 1957 when it remarked that "the full burden of avoiding price inflation cannot be successfully carried by fiscal and monetary restraints alone. To place this burden on them would invite the risk of producing effects on the structure and functioning of our economy which might, in the years ahead, impair the vitality of competitive enterprise."

If we were to rely on self-restraint by the parties to wage agreements which produce "cost push" inflation, our defense against it would also be doomed to failure, at least over much of the time span with which we are concerned in this volume. This is true if for no other reason than that there is violent controversy between these parties as to which one of them should be exercising the restraint.

Employers take the general position that "cost push" inflation is the creature of monopolistic unions that force them to grant wage increases with which they can survive only by making compensating price increases. Completely on the contrary, union leaders commonly plead innocent and charge the employers with pushing prices up independently of cost increases. According to Solomon Barkin, Director of Research, Textile Workers Union of America, "The declared policies of the large industrial corporations is to administer their prices in an inflationary way." *

As a matter of *fact*, as opposed to debate, there have in recent years been clear-cut cases of "cost push" inflation

* "The Politics of Rising Prices," *The New Leader*, Dec. 1, 1958, Vol. XLI, No. 44, p. 13.

caused by agreement to pay wage increases which, if profit margins were to be maintained, could only be accommodated by offsetting price increases. One of many available examples is to be found in the steel industry. There, according to a study by the U.S. Bureau of Labor Statistics, output per man-hour increased about 14 percent from 1951 through 1955.[*] But increases in hourly wage rates, not including the added cost of fringe benefits, increased by almost twice as much. Not surprisingly, the price of steel increased a little over 14 percent. No doubt, there have also been cases where prices have been "administered" upward more than increases in wages and costs would have justified.

The power of our great unions to produce "cost push" inflation is, of course, enhanced by their exemption from prosecution under the Federal antitrust laws. Thus, elimination of this exemption would remove one potential and, at times of late, actual source of "cost push" inflation. However, the very rise of the unions to transcendent economic power in many of our basic industries has carried along with it a rise to political power, which makes removal of their exemption from antitrust law prosecution (as the monopolies they clearly are) an unlikely political development, at least for some years.

In the meantime, there seems little likelihood that labor unions in the U.S. will clarify the issue of "cost push" inflation as it was clarified some years ago by the leaders of the Swedish Federation of Labor. In 1951 the Swedish labor leaders recognized that the granting of wage demands they had made for their constituents would, by the route of increasing costs, lead to an increase in prices and the cost of living. So they demanded, and received, a supplemental wage increase to recompense the members of the Federation

[*] BLS Bulletin 1200, 1956 and article in *Monthly Labor Review*, November 1956 by M. Haven and A. D. Searle, p. 1276.

for the loss of purchasing power caused by the inflationary impact of the original demands.*

Until the issue is clarified, both by better reporting and analysis of the myriad facts involved, our Presidents can be expected to call eloquently for restraint on the part of both unions and employers in raising prices through cost-increasing agreements. It is also possible to hope that heed will be given to such requests. But it must be observed that the record of "jawbone control" of either wages or prices, as it has been characterized, is not one of notable success in the United States.

Still, the case is something less than hopeless. There are powerful new forces at work, and in prospect, which promise to exercise a restraining influence on the future course of "cost push" inflation. In summary form, they include:

1. Attainment of ample capacity in almost all lines of industrial production, a development already stressed in Chapter 2, and hence increasing intensity of competition.

2. Rapid increase in the output of industrial labor per manhour.

3. Waning political enthusiasm for maintaining farm prices at artificially high levels, and increasing technical difficulty in doing it.

4. Growing unpopularity of inflation.

NEW GAINS IN PRODUCTIVITY

Coming out of the recession of 1957–1958, the productivity of industrial labor has increased very rapidly. A development of this kind is a standard phenomenon of recovery from a recession and for standard reasons. The less competent

* "The Role of Cost-of-Living Anticipations in Swedish Collective Bargaining," an unpublished memorandum by Ludwig Wagner for the McGraw-Hill Department of Economics, 1954.

workers tend to be laid off; those remaining have a tendency to work a little harder; and, with excess capacity quite generally available, the best of the producing facilities are used. However, there is reason to believe that the speeding up of the productivity of industrial labor which has characterized the recovery from the 1957–1958 recession will prove to have a new element of vigor and carry-through. The reason is found in the continuing boom in research and development, dealt with in Chapter 3, which carried right through the recession on an ascending curve and which is leading to a flood of new and improved industrial processes and equipment.

Any gain in industrial productivity would, of course, reduce proportionately the "cost push" power of industrial wage increases—just as the absence of much of any gain made a key contribution to the "cost push" inflation between 1956 and 1958. For example, in analyzing the inflationary experience in 1956, when the average of wholesale prices went up over 3 percent, the President's Council of Economic Advisers observed: "It would appear that the improvement in output per employee manhour which occurred in 1956 was not only less than the rise in 1955 but less than the average for the postwar period ... [The] smallness of the 1956 gain contributed to the rise in unit labor costs and, in turn, to the increase in prices." *

The small increase in productivity in 1956 appears to have been due, in part, to a sort of industrial indigestion resulting from a great rush to install new and better plant and equipment.† In 1956 the dollar volume of business invest-

* *Economic Report of the President,* January 1957, p. 34. In May 1957 the Bureau of Labor Statistics released figures showing that unit costs went up 4.4 percent in 1956.

† A contribution to low productivity also seems to have been made by the incorporation of an abnormally large number of new workers, many of them unskilled, part-time workers attracted by an abundant supply of jobs

ment in new producing facilities jumped about 22 percent above that in 1955, which itself had constituted the all-time record-breaking dollar total, and went up again by 5 percent in 1957. Now (in 1959) the rapid rise in industrial productivity is due in part to the shakedown of the record-breaking new equipment installations of those earlier years.

THE ROLE OF FARM PRICES

The precise part which the future course of farm prices may play in determining how much, or little, "cost push" inflation will be our lot is as uncertain as next year's weather. But there are forces, both political and technical, at work which permit at least the suspicion that farm prices will exert a moderating influence on any general upward tendency of the general price level.

This was clearly not the case in the period 1956–1958 when an increase in consumer prices of about 3 percent a year gave "cost push" inflation major status as a matter of national concern. Until mid-1958 (see chart on page 184) farm prices not only shared in the general movement of prices, but actually had a multiplier effect through escalator wage agreements which provided for increases in wage rates to match increases in the cost of living which farm prices had a large part in shaping. Between January 1956 and July 1958 the Bureau of Labor Statistics Consumer Price Index rose 9.3 points (from 114.6 to 123.9, the average for 1947–1949 being equal to 100), largely because of an 11 percent increase in food prices. The way this affected wages may be seen in the

of a kind they could handle. A total of about 600,000 had been estimated as a likely increase in the labor force for a year in the mid-fifties. But in the year between June 1955 and June 1956 no less than 2,600,000 new workers took jobs, many of them inevitably of the relatively ineffective type indicated.

operation of the cost-of-living provision of the contract between General Motors and the United Auto Workers, which
required GM to increase the hourly wage rates of its employees by a total of 19 cents an hour—apart from increases
for productivity and other reasons.

Since mid–1958, the movement of farm prices has been
downward. And both the prodigious plenty created by the
continuing technological revolution on the farm and a growing political indisposition to have the Federal government
support key farm prices at very high levels could well result
in at least not having the trend sharply reversed. As will
be shown in Chapter 9, there is no reason to believe that the
Federal government will fully withdraw its financial assistance from agriculture for years to come. But there is good
reason to believe that the assistance will take the form of
lower rather than higher support prices, perhaps accompanied by direct subsidy payments to farmers. This would
permit *market* prices of some farm commodities to decline,
and so reduce, in some degree, the cost of food and textile
products to retail consumers.

Operating through the consumer price index and escalator
wage agreements tied to that index, a lowering—or even
leveling off—of farm and food prices would be echoed in
reduced "cost push" inflationary pressure. And since the
lowering of farm support prices might well be attended by
lower Federal expenditures for surplus crop storage, lower
interest payments on money tied up in surplus crops, and a
reduction in the number of personnel required to administer
these programs, one further result could be a considerable
lightening of the load agriculture now places on the Federal
budget. Such budget lightening would, in itself, amount to
a reduction in inflationary pressures.

Thus there is in a revamping of the Federal farm program,
at least in the direction of lower support prices, and con-

ceivably with considerable further economies, the possibility of taking quite a bit of the steam out of "cost push" inflation. This is a process to which the spectacular increase in farm productivity can make a decisive contribution—especially if, through revision of the support program, the gains in productivity can be concentrated on such consumer items as meat and dairy products. (The existing support program provides strongest incentives for production of nonfood items, such as cotton and animal feeds.)

THE BUYERS STRIKE AT LAST

The conventions of respectable economic discourse in the United States call for condemnation of inflation, "cost push" or otherwise. Hence, what is said or written about it is a very fallible gauge of what people either think or are disposed to do about it.

However, there are some indications that inflation—creeping, trotting or galloping—is becoming more unpopular in the United States. One of the more persuasive indications comes from the Survey Research Center at the University of Michigan, whose studies show that, by and large, rising prices would do very badly in a popularity contest and, much more important, that rising prices—particularly for durable goods—tend to discourage buying.* (Consumers may, of

* "The prospect of rising prices is viewed unfavorably by most people. A small minority said this October that rising prices are to the good because they are indicative of active demand; but far more people said that rising prices are 'to the bad.' Their most common arguments are that wage increases tend to lag behind price increases or that high prices prevent people from buying anything but necessities. . . .

"The resentment against inflation revealed by these data is important, since past reinterview data suggest that people who expect rising prices and say that 'this is to the bad' make fewer major expenditures than others with similar incomes." George Katona and Eva Mueller, "The Consumer Outlook," papers presented at the Sixth Annual Conference on the Economic Outlook, University of Michigan, Ann Arbor, Michigan, Nov. 3–4, 1958, p. 52.

course, resume a strong rate of buying once prices level off, even though the level remains high, as it has in most of the postwar years.)

The conventional doctrine has been that inflation spurs buying because people, seeing their money losing its purchasing power, hurry to get rid of it. But the Survey Research Center's studies find that, at times when money is rapidly losing its purchasing power, consumers actually are more inclined to hold back in hope that later on will prove a better time to buy. This finding, it should be noted, brilliantly underlines the importance of going into the field to find out directly about consumer or other economic behavior, as well as doing armchair theorizing about it.

Whatever the popularity of inflation now, it seems to be an entirely safe prediction that it will diminish in the years immediately ahead. As indicated in Chapter 4, the proportion of our population composed of older people is mounting steadily and rapidly. With most of them living on retirement incomes fixed in dollar amounts, the votes against inflation will rise as their numbers do. And there are many methods, ranging all the way from not buying to changing Congressmen, to give these votes economic effect.

The considerations which have been outlined are not designed to suggest that "cost push" inflation is or soon will be entirely a thing of the past. We have created and tolerate an institutional framework which in some particulars positively fosters it. But these considerations also provide substantial foundations for the expectation that creeping "cost push" inflation will be held within tolerable limits and will not graduate into—or, rather, degenerate into—trotting or galloping inflation.

This, of course, raises the question of what are tolerable limits. There are those who would argue that, in perspective, there is really nothing to get very excited about in the rate

at which the general price level has increased during the past
decade. Among them, Professor Emeritus Alvin H. Hansen
of Harvard University calculates this rate of increase, compounded, to have been 1¼ percent a year for wholesale
prices, and 1¾ percent for consumer prices.* "In contrast,"
he remarks, "in the sixteen years of peacetime prosperity
from 1897 to 1913 the compound rate of increase per annum
was much higher—2½ percent. Taking the longer view
covering six decades from 1897 to 1958, the per annum rate
of increase of prices (wholesale and consumer) was 2⅓
percent. . . . Yet when anyone suggests a possible increase
of around 2 or 2½ percent per annum over the next two or
three decades alarmists are apt to cry 'ruin and disaster.' This
rate of increase is, however, precisely what the United States
in fact experienced during the last sixty years."

Without taking up with the alarmists who alarm Professor
Hansen, it can be pointed out that it is not "a possible increase of around 2 or 2½ percent per annum" which is the
basic cause of the perturbation of most of them. To be sure,
such an annual rate of price inflation would make savings
deposits and investments in fixed income securities at traditional rates relatively bootless. Recognition of this fact by an
increasingly sophisticated investment public could involve
at least temporarily disturbing financial adjustments, both
public and private. In fact, it was in substantial measure fear
of creeping inflation as our steady companion in the years
ahead which prompted the rush into common stocks and the
retreat from government bonds in 1958–1959, with attendant
difficulties in Federal financing.

However, as between assurance of a slowly declining price
level and a slowly rising one, the latter is much to be preferred
as a tonic to business expansion and growth. With prices
slowly but steadily declining, costly miscalculations by busi-

* In a letter to *The New York Times,* Jan. 23, 1959.

ness managers tend to stand out like beacon lights, whereas such mistakes tend to be submerged and blurred by rising prices. The influence on the disposition to be venturesome is obvious. Even more obvious is the fact that with steadily declining prices in prospect boards of corporate directors tend, on cost grounds, to postpone and postpone and postpone new installation of producing facilities which are of the very essence of growth and expansion.*

No, what most of the alarmists to whom Professor Hansen refers are alarmed about is the possibility that, even in the absence of wars, the sort of creeping inflation he finds we have had for the past sixty years will turn into galloping inflation or, as a variant of it, lead to a wild speculative spree, centered in the markets for investments which may serve as a hedge against inflation, with a disastrous crash to follow.

If, however, this chapter has done its work tolerably well, the conclusion must be that inflation, "cost push" or other, while not a thing of the past, is unlikely to attain destructive proportions in the decade ahead.

There may well be times when, under specially propitious circumstances from a union bargaining point of view such as those prevailing in the spring of 1955, powerful unions may be able to exact such large wage increases (and employers be able to pass them along) that, even with the most stringent monetary policy possible, prices are forced up sharply in the industries involved. In 1955, the United Automobile Workers, helped by a boom which resulted in all-time record-breaking sales of about 7.2 million passenger cars that year, obtained an increase in wages and fringe benefits of more than twenty cents an hour, which set the pattern for similar agreements in other basic industries. This was such a complete "break-

* There is a useful discussion of the relationship between inflation and economic growth in a volume, *The New Inflation*, by Willard L. Thorp and Richard E. Quandt, to be published by McGraw-Hill in 1959.

through" of the established wage pattern that it put almost irresistible upward pressure on the price structure.

There may also be times (we have not had one for so many years that fingers should be kept crossed) when crop failures will give the inflationary ratchet, with its gearing of the cost of living and wage rates in many wage contracts, a specially lively twist. And the same thing may happen as a result of a sort of traffic jam in a high-speed movement to install more and better industrial plant and equipment, such as that which occurred in 1956 and 1957.

But we have effective instruments for monetary control, and a demonstrated determination by those in command of them to use them courageously to contain inflation. And working on their side in crucial sectors such as those of food supply and industrial equipment we have the most basic enemy of inflation, abundance. With this line-up in an economic arena where inflation is increasingly unpopular, the odds are good that over the next decade it will be held within safe limits.

CHAPTER NINE

Are Agriculture's Aches Contagious?

The notion that our depressions generally are "farm led and farm fed" has long been an article of faith among a substantial number of people who might be called, with respect to their economic viewpoint, agricultural fundamentalists. The principal basis for this notion seems to be their recollection that agriculture went into a depression of its own in the early 1920s, long before the collapse of the stock market or even of the Florida land boom. The drop in farm incomes, the argument runs, meant that farmers had to cut down on purchases of tractors, automobiles and other manufactured goods. This, in turn, reduced job opportunities and held down incomes of factory workers. Eventually, as the effects compounded and worked through the economy, a general depression resulted.

If correct, this diagnosis would make the recent course of U.S. agriculture an ominous sign for the future of the American economy. With rare exceptions like 1958, farm income has been slipping almost steadily since 1951.* Net farm income in 1957 was 29 percent lower than in 1951. If falling farm income were indeed a portent of a general economic slump, then the support of farm prices and incomes through the expenditure of Federal money at a rate of some $7 billion

* See Appendix II for a discussion of recent trends in farm income.

a year might be pretty cheap insurance for the rest of us.

The evidence suggests that agriculture does not now have this capacity to put the entire economy into a tailspin—if it ever did. Nevertheless, agriculture does present a serious problem with which we must deal far more effectively than we have done so far, if our economy is to show a really satisfactory record of performance.

ARE DEPRESSIONS FARM LED?

The relationship between agriculture and the general economy has been studied carefully by a number of investigators, including the National Bureau of Economic Research, to determine whether agriculture actually does run ahead of other industries in recession or recovery. These investigations have failed to uncover any such relationship. In fact, the sequence seems to run the other way—a general economic slump means a declining market for farm products and declining income for the farmer.

On close inspection, the history of the 1920s does not provide any unequivocal support for the belief that distress on the farm touched off the Great Depression. The collapse of farm prices came early in the 1920s, following World War I, and the collapse was abrupt. According to one prominent agricultural economist, "by the spring of 1921, American agriculture found itself in a more unfavorable position than it had experienced at any time in the memory of men then living, or possibly at any time since the nation's beginning. The purchasing power of farm products in terms of non-agricultural products was down to 63 percent as compared to prewar." * After 1921, however, farm prices and incomes gradually recovered and remained relatively strong through

---

* Murray R. Benedict, *Farm Policies of the United States, 1790–1950*, New York, Twentieth Century Fund, 1953, p. 172.

the late 1920s, as the following figures on average net income
of farm operators show:

1920	$1,085	1925	$979
1921	597	1926	913
1922	677	1927	907
1923	781	1928	901
1924	818	1929	962

It is easier to defend the proposition that "the prosperity
of agriculture depends heavily upon the buying power of
nonfarm people." * Professor Dale E. Hathaway of Michigan
State University—the agricultural economist assigned by the
Congressional Joint Economic Committee to report on "Agriculture and the Business Cycle"—found that in ten periods
of business expansion between 1910 and 1956, net farm income rose in all but one. And in ten periods of business con-
traction, net farm income declined in all but two.†

As we have learned in the last few years, it is also possible
for agriculture and general business to be moving in opposite
directions at the same time. Farm income in the years 1955–
1957 was lower than in 1954, though business generally was
enjoying a boom during this period. In 1958, by contrast,
farm prices and incomes rose sharply despite a severe, if
brief, recession in general business. Because the rise in prices
of some farm products in 1958 was the result of freakish
weather conditions and a low point in the cattle and hog
production cycles,‡ farm incomes were declining and again
moving counter to the nonfarm economy in early 1959.

---

* *Ibid.*, p. 241.
† *Policy for Commercial Agriculture: Its Relation to Economic Growth and
Stability,* papers submitted by panelists appearing before the Subcommittee
on Agricultural Policy, Joint Economic Committee, 85th Congress, 1st
Session, Washington, Government Printing Office, 1957, p. 54.
‡ See "The Surge in Farm Income," *Business Conditions,* Federal Reserve
Bank of Chicago, December 1958, pp. 6–10.

Certainly, agriculture's potential for disturbing the rest of the economy has diminished as agriculture's relative position in the economy has declined. In 1929, farm people accounted for 25 percent of the total population, and 10 percent of our national income originated in agriculture. Now only about 12 percent of our population live on farms, and only 5 percent of our national income originates in agriculture. In addition, income of farm people from nonfarm sources—such as part-time and off-season factory jobs—has risen to be half as large as their income from farming. So, as consumers, farmers are becoming less vulnerable to changes in farm income.

There is one important exception to this general observation that farmers now occupy a less prominent place in our economy and consequently have less potential for generating disturbances elsewhere. This exception is in the area of fixed investments in buildings and equipment. Farmers now account for about 7 percent of total fixed investment, which is a slightly higher proportion than in 1929 and is a reflection of the increased mechanization—and smaller labor requirements—of U.S. agriculture. In the 1958 recession, farmers put some of their increased incomes into machinery; and agricultural machinery shipments, contrary to the trend in machinery generally, were substantially higher than in 1957. In this instance, farmers were able to lend support to a sagging industry. But in severe depressions, when farm income fell sharply, one of the most pronounced effects was a steep drop in sales of farm equipment.*

Although instability in agriculture can have a large impact on agricultural machinery and certain other industries supplying farms and farm people, it does not appear to involve more than marginal consequences for the rest of the economy. In any event, it would be difficult to represent agriculture as a

* Hathaway, *op. cit.*, pp. 64–69.

serious threat to general economic prosperity, or stability, in the years ahead. This is particularly the case if, as seems likely, government programs continue to limit the variations in farm prices and incomes.

These observations should not, of course, be taken to mean that agriculture has lost any of its obvious and basic importance to the nation as a supplier of food, fibers and other everyday necessities. It is a tribute to U.S. agriculture that it has been able to carry out its essential function of producing for a growing population while requiring smaller quantities of such resources as land and labor.

TOO MANY RESOURCES

The potential of agriculture as a breeder and feeder of depressions clearly has declined. However, we are still faced with a serious farm problem which may be regarded as the consequence of too much success coming too fast. This problem is revealed in several ways: a costly and singularly ineffectual Federal farm program; the failure of farmers in recent prosperous years to share in the prosperity despite huge government subsidies; the prevention of healthful readjustments in the use of our agricultural resources. Basically, we have failed to come up with any politically palatable way of coping with the prodigious rise in productivity in agriculture during the last two decades.

The effect of mechanization, and of new developments in fertilizers, insecticides and genetics, can be seen most dramatically in the chart showing the number of persons supported by the production of one U.S. farm worker. In 1820 the average number of persons supported by each farm worker was 4.12. By 1940, each farm worker produced enough food and other farm products to meet the needs of 10.69 persons. But by 1957, each farm worker was supporting 23.55

persons. Thus, in the seventeen years 1940–1957 the increase in the number of persons supported per farm worker was twice as great as in the preceding 120 years. The gains in productivity per acre have been almost as spectacular—crop yields per acre in 1958 were 43 percent higher than the average for 1947–1949.

The principal result of these gains in productivity has been the creation of staggering surpluses of farm products, particularly of the six so-called "basic crops" that have been the object of special solicitude in government programs. These six crops—corn, wheat, cotton, tobacco, rice and peanuts—

Persons Supported by Production of One Farm Worker

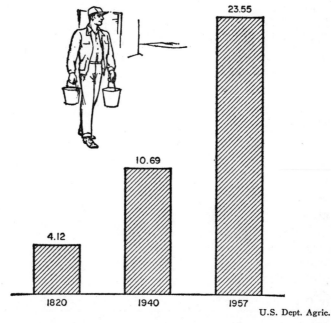

U.S. Dept. Agric.

Productivity on the farm has been increasing faster than productivity in the factory. Today nearly six times as many persons are supported by one farm worker's production as were supported by one farm worker nearly 140 years ago, and nearly twice as many as were supported by one farm worker before World War II.

owe their selection partly to political considerations. But they were also designated for government support programs in the depression period because they can be stored longer than most other crops. The theory, when the farm legislation of the 1930s was passed, was that if some of the crop could be held off the market during the temporary periods of surplus, it could be sold later on for a better price when market conditions improved. During the war there was the additional motive of using a price guarantee as an incentive to farmers to increase production.

Developments during the war drastically changed the nature of our problem of farm surpluses. With guaranteed prices and assured markets in the U.S. and allied countries, farmers expanded their production rapidly. Their incomes soared, net farm income being three times as large in 1945 as it was in 1940. They built up their financial resources from $4.2 billion in 1940 to $12.5 billion in 1945. Much of this money, during and after the war, went into purchases by successful farmers of more farm land and more equipment. The value of machinery per farm (expressed in constant 1947–1949 dollars) rose from only $646 in 1940 to $1,293 in 1949 and to $2,126 in 1958. The average farm was becoming larger, better financed, better equipped—in short, more productive—during the war and immediate postwar years. But as foreign agriculture recovered in the late 1940s, our export market suffered. And the problem of U.S. agriculture became one of chronic, not temporary, surpluses.

The devices used by the government as ways to reduce surplus production have been singularly ineffectual. Direct controls have taken the form, for the most part, of acreage restrictions—that is, programs designed to limit the amount of land planted to a supported crop. But farmers have simply cultivated more intensively, planted high-yield hybrid seeds and used more fertilizer and insecticides on the reduced acreage. Also, farms outside the primary areas of production of some basic crops, particularly wheat, have been drawn into the market by the assurance of a guaranteed price, although they are largely beyond the reach of the control program. And land taken out of production of basic crops has often been planted to other crops, merely transferring the surplus problem.

The actions by Congress to move in the direction of lower price supports have been limited. And such reductions as have been put into effect have not increased consumption appreciably nor reduced production. It is a characteristic of most farm products that demand for them is inelastic—that is, a reduction in price will not induce a proportionate increase in sales. Lower prices, in such cases, do not stimulate much increase in consumption and actually result in a decrease in total income from marketing the crop. On the supply side, because of the increase in productivity on the larger farms, it takes extremely sharp price cuts to induce lower production—price cuts of a size that would put many small farmers in real distress. One of the ironies of our farm program is that, while the preservation of the moderate sized "family farm" has been among its principal purposes, its benefits have gone in large part to the highly efficient big commercial farms.

The government's farm price support programs have become increasingly expensive. During the 1959 fiscal year, total Federal expenditures for agriculture are estimated at about $7 billion—more than for any other purpose except defense and interest on the public debt. And about $5 billion of this total is for support of farm prices and incomes. Surplus farm commodities in government inventory and under loan by July 1959 will amount to over $9 billion. The cost of interest and storage alone on these government stocks is running about $1 billion a year.

The *net* cost of the farm program to the government is, of course, not as large as these figures might suggest, for some of the crops under government loan eventually are sold. And some of the government expenditures that directly or indirectly aid agriculture have other objectives, such as the $17 billion spent for farm products used in war and post-war relief in other countries. Leaving such programs out, however, the Department of Agriculture estimated that the *net* cost to the government of stabilizing farm prices and income over the period 1932–1958 (fiscal years) was $15.7 billion.* And the net costs of these efforts since 1956 have been averaging nearly $2.7 billion a year.

Despite these heavy expenditures, *average* farm income has been maintained only because the farm population which shares the income has been declining, and also has been earning more nonagricultural income from part-time and seasonal jobs. This economic readjustment is necessary if agriculture is to provide a decent livelihood for those who remain on farms. But it still has a long way to go. As of 1954, one-third of the 3.1 million commercial farms in the U.S. had annual sales of less than $2,500.† One danger of Federal price and income support programs is that they will encourage many people to stay in farming who might be better off in other occupations. And even within agriculture, these programs have kept too large a proportion of our agricultural resources tied to the production of crops that consumers don't want.

It is, of course, easy to exaggerate the cost of the Federal farm programs and also the apparent hopelessness of the

---

* *Realized Cost of Agricultural and Related Programs, by Function or Purpose,* Fiscal Years 1932–1958, U.S. Department of Agriculture, January 1959.

† These one million small commercial farms are defined as farms where the operator was not working off the farm as much as 100 days in the year and the amount of farm sales was greater than the income of family members from off-farm sources.

farm problem. The cost of all Federal farm programs in the 1959 fiscal year amounts to about 1.5 percent of our gross national product. But in 1939, the agricultural budget came to 1.3 percent of the gross national product of that year. So it is not evident that agriculture is responsible for an appreciably heavier drain on the rest of the economy now than it was twenty years ago. Nevertheless, Federal spending of $7 billion for agriculture may be regarded as an inflationary threat if it makes the difference between surplus and deficit in the Federal budget.

Furthermore, the trouble in agriculture is concentrated heavily in a few crops; more than half of our total agricultural market sales, including all meat and citrus products, are not covered by any price support program. Significantly, perhaps, the most serious trouble is in the crops that have been under special protection.

Nevertheless, there can be no doubt that the problems of agriculture will remain among the most important economic

Per Capita Income, Farm and Nonfarm Population

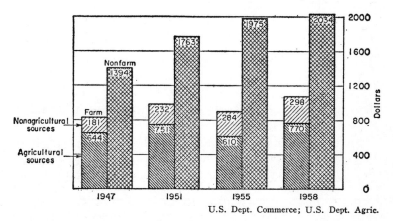

U.S. Dept. Commerce; U.S. Dept. Agric.

Per capita farm income (including income from both farm and nonagricultural sources) is just a little more than half as much as the per capita income of the nonfarm population.

problems we shall have to face in the years ahead. The Congressional committee that studied these problems recently was confronted during its hearings with a universal opinion of farm experts that there was nothing in view in the supply and demand factors affecting agricultural products that would appreciably alter the surplus situation in the next five to ten years.*

WHAT SHOULD BE DONE?

The central problem, over the long pull, is to encourage agriculture to show continued improvements in productivity and furnish adequate production for a growing population—a job it has performed superlatively in recent years—but without having it either a sick industry or chronically wet-nursed by the Federal treasury.

Perhaps the most hopeful sign in current deliberations on our farm problems is the increasing appreciation that continuation of the high-level price supports adopted during World War II will not solve these problems. This feeling has been accompanied by resentment among consumers over having to "pay twice" for the cost of farm price supports, once as taxpayers and a second time as consumers who are charged more than they would be in a completely free market. It is to be hoped that this resentment will not blind consumers to the vital interest of the nation generally in the development of a workable farm program and in economically healthy agriculture.

We do not profess to be qualified to lay down the specifications for a satisfactory farm program. And we doubt seriously that any revolutionary new program can, or should, be in-

*Policy for Commercial Agriculture: Its Relation to Economic Growth and Stability, Report of the Subcommittee on Agricultural Policy to the Joint Economic Committee, Congress of the United States, 85th Congress, 2nd Session, Washington, Government Printing Office, 1958, pp. 7–8.

troduced overnight. This includes notably the revolutionary proposal that agricultural markets be made completely "free" at once. At the other extreme, it includes also any proposal for controls that are stringent enough to make the present farm program work. Neither of these extremes is in the cards politically; and it is far from certain that either would be desirable economically.

The best bet seems to be to work toward gradual reduction of extravagant support programs for "basic" crops and try to limit price and income support measures to situations of temporary distress—as was originally intended. We must also frankly recognize the politically unpopular truth that we have too many resources, including people, engaged in producing farm products.

Meanwhile, the process of easing a painful adjustment for agriculture will continue to involve substantial government outlays. The sensible approach is to see to it that these outlays do not continue to rise under "open-end" programs —in which the government is obligated to make some payments without limit—and that they are directed toward the solution, not the perpetuation, of our farm problems.

Over the next few years, we should be able to do more in the way of disposal of our surplus crops through aid to impoverished foreign nations, whose food problem is just the opposite of ours. (This is, and will become increasingly, a delicate diplomatic matter, because of the possibility that these aid programs will compete with normal exports of farm products by friendly nations such as Canada.)

Another idea to which more attention might be given is the substitution of direct income payments for present price support payments. This idea was incorporated in the Brannan Plan, the controversial program offered by President Truman's Secretary of Agriculture in 1949, as a means of aiding producers of perishable crops. It was dismissed peremptorily by many people largely because of its association with the costly high-level support program and rigid controls of the Brannan Plan. But an income payment has the rational appeal of giving the consumer the benefit of lower market prices and thus the impression that he is paying only once for his aid to farmers. It would also be easier to avoid huge subsidies to large commercial farms under income payments (with a top limit per farm) than it is now under price supports.

CONCLUSION

We see no reason for worry that agriculture will drag the nation into depression. Indeed, a good case could be made for the contention that a continually increasing drain on the Federal treasury through our present farm program makes the threat of inflation far more worrisome. For the good of both agriculture and the economy at large, we would like to see some progress made toward reducing the burden on taxpayers and encouraging the growth of agriculture in the right directions. But—as one agricultural expert we know has remarked—"there are worse things than an overabundance of farm products."

CHAPTER TEN

U.S. Business and the World Overseas

If this book had been written ten years ago, the authors might have been considered foolish for suggesting that support for growth and stability in U.S. business might come from the world beyond our shores. Few businessmen, in those early postwar years that included the Berlin blockade and the Korean War, were thinking about foreign developments as anything but sources of trouble. Our concerns abroad were largely military. World trade was at a low level. And in general, this period of international violence, which lasted from 1948 to 1953, was one in which large defense expenditures, high tax rates and controls over specific commodities seemed to be the main results of what happened overseas. The Marshall Plan, inaugurated in 1948 to assist economic recovery in Europe, was widely attacked as a "giveaway" that would not profit U.S. business.

Today, however, it is a part of the "standard forecast" on U.S. business to include a plus factor for growth in overseas markets. The world has not completely quieted down by any means. There are enough military problems, particularly around Berlin and in the seething areas of the Middle and Far East, to require a large U.S. defense program and taxes high enough to pay for it. (See Chapter 6.) But in the last five years, *economic growth* has become as important as military security among our concerns abroad.* Enough of

* For example, in a statement to the Senate Foreign Relations Committee on Jan. 14, 1959, John Foster Dulles listed the three basic purposes of

the world is now at peace (or close to it) and enjoying economic revival to furnish growing markets abroad for U.S. business. And it is American goods and services, rather than American military protection, that our friends abroad increasingly seek.

In particular, Western Europe—restored to economic vigor by the Marshall Plan of U.S. aid and its own considerable efforts—has been enjoying since 1954 something resembling our own (earlier) postwar boom, with surging demand for both capital goods and consumer durables. A slower, but still impressive, resurgence has occurred in Japan and other nations of free Asia.

This economic revival of the free nations has made the world overseas a considerably more congenial place for U.S. business. It has lessened the danger of Communism in many countries of Asia and removed it, at least for the present, in Western Europe. Economic strength has bolstered the Western military alliance, NATO, and thus reinforced the deterrents to military aggression by the Communist powers. Indeed the Premier of the Soviet Union (at this writing), Mr. Khrushchev, has stated that the future contest between the Communist and capitalist systems is to be one of peaceful production—clearly the sort of contest that an expanding American economy should welcome. Perhaps most important of all, from a strictly business viewpoint, economic revival abroad has permitted a gradual relaxation of tariffs, currency restrictions and other barriers to our trade.

The trend of U.S. exports reflects this improved economic environment. Since 1953, merchandise exports have gained over 30 percent, maintaining a level of more than $16 billion in 1958 despite the general business recession and a sharp

---

American foreign policy as: (1) a stable world order, (2) the spread of responsible freedom and personal liberty, (3) the attainment of a more rapid rate of economic growth by the free nations.

drop in oil exports from the 1957 level.* An increasing number of U.S. firms are building plants abroad. Our total capital investment in foreign countries is now somewhere around
$28 billion, compared with only $12 billion in 1950.† And
the recent rate of investment is over $3.5 billion per year.
Together, our rapidly increasing overseas trade and investment support an estimated 4.5 million jobs in this country.
By 1968, if present trends continue, there will be jobs for
over 6 million persons in producing or servicing goods for
overseas shipment.

How good really are the chances for thus expanding our

U.S. Commercial Exports, 1950–1958

Commercial Exports as Percent of
Gross National Product

1950	3.5%
1955	3.6%
1958	3.7%

U.S. Dept. Commerce

U.S. commercial exports hit an all-time peak of $19.6 billion in 1957. They dropped in
1958 to about $16.5 billion. Commercial exports have been accounting for a slightly
larger share of the national economy since 1950.

* In 1957, U.S. merchandise exports were $19 billion, but this figure was
inflated by emergency oil shipments during the Suez crisis.
† "U.S. Industry Migrates Abroad to Tap Markets of the World," *Business
Week*, Jan. 3, 1959, p. 29.

overseas trade and investment? Will it provide a growth stimulus to the domestic economy in the next ten years, as it has for the past five years? We frequently hear the assertion that U.S. business has got its costs too high and priced itself out of world markets for the future.

Some experts have also expressed fears of our capacity to cope successfully with Russian economic competition. One of these fears is that, without regard to cost or price, the Soviet communist dictatorship can dump goods in the free world in such a way as to demoralize orderly marketing processes upon which successful free world trading depends. Another worry is that this dictatorship will force a growth rate in the U.S.S.R. so fast that the American free economy will appear a sorry second best in production of goods and services, and the uncommitted countries will then flock into the Russian camp, accepting the U.S.S.R. as world economic leader.

If for no other reason than the remarkably confident quality of the rhetoric used, we have carefully looked into how much there might be in Soviet boss Khrushchev's threat that "we will bury you ... in the field of peaceful production." The short answer is that there is not much substance to this boast. Because it is growing on a relatively small industrial base, the Soviet economy may, for some years to come, show an annual percentage growth rate considerably above that of the American economy. But in terms of actual volume— in the output of goods and services—there is little likelihood that the Soviets will overtake us in this generation. In fact, as they approach a comparable stage of economic development, their growth rate, calculated on their own larger base, seems likely to slow down.*

There is much more to worry about, we have found, in

---

* "The Soviet Economic Threat," a McGraw-Hill Department of Economics Report by Martin Kohn, Sept. 2, 1958.

the adroitness of the Soviet dictators in mobilizing their foreign aid, their propaganda and, on occasion, their disruptive dumping of goods. But, so far as their dumping is concerned, it does not seem too much to expect that the nations of the free world will have economic ingenuity enough to devise arrangements (perhaps something in the nature of an economic NATO for the western world) for absorbing any products which the Russians wish to provide at giveaway prices. And there is also reason to doubt that the Russians, needing almost everything badly, will have much sustained appetite for such operations. Indeed the excitement caused by their operations of this type thus far has been out of proportion to their impact on free markets.

Some of the other threats to expansion of trade in the free world are real and pose special problems that we shall deal with under appropriate topics below. However, given escape from atomic, as opposed to economic warfare (our most basic assumption) the general outlook is for continued rapid growth in that sector of the American economy which looks overseas for its potential. In elaborating this thesis, we shall have occasion to look first at the rapid rates of growth, in population and national production, that are in prospect for the rest of the world. We shall also deal with the revolution in living standards that is creating markets abroad for many U.S. goods. Finally, we shall touch on some of the special financial arrangements that have been made to facilitate world trade, and on the emergence of great regional trading areas—notably the European Common Market—in which production and living standards can more nearly approach U.S. levels. In each case, we shall note unsolved problems. But the over-all trend is toward greater progress.

THE EXPLOSIVE RISE IN POPULATION

Since 1920, the population of the world has increased by roughly 800 million. This is more than the entire world population in 1750.* In the next generation, if present trends continue, population will rise another 1 billion persons, all of them needing food, clothing, shelter and medical services, and most of them potential consumers for at least the simpler types of household goods. This rapid growth of population is likely to strain the resources of nations in Asia and Latin America where production is now barely adequate to support tolerable living standards. And it may pose insoluble problems for Russia and China, where the basic needs of growing populations seem too great for these economies to continue building massive war machines—or to concentrate on showy projects in heavy industry. In fact, population growth is not an unmixed blessing for any country. But for the United States (and also for Western Europe), population growth around the world means an opportunity to export, and by exporting to utilize some of the expanding capacity of our own industry and agriculture.

The U.S. is already providing less fortunate nations with many of their day-to-day necessities: food and fiber, coal, oil and fertilizers, drugs and medicines. But increasingly, the rest of the world needs durable items: capital goods to raise production in the undeveloped nations, and consumer goods for those already able to improve their living standards. Many of these items could be (and within a decade, well may be) sold to both China and Russia to make good their own deficiencies, if they would join us in the community of world trade. Eventually, the hunger of large populations, for both necessities and the simpler luxuries of life, may be the force

* W. S. Woytinsky and E. S. Woytinsky, *World Population and Production,* The Twentieth Century Fund, New York, 1953, p. 34.

that breaks down barriers between Western and Communist blocs. Meanwhile, the United States—as the largest producer of both farm and industrial commodities—faces a challenge to supply the deficiencies in the rest of the free world.

Just how large these deficiencies are may be seen from the following comparison:

In the United States, annual production of goods and services comes to roughly $2,500 per capita. But in some other *industrialized* nations of the free world per capita output is under $1,000—or less than half as much. Statistics for less developed areas are necessarily rough. But it appears that in the less industrialized free nations, which have a total population of over 1 billion (or 42 percent of the entire world population) output per capita is about $120 per year— only about a tenth of the figure for industrialized areas! *

The Communist bloc nations, with 900 million people, produced $300 per person in 1956, the last year for which we have any figures. Although this is low by Western standards, it is more than twice the per capita output of the undeveloped nations—quite enough to be impressive to Asians or Africans who have never visited the West. In fact, a key part of the Communists' propaganda appeal is that *they* (and they identify themselves as Asians) have found a way to raise output faster than population.

Their way, of course, is largely forced labor, the sacrifice of living standards (and even lives) for a generation, to build massive industrial plants. We can offer a much better solution—better in economic, as well as in humanitarian terms. Our way, which has already worked in expanding the economies of America and Europe, is to build up the undeveloped countries as suppliers of raw materials which they have in abundance, and which our industry badly needs. This has

* *Foreign Economic Policy for the Twentieth Century,* Report of the Rockefeller Brothers Fund Special Studies Project III, Doubleday and Company, Inc., New York, 1958, p. 46.

been a primary purpose of our "Point Four" Program, which provides technical aid and development loans in Asia, Africa and Latin America.

In 1957, the United States imported $6 billion of raw materials from these areas; within ten years we shall need to import $10 billion or more. As we pay for these raw materials, the overseas nations will acquire an increasing supply of dollars with which to buy capital goods and consumer goods in America.* These are things we can often supply to them more quickly and cheaply than if they sacrificed themselves cruelly to build their own industries.

In the immediate future, many nations abroad will continue to need food and semi-finished manufactures from the United States, for it will take time to build up their own resources. We can expect to keep shipping large quantities of wheat and corn, cotton and textiles, coal and some metals. These shipments will be a considerable aid in stabilizing our own mining and agriculture. But the next logical step will be to help undeveloped countries start their own basic industries. Perhaps within five years, and almost certainly within ten years, the urgent demand from overseas will be for capital goods—for better tools of production that will enable these countries to supply their own food, fuel and light manufactures.

GIVE US THE TOOLS

Without better tools, there is little hope that output per worker in the undeveloped nations will rise as fast as population (which in the case of countries like Egypt or India is not expected to stabilize for at least fifty years). Under such

* Gilbert Burck and Sanford S. Parker, "America Becomes A Trader," *Fortune*, October 1957, pp. 123–127. See also: David Rockefeller's address to the Omaha Chamber of Commerce, "U.S. Business in an Expanding World Economy," reprinted by the Chase Manhattan Bank, Nov. 13, 1958, pp. 5–6.

conditions, the gap between rich and poor nations would simply increase, to the delight of Communist agitators. But with better capital equipment—financed, where necessary, with U.S. government loans or by private investments of U.S. business firms—these nations can hope for a better life.

Indeed this has already occurred in some cases. One such case is Venezuela, where investment by U.S. oil companies has raised production and incomes enough to give much of the population first-class food, housing, medical care and even such recreation as films and TV.* Another is Formosa, where decent living standards have replaced primitive toil and poverty, thanks to shipments of U.S. farm equipment under our foreign aid program. In other nations, wherever we have provided the tools, output and living standards *are already increasing*. This sort of tangible accomplishment is our best answer to Communist propaganda claims.

For the undeveloped nations as a group, manufacturing production has more than doubled since prewar. Since 1948, there have even been modest increases in output of goods *per capita:* 6 percent in Latin America, 15 percent in Southeast Asia and 32 percent in the Middle East and Africa.† If we can maintain or increase these growth rates, we can hope for some degree of political stability in the undeveloped areas, and so for their continuing friendship with the West.

Moreover, the development of higher living standards abroad—the "revolution of rising expectations," ‡ as it has been called—can be a major growth impetus to our own

---

* Reuel Denney, "Oil Town: New Style," *The Lamp,* Standard Oil Company (New Jersey), Fall 1958, pp. 6–17.
† "Growth Situation: The World," *Fortune,* October 1957, p. 122. The figure for the Middle East is somewhat exaggerated by the inclusion of oil output.
‡ Foreign Economic Policy for the Twentieth Century, Report of the Rockefeller Brothers Fund Special Studies Project III, Doubleday and Company, Inc., New York, 1958, p. 6.

economy. The products associated with high living standards are, in many cases, of American design or manufacture— from Coca-Cola to X-ray machines. Whether specific goods are made here, or made abroad in imitation, the U.S. economy will benefit.

In particular, our capital goods industries hold a key position in the effort to raise per capita output around the world. To provide even a start toward adequate capital equipment for the underdeveloped countries, we could well export enough to take up most of the spare capacity created by swings in the domestic demand for new plant and equipment. It has been estimated, for example, that capital investment in the overseas petroleum industry (much of which depends on equipment shipped from the United States) will increase by 140 percent in the next ten years compared with the past decade.* And the United States is the logical supplier for other capital goods, from processing machinery to high-speed computers that will be in demand overseas.

Today this demand is more potential than actual. There are problems of cost, and the availability of dollar exchange —and others that we shall deal with below. But in the long run, it is capital goods demand that will be most affected by the rise in world population, as each nation strives to produce its own food and light manufactures.

NEW INSTITUTIONS FOR WORLD TRADE

Before demand abroad can materialize fully into business for American companies, many improvements are needed in the structure of world trade—both in the arrangements for financing this trade and in the regulations under which goods

* F. G. Coqueron, H. D. Hammar and J. G. Winger, "Future Growth of the World Petroleum Industry," Petroleum Department of the Chase Manhattan Bank, November 1958, p. 43.

are shipped between countries. Although other nations may want American goods, this does not always mean they can pay for them. Consequently, one essential for expanding trade is a set of financial institutions that can loan money—particularly U.S. dollars—to support rising trade volume. Another essential is to reduce the maze of tariffs and import quotas that now limit shipments from one nation to another. (The U.S. itself imposes some of these restrictions, although not as many as in most other countries.) Great progress has been made since World War II in easing trade barriers and improving financial arrangements. But we must do more if we want to accelerate the volume of exports and imports.

Most of the present restrictions on trade result from the chaos that enveloped Europe (and the Far East) during two world wars. These disrupted the old economic order that had governed trade during the nineteenth century and early twentieth century, when Europe was the principal center of world trade—most of it financed with gold or with the British pound sterling. During this earlier period, Europe drew raw materials from its colonies in Asia and Africa and shipped back manufactured goods. There were few tariffs on such trade, and few tariffs between manufacturing countries. Men and goods moved freely between the nations of Europe, and so did capital. When one nation imported more than it had exported, the balance was adjusted by the shipment of gold. And although gold movements affected price levels in various countries, no government was sufficiently concerned about domestic inflation to interfere with the processes of trade.

Two world wars shattered this old system. Colonial empires disappeared, and the former colonial nations began their own light manufacturing industries—usually with tariff protection. Nations at war, or preparing for war, adopted tariffs and import quotas to protect their vital industries.

Then, as war exhausted financial reserves, many countries experienced severe inflation. Currencies were shaky, and it became impossible to settle trade balances in gold or to allow free conversion of one currency into another. Immediately after World War II, large amounts of sterling and other currencies were "blocked" so that they could not be converted into gold or U.S. dollars.

In the past ten years, the United States, which is now the largest trading nation, and the European countries have been endeavoring to develop new institutions that would permit a vigorous revival of world trade. The first steps after World War II were to provide U.S. dollars where they were most needed to expand production and as backing for weaker currencies. The U.S. took the lead (and subscribed the largest share of the funds) in formation of the International Bank for Reconstruction and Development and the International Monetary Fund. The Bank is a long-term lending institution to furnish capital for basic resources and industrial development. The International Monetary Fund makes short-term loans (in the appropriate currency) to nations whose trade is temporarily unbalanced—and also provides expert counsel on the control of inflation and other measures needed to strengthen particular currencies.

In addition to these international financial agencies, the U.S. itself has made substantial capital loans (and outright grants) under reconstruction programs, the Marshall Plan and subsequent aid programs, and has financed a large volume of trade through our own Export-Import Bank. The total result of these international lending programs (plus the rise in U.S. private investment and imports) has been a large flow of dollars abroad—enough to support an encouraging rise in world trade over the past decade.*

* As an example, Export-Import Bank loans provided $3.5 billion of dollar exchange to Latin America in 1948–1958. The International Bank provided

But although these emergency aid programs have remedied the complete paralysis of trade that prevailed after World War II, they are not sufficient for a full restoration of the free and vigorous trading community that existed earlier in this century. (Most currencies are not yet strong enough for the ups and downs that would accompany completely free trade between nations. And the international lending institutions do not have sufficient capital to finance the spectacular growth that might occur if there were no trade barriers.) The International Bank and Monetary Funds and also the special U.S. government aid programs were set up with the idea that the world shortage of dollars was temporary and could be remedied with limited amounts of new capital. There was not, at the time, any way to foresee that former colonial areas would develop so rapidly into markets for capital goods or that European recovery would be so vigorous as to outstrip the supply of capital funds within a decade. Many of the largest dollar aid programs have been voted by Congress in particular years, to meet temporary emergencies—like the war damage in Europe or the recent food shortage in India—and cannot be counted on for long-range development.

In 1958, the U.S. government outlined several new programs to provide more long-term capital for international economic development, and to put such development on a long-range basis, without repeated reliance on annual appropriations by the U.S. Congress. The first step would be

---

$1 billion. U.S. private investors (who are more important in Latin America than elsewhere) furnished $9 billion. U.S. exports to Latin America rose from $1.9 billion in 1948 to over $2.5 billion in 1957.

In the same period most European nations acquired substantial gold and dollar reserves, and at the end of 1958 the leading European currencies were made convertible into dollars for trading purposes (i.e., any nation holding British sterling or French francs can exchange these for dollars and buy American goods if it so chooses). Formerly the Bank of England or the Bank of France would not make such exchanges.

an increase in the authorized capital of the International Bank from $9.5 billion to $20.5 billion, of which increase $3.2 billion would be pledged by the U.S. Our government has also recommended a new affiliate for the Bank (the International Development Association) that would make loans repayable in local currencies. And we have begun our own Development Loan Fund to make long-term and local currency loans that would not be suitable for the U.S. Export-Import Bank. Loans of this type, which have been designated in financial parlance as "soft loans," will be particularly helpful to the underdeveloped nations.

The U.S. is supporting efforts to form regional banks (for development loans) in the European Common Market—including its members' African colonies—Latin America, Southeast Asia and the Middle East. Eventually such banks may be able to make a substantial number of loans, of a specialized type not suitable for the International Bank. And they will more nearly enable the members of each region to help themselves. The U.S. foreign aid program appropriately is shifting its emphasis from direct loans to individual countries toward larger participation in the sort of international and regional institutions just described. For example, the U.S. expects to play a leading role in the establishment of a new development bank for Latin America.

Finally, the U.S. and other nations are enlarging their contributions to the International Monetary Fund. The Fund's total capital will soon be increased from $9.2 billion to $14.3 billion, thus enabling it to give stronger backing to countries whose currency reserves are strained by fluctuations in trade.

Altogether, these new institutions will offer support for a greatly expanded volume of foreign trade and investment. Not only will they have larger capital resources than have been available in the early postwar period. They will also have much greater flexibility in dealing with local needs (for example, by making local currency loans). And through the regional arrangements, they will be closer to the special problems that prevail in some sections of the world, but not in others. If we can manage to remove tariffs, and other trade impediments, as rapidly as we are improving financial arrangements, we shall near a solution to the largest problems of world commerce.

CAN WE COMPETE IN FREE MARKETS?

As our story has unfolded up to now, it seems clear that prospects are bright for expanding world trade over the next decade. Population and living standards are increasing abroad even more rapidly than in the U.S. The flow of capital to support world trade and investment promises to be more adequate in the next ten years than in the past. And with this increased financial strength, the great trading nations can make substantial cuts in tariffs. Thus, in the 1960s we may be approaching something resembling a free flow of goods in world commerce.

But will the U.S. share in the prosperity created by free markets? As the largest industrial and agricultural producer in the world, we certainly should. As the traditional leader in technical progress and low-cost production techniques, we ought to. But lately the ability of the U.S. to compete in world markets has been seriously questioned by knowledgeable people—many of them executives in U.S. export industries.

The reasons for these new fears about our ability to compete are described as follows:

1. The U.S. is already getting a flood of imports from nations where labor costs are lower—Belgian glass, German steel, Japanese textiles, British and Swiss machinery, not to mention

the imported cars from Germany, France and Britain. These imports are concentrated in markets close to our seaboard, and the number of products affected is a minority of all U.S. industrial products. But there is no question that the flow of imported goods is increasing. Costs are generally 10 percent to 15 percent below those of comparable U.S. products.

2. At the same time, we are losing export sales to European manufacturers—both in Europe itself and in "third markets." They offer lower costs and easier credit terms. And European countries can probably cut their costs of production even more as they develop mass markets on the continent.

3. Furthermore, so the argument goes, the U.S. is rapidly becoming a high-cost nation because of the strong push on costs that is exercised by our powerful labor unions. As long as this "cost-push" continues, we shall be priced out of our share in world markets.

All of these factors, so the argument runs, put us in an unfavorable position to negotiate further reciprocal cuts in tariffs with the nations of Europe (and Asia). In fact, many of our industries want more protection, not less. It is easy to understand such fears on the part of American producers who are faced with the increased competitive strength of British, German or Japanese companies.

Nevertheless, a careful analysis of the facts indicates that the U.S. *can compete effectively* in most of the world's markets, and that therefore it will gain business (on balance) from the general expansion of free world trade. As noted above, a large share of foreign manufactures sold in the U.S. are specialty items, or else industrial products that are competitive only on the seacoast, where shipment does not involve much freight. Even if our tariffs are lowered further, it seems unlikely that the bulk of the U.S. market will be affected. Similarly, in the case of raw materials—lead, zinc, copper, crude oil or cement—our domestic market is so large and has such imposing growth prospects relative to our own supplies that we stand to benefit from the greater availability of foreign products. The "flood of imports," while it may be just that when measured in tons or gallons, will hardly be so large relative to the U.S. domestic market as to pose a serious threat to the growth of our own production.

When it comes to selling abroad, there is no doubt that U.S. business has adjustments to make. Revival of European industry means that it will be more difficult to ship many types of manufactured goods to that area. Many U.S. firms are already adjusting to this situation by setting up manufacturing plants in Europe. (The cutting of tariffs between European nations, and the easier convertibility of currencies, make this a much more attractive proposition than formerly.) There is nothing to stop a U.S. firm from taking advantage of low labor costs in Europe to manufacture there and serve what is now a wide area within the European Common Market. In fact, many of our future imports from Europe may represent the sales (and profits) of U.S. firms operating there, as is already the case with automobiles manufactured by British and German subsidiaries of Ford and General Motors.

In third markets also—i.e., in the less developed nations of Asia, Africa and South America—European competition will force many U.S. companies to review the quality, price and credit terms for the merchandise they offer. But in these areas the U.S. has strong advantages. The first of these is our great manufacturing capacity—of which we have far more in reserve than Europe or Japan. In fact, as demand rises within the European Common Market area, manufacturing capacity there may well be taxed to the limit. Thus, in many cases the U.S. will continue to be the primary source of supply for other nations.

Moreover, the U.S. will continue to finance (through the public and private investment programs already described) a major share of world trade, so that many countries will find it easiest to make their purchases in dollars. This is particularly true of those countries supplying us with raw materials, of which the U.S. is the largest consumer in the world. Also, the U.S. continues to enjoy technical superiority in many fields, from motion pictures to atomic energy equipment and electronic computers. With our $9 billion-a-year program of research and development, it seems reasonable to expect that American companies will continue to find new and unique products that are for sale only from the U.S.

Finally, we can hope that the U.S. will do far better than the pessimists predict at holding down our costs. Although prices have risen rather sharply in the U.S. since 1955, our record over the entire past decade has been considerably better than that of most other industrialized nations. If, as outlined in Chapter 8, we take reasonable measures to keep general inflation under control, there is no reason to believe we shall price ourselves out of export markets. In fact, it seems more likely that foreign nations may themselves experience a considerable dose of "cost push" inflation, as labor abroad seeks wages that will support better living.

To sum up, the U.S. is still in a position of strength that will enable us to support, and benefit from, a continuing reduction of tariffs and other trade obstacles. Despite strong foreign competition, the following comment seems to state the prospects correctly.

Every serious study that has been made in this field to date indicates that the preponderant bulk of American industry is well able to meet such competition. Indeed, one of the most important arguments in favor of trade liberalization is that it will broaden competition and thus increase the competitive discipline that is a major safeguard against inflation. Especially when consumer demand in the United States is pressing against our capacity output, freer access of foreign producers to our market will help to keep prices from rising. Under any gradual progression toward tariff liberalization, the displacements are not likely to be on a broader scale or of deeper dimension than those that are continuously occurring through domestic competition within and between industries.*

Thus, although some export industries may suffer in the development (and realignment) of world trade, our over-all exports will rise and contribute to growth in the general economy. It is important to recognize this, because a U.S. tariff policy designed to give complete protection to all our domestic products could hold back the development of other areas that depend on export trade more heavily than we do. And the development of regional trading areas in Europe, Latin America and elsewhere is one of our bright hopes for free world prosperity.

EUROPE'S COMMON MARKET

A full discussion of regional markets is beyond the scope of this volume. But the potential for U.S. trade may be illustrated by a brief description of the largest and most advanced of these regional concepts, the European Common Market. On January 1, 1959, six industrial nations on the continent of Europe—France, Germany, Italy, Belgium, Netherlands and Luxemburg—began to integrate their economies. According to present plans, these nations will eventually form one big market like that of the fifty United States, in which there are no tariffs, import quotas or other obstacles to the free movement of goods, manpower or investment capital.

---

* *Foreign Economic Policy for the Twentieth Century,* Report of the Rockefeller Brothers Fund Special Studies Project III, Doubleday and Company, Inc., Garden City, N.Y., 1958, chap. 10, p. 41.

The entire Common Market area—again like the United States—will have a common tariff and a common trading policy toward the rest of the world. Great Britain, Austria, Switzerland and the Scandinavian countries may later join in this arrangement, thus enlarging the free trade area in Europe to a market roughly two-thirds the size of the U.S. (as measured by gross national product).

This integration is scheduled to come about very gradually. The treaty bringing about the six-nation Common Market is to go into effect over twelve to fifteen years. However, the eventual importance of the movement toward one regional economy is beyond doubt. With any degree of success, it will create a mass market for goods such as Europe has never known in its centuries of division into small nations. And with mass markets will come mass production and greater industrial efficiency.

Increased efficiency, plus the removal of tariffs between the six nations, will give European companies advantages in this area against American firms. This may cause some re-shuffling in our trade with Europe over the next decade. Roughly one-third of our present exports to Europe are in lines that may be adversely affected—mainly machinery and chemicals. But other items, mainly fuels and raw materials, will be in greater demand, and the net effect will be expansionary. On balance, Europe seems likely to increase its *total* purchases of American goods once its tremendous potentials for growth, under the new system, are fully realized.*
Furthermore, American companies, many of which are already operating in the Common Market area, will have the opportunity to increase sales and profits of their European subsidiaries.

Perhaps most important, nations in other parts of the world

* Howard S. Piquet, "The Impact of Euromart on United States Trade," *Export Trade*, Dec. 1, 1958, p. 13.

are watching Europe's experiment in regional integration. Although, in some vital particulars, the idea may be easier to apply in an industrial area like Western Europe, the development of stronger regional economies would be of great benefit in Latin America, the Middle East and elsewhere. Several nations of Central America have held discussions on such a plan, and the United States has offered its backing. To the extent that any region is able, by integration, to increase its industrial efficiency and economic growth rate, it will become a better market for American products.

WORLD TRADE IN 1968

What will world trade be like at the end of the next decade? And what will be the place of the United States in this trade? If the preceding sections are correct, trade will be bigger and freer. Goods will move with less impediment from tariffs or import quotas. Currencies will be more freely exchangeable.

This does not mean that trade will return to the pattern of the nineteenth century. The industrialized world has grown too much since those days. It now includes sections of Asia, Africa and other lands that once belonged to the colonial trading system, but now are developing their own economies. These areas are too diverse to fit under one economic tent, as the civilized world once fitted into the economy of Europe. Rather, the new world of free trade will be made up of great regional markets, like those we have just described in Europe and Latin America. Within such markets, tariffs will be minimal or nonexistent. But some tariffs will remain between regions, to be progressively reduced as the less developed regions build up their export potential.

In each area, industrial development will be promoted by regional development banks and by a larger flow of international (or in the new terminology, interregional) capital, as described in the preceding section. An important result of such developments will be a larger world market for capital goods, which—because of their key importance to U.S. business—will be a strong aid to U.S. economic growth and stability.

How can we relate all this specifically to the U.S. business picture? One way to gauge the impact of expanding world trade on U.S. business is by the figures on our export sales. These rose from $12 billion in 1949 to over $16 billion in 1958. Estimates for 1968 range around $25 billion—or over 50 percent higher than in 1958.* And the rise in capital goods sales is likely to be even sharper, once sufficient demand builds up in the now undeveloped countries. From below $6 billion in 1958, exports of capital goods may well reach $9–10 billion by 1968.

This special factor of strong demand for capital goods will boost our exports to the regional markets of Asia and Africa more sharply than to our traditional customers in Canada and Latin America, who buy more consumer products. It also seems likely that the U.S. will be exporting large quantities of food, cotton and other farm products to the swelling populations of Africa and Asia. To the European Common Market, we shall be shipping much greater quantities of chemicals, coal and other raw materials, and larger amounts of specialized machinery.† But over-all, our trade will veer toward the less developed regions.

* In its calculations for the "American Economy, Prospects for Growth to 1965 and 1975," the Department of Economics of the McGraw-Hill Publishing Co. estimates commercial exports at $26 billion for 1968 if exports account for only the same percentage of gross national product in 1968 as in 1958.

† For a detailed discussion of future export markets by commodity and country of destination see Burck and Parker, *op. cit.*, pp. 125, 298–300.

Rising exports will be only one part—and perhaps the minor part—of the U.S. role in expanding business abroad. American companies now have about $28 billion invested in plants overseas, whose sales are not counted in our export data. These sales are growing more rapidly than are shipments from the U.S. From a level of $12 billion in 1949, they rose to $30 billion in 1958, and could double to reach $60 billion in 1968.* The profits returning to the U.S. from such operations will be in the vicinity of $5 billion, and this does not count the remaining profits that will be reinvested overseas to build up still more business. Altogether U.S. exports plus the sales of overseas subsidiaries may be nearing $100 billion ten years after this chapter is written, with profits to American companies of $5 to $10 billion.

This prospect is a happy ending to the story that began with U.S. aid to devastated Europe in 1948. By helping others, we have helped our own economy to acquire a new source of growth and profits. And we have begun an experiment in international cooperation to prove, more convincingly than any propaganda, that political freedom and private enterprise are compatible with rapid economic progress in all lands. Undersecretary of State C. Douglas Dillon expressed this thought in ringing words when he said that this is "a time of great opportunity that challenges us to prove that our system of democratic freedom can yield the greatest material benefit to the individual as well as the greatest spiritual benefits. Here on the American continent we ... have already accomplished much. ... If each [nation] does his share, and if we work cooperatively for an integrated program of development, we can demonstrate that free peoples can out-produce enslaved peoples and can do so

* "U.S. Industry Migrates Abroad to Tap Markets of the World," *Business Week,* Jan. 3, 1959, p. 29.

without sacrificing their way of life." * There could be no
better task for U.S. business in the years ahead. Moreover,
as the various sections of this chapter have indicated, the
actual trend of business abroad is in a direction that will contribute both to our international objectives and to the sustaining of economic growth and prosperity.†

* C. Douglas Dillon, "The Role of the United States in Latin American
Growth," an address to the Special Committee of the Council of the Organization of American States, Washington, D.C., reprinted in the *Commercial and Financial Chronicle*, Dec. 11, 1958, pp. 6–7.
† *New Light on Overseas Investment*
  Estimates of overseas investment by U.S. business firms, as presented in
this chapter, are derived from a survey conducted by the U.S. Department
of Commerce on actual investment in 1957. The first comprehensive survey
of *plans* by American firms for capital expenditures overseas conducted in
July 1959 by the McGraw-Hill Department of Economics indicated that manufacturing and petroleum companies reporting would spend $2.1 billion
overseas in 1959 for new plants, equipment and property. Expenditures
on this scale in 1959 would be consistent with the trend shown by previous
data.
  According to the McGraw-Hill survey, foreign capital expenditures of
U.S. industrial companies are expanding more rapidly in Western Europe
than in any other area, reflecting the development of the European Common
Market as discussed above. In 1960 U.S. manufacturers plan to invest more
in new facilities in Europe than in Canada and Latin America combined.
The survey also confirms the trend among U.S. companies to do a greater
proportion of their overseas business through subsidiaries in the overseas
countries, rather than merely by increased export shipments from the United
States.

CHAPTER ELEVEN

The Last Round-up

In a speech in Washington, D.C., not long ago, former President Herbert Hoover said:

Secretary Humphrey [then Secretary of the Treasury] says that unless we change some of our ways, we will see "a depression that will curl your hair." Mine has already been curled once—and I think I can detect the signs. The obvious sign of inflation is the advance in prices, wages and the cost of living. But another sign is the temperament of some of our economists. Again you hear the same expressions as in the inflation period thirty years ago—that "we are in a new economic era," that "the old economic laws are outmoded." *

This statement by an eminent elder statesman, who certainly has impressive credentials as an authority on depressions, highlights the special risks to professional reputations run by economists who advance and defend the proposition put forward in this book—that there are strong foundations for the belief that general prosperity rather than recurring boom and bust promises to be the general rule over the next decade. We have so far as we can recall avoided the phrase "new economic era" which rouses peculiarly noxious recollections for those old enough to remember how the "new economic era," discovered by some economists of eminence at the time, dissolved into the worst of all depressions.

* From an address to the Third National Reorganization Conference of the Citizens Committee for the Hoover Report, Feb. 4, 1957.

Neither have we found that "the old economic laws are outmoded."

Even more important in the list of what we have not done, we have not envisaged a smooth and steadily sustained level of prosperity over the years ahead. Quite on the contrary, we have definitely envisaged the possibility, and indeed the probability, of continuing ups and downs in business which may at times result in short periods of unemployment of as much as 6 or 7 percent of the nation's labor force, and comparable declines—and recoveries—in other key elements of the economy. In an economy with a gross national product running up toward $500 billion a year, the actual magnitude of a decline of even 4 or 5 percent—$20 or $25 billion— would, unless seen in true perspective, have considerable hair-curling capacity of its own.

Also, in our explorations we have indicated many remodeling and improvement jobs that must be done on the institutional framework of our economy before it can even be slightly suspected of being anywhere near as good as it should be. These jobs have ranged all the way from providing better arrangements to govern life down on the farm to those for widening markets in the remote reaches of the world, and perhaps presently on the edges of outer space.

But we have argued that since the Great Depression of the thirties there have been changes in the American economy and the forces shaping it which provide firm foundations for the faith there will be no recurrence of any such devastating economic plunge again any time soon. Having argued as much, we are fully aware of the possibility that the course of economic events may undo us and permit some elder statesman a generation hence to dwell on our deficiencies. Perhaps, keyed to current economic terminology, he may be talking about "built-in stabilizer" bunk as a midcentury companion piece for the "new era" of the twenties.

So what to do? Play it safe professionally by waiting to see what has happened and then reporting that it has happened, and why? We think not. Sighting new forces making for more steadily sustained growth and prosperity, we think it would be positively derelict of us not to array them, lest through inadvertence they be dissipated or destroyed. We much prefer the risk of being destroyed by perverse events rather than by timidity. Also, taking this risk befits us in our roles as business economists.

It really should not be necessary, but to be surely on the safe side perhaps we should re-emphasize the fact that the forces we see making for sustained growth and relative stability in the years ahead are by no means foolproof forces. Such vast and impersonal forces ultimately get involved that it is easy at times to forget that our economy is run by people. But that fact remains. And if people are foolish enough, they can wreck it. We are always aware, and at times rather painfully aware, of this fact. But by having a clearer understanding of the forces making for the prospect that prosperity will be the general rule, the chances of having foolish decisions dissipate them should be reduced.

On our way to our cheerful conclusion about our prospects for prosperity, the first, and many would feel the most forbidding, hurdle we had to clear was that put in place by the proposition that it is impossible to escape the boom-and-bust pattern in business investment. This proposition is firmly embedded in the standard pattern of both professional and lay thinking about the movement of the American economy along the path of time—first an enthusiastic expansion of investment and along with it expansion of producing capacity, rising to a dizzy climax, and then a crash and recession or depression while the country grows up to its overbuilt producing capacity.

Here we won't undertake to review the detailed considera-

tions, set forth in Chapter 2, which support our expectation
that it will be possible to keep business investment on a
tolerably even keel over the next decade, while the volume
of investment moves upward. These considerations include
the prospective shortage of manhours relative to expanding
production requirements; the needs of increased investment (1) to overcome old age and obsolescence of producing equipment and (2) to cope with the increasing difficulty
of obtaining some key raw materials; the increased stability
imparted to the investment process by the development of
long-range planning; and some improved prospects of having adequate funds to carry out a steadily expanding investment program.

The tremendous expansion of industrial research and development since the end of World War II plays a crucial
part in shaping our expectation that business investment can
be kept relatively stable and rising. In fact, it plays such a
crucial role that we have devoted Chapter 3 to research and
development and its dynamic role in creating a flood of new
and better products, processes and equipment, and thus both
calling for and accommodating a steadily expanding volume
of investment without having it lead to excess capacity.*

Of course, business investment in new producing facilities
is not a free-wheeling operation. If it is to have relatively
steady growth, it must have as a companion growth in the
volume of consumption.

Hence, logically enough, we moved on to a consideration
of (1) the prospects that the consuming public will have
what it takes in the way of income to sustain an expanding
volume of production at a high level, and (2) whether the
arts of marketing have what it takes to see that this income
is steadily devoted to this purpose. On the adequacy of the

* See "Do We Have to Bust When We Boom?" by Dexter M. Keezer, *Saturday Review*, Jan. 19, 1957, p. 24.

flow of income to consumers we believe that the facts warrant the optimistic conclusion reached in Chapter 4. Thanks to what also has been correctly characterized as a revolution in its distribution, consumer income is distributed in a width and depth which makes possible both a broad and steady flow of consumer buying. There are also new arrangements, such as built-in provisions for regular wage increases, which serve to sustain an increasing flow of consumer income.

The very fact that, as a whole, the American consuming public has become so rich puts a special burden on the arts of marketing. It is the historically unique burden of persuading people who, so far as their immediate comfort and convenience is concerned, are under no compulsion to do so, to continue to purchase an expanding volume of goods and services. Although it does not seem to us by any means an open and shut proposition, our review of the developments in the arts of marketing in Chapter 5 permitted us some hope that they will be adequate to the crucial role assigned to them by the coming of age of abundance—a development which gives marketing the status of an absolutely basic economic process.

At any time appraisal of the economic outlook involves a whole series of judgments about how the various governments—Federal, state and local—will perform the roles assigned to them. Even in the days when there was wide popular support for the proposition that "that government is best which governs least," the various governments made rules which had a decisive bearing on the course of economic life. But in times like these when these governments collect through taxes and spend no less than about one-fifth of the national income, they play an overshadowing role in shaping the course of economic life.

In deference to these realities, we devoted detailed attention to government in its role as tax collector and spender, as guardian of fair competition, and as an economic and financial stabilizer.

Although, on many grounds, the fact that government handles about one-fifth of the national income is to be deplored, this state of affairs does contribute an element of economic stability of sorts. In Chapter 6 this element was analyzed, as was the capacity of government to contribute further to both growth and stability by well-designed and executed tax policies.

We could find little support in the recent record for the fear examined in Chapter 7, that with the growth of "big business," monopoly is growing apace. Some difficult problems are involved in working out a constructive set of interactions between big and small business in manufacturing, but, as a whole, American business, big and little, is not only competitive but tends to get more, rather than less so. This is a fact of major importance in the outlook for both economic growth and stability.

Because it is currently one of the most pervasive fears for our economic future, we dealt at some length with the fear that the monopoly power granted by Congress to trade unions will be used to exact wage increases which, through cost and, hence, price increases, will take us on a disastrous inflationary ride, to be followed by an even more disastrous fall. In Chapter 8 we reached the conclusion that, while surely not fanciful, the fear here tends to be excessive, and that there is reason to hope that over the span of years with which we are concerned price inflation can and will be held within tolerable bounds.

It is a well-worn economic dictum that economic depressions in the U.S. begin and end down on the farm. There is also a very deeply worn path to the U.S. Treasury to get money to keep key farm prices propped up. Hence we felt it necessary to determine whether what has become the chronic inability of our agriculture to stand on its own (or at any rate free-market) feet, is a major menace to relatively sustained growth over the decade ahead. We were comforted to find in Chapter 9 that "it ain't necessarily so."

In Chapter 10 we took a broad look overseas to see what the developments in prospect there promise to do to relatively sustained prosperity in the U.S., or the lack of it. And, where a decade ago any such conclusion would have been regarded as completely fanciful, we found that foreign economic developments promise to make a positive contribution to relatively sustained economic growth in the U.S. over the next decade.

Along with the things which were done in some detail in moving toward our cheerful conclusion about the prospects for sustained prosperity, a number of things having some significant bearing on this conclusion were left undone, either because we did not feel we knew enough to do them or felt compelled by limitations of time to postpone doing them. For example, we did not deal with the important question of whether or not the arts of corporate management have been advanced to a point where there is assurance that our very large business units won't make managerial mistakes proportionate to their size and, thus, create economic disturbance of a generally destructive type.

Experts in the arts of management with impressive credentials tell us not to worry on this score. In support of their good cheer they cite: (1) the greatly improved means of communication in corporate management, including those provided by electronic calculating gear, (2) large strides in the effective decentralization of very large corporate units, and (3) great advances in the educational development of executives, including that provided by a large array of courses which take executives back to the universities for special advanced training. Developments such as these, they assure us, make obsolete the remark prompted by a really magnificent managerial bloomer by officers of one of our largest corporations, that it takes a really big company to make a really big mistake. We are willing to believe that they are right, but the limitations of our present knowledge of the subject matter make this an exercise of faith.

As noted in our opening chapter there are a number of other key questions about our economic future which we ruled out of consideration simply by making comfortable assumptions about them. The most fateful of these assumptions was, of course, that we shall not have World War III fought with atomic weapons during the period with which we have concerned ouselves. We shall, we are sure, be engaged in a rugged economic contest with the U.S.S.R. over the years ahead. But, given a modicum of good management, we are confident of the capacity of the American economy to hold its own, and then some. Another assumption is that we shall not encounter any debilitating shortage of basic resources, an assumption which relieved us of the necessity of exploring prospects of areas overseas which are the sources of many of these materials. There is good reason to believe that this is a sound assumption. Joseph L. Fisher, Associate Director of Resources of the Future, and one of our leading authorities on resources, has recently remarked that "the answer to the question: Is there likely to be a general resource and material shortage, must be no." *

In spite of omissions of the type indicated, we believe that our analysis has been comprehensive enough and searching enough to give stout support to our conviction that, as it moves into the sixties, the American economy is a very robust creation. Even if you find our conclusion too bold or too cheerful for your taste, we shall have served a large and

---

* From an unpublished manuscript, "Outlook for Natural Resources and Problems of Their Development."

satisfying part of our purpose if we have prompted you to consider carefully the potentialities we have arrayed in looking down the economic avenues ahead. There we expect to have events validate the proposition, advanced at the outset of this exploration, that, "short of some cataclysmic development, such as that of world atomic war, the American economy has undergone basic changes since its catastrophe of the thirties which give powerful support to the expectation that relatively steady growth and prosperity will be the general rule, rather than the nervously embraced exception, over the next decade."

APPENDIX I

Development of the McGraw-Hill Index of Manufacturing Capacity

The McGraw-Hill Index of Manufacturing Capacity is constructed from year-to-year percentage changes in physical capacity, as reported by companies cooperating in the McGraw-Hill Annual Survey of Business' Plans for New Plants and Equipment. The Index is a measure of manufacturing capacity as compared with capacity in the base period, December 1950.

The McGraw-Hill Index is solely a measure of capacity in terms of plant and equipment. It does *not* measure capacity in terms of available manpower or materials, which may also at times limit producing ability. Individual companies report changes in capacity in accordance with their own definitions, though most companies in any given industry tend to follow the same practice in defining capacity.

The Department of Economics has secured information on increases in manufacturing capacity through its annual surveys since 1948. Since 1955 it has also asked companies to report the rate of capacity at which they were operating at the end of the preceding year. According to the latest McGraw-Hill Survey, at the end of 1958 manufacturing capacity was 57 percent greater than in 1950, and manufacturing companies were operating, on the average, at 80 percent of capacity.

CRITICISMS OF THE INDEX

Criticism of the McGraw-Hill Index, suggesting that it overstates the growth of manufacturing capacity, has come recently from two sources—Sumner H. Slichter (Lamont University Professor, Harvard University) and *Fortune* magazine. Professor Slichter bases his criticism on a comparison of the McGraw-Hill Index with the Federal Reserve Board Index of Manufacturing Production. *Fortune* has calculated its own index, showing a smaller increase, from a variety of financial data.

Professor Slichter finds support for his contention that the McGraw-Hill Index overstates the rise in manufacturing capacity in "the change in the actual rate of factory output between two periods when factories as a whole were producing at about capacity—May and July 1953 and December 1956." He continues:

> In May and July 1953 the index of factory output reached 139; the index of durable goods manufacturing reached 156 in May and 157 in July and August. At this time the manufacturing industries must have been operating fairly close to capacity because weekly hours were 40.7 in May and 40.3 in June. In durable goods manufacturing hours were 41.5 in May, 40.8 in June and 41.1 in August. In May 1953 the steel industry, a key determinant of general industrial capacity, was operating at 100.1% of theoretical capacity.
>
> The next peak in factory output occurred in December 1956, when the index of factory output reached 149, and the index of durable goods output, 167. In December 1956 average weekly hours in manufacturing were 41.0, and in durable goods manufacturing, 41.9. The steel industry was operating at 99.6% of capacity. Hence, factory output in December 1956 must have been pretty close to capacity. The increase in factory output between the two periods of capacity operation—May and July 1953 and December 1956—was only 7.2% for all manufacturing and only 6.4% for durable goods manufacturing. These amounts are less than half the increase in capacity estimated by McGraw-Hill and well below the long-run 3% annual rate of rise in the real expenditure for goods.*

* Sumner H. Slichter, address at the Annual Meeting of Associated Industries of Cleveland, March 3, 1958.

Fortune's September 1958 issue contends that the "real" over-capacity in U.S. manufacturing is "considerably less than has generally been assumed." To back up this contention, *Fortune* "developed a new measure of manufacturing capacity that shows 3% less increase in capacity, from 1953 to 1957, than does the McGraw-Hill Index." *Fortune's* index is based on financial data—specifically, capital stocks for major industries as reported in income tax returns and estimates of manufacturers' purchases of plant and equipment, less retirements. It does in a complicated statistical fashion what the McGraw-Hill Index attempts to do directly through a survey.

Neither *Fortune* nor Professor Slichter, in suggesting that the McGraw-Hill Index exaggerates the amount of excess capacity in manufacturing, takes up the matter of the declining rate of operations reported in the McGraw-Hill Survey. Between the end of 1955 and the end of 1957, the average operating rate in manufacturing declined from 92 percent to only 78 percent of capacity. By the end of 1958 the operating rate was still only 80 percent after eight months of recovery. In these figures—contrasted with the 90 percent preferred operating rate—we have manufacturers' own estimate of unused capacity.

Several other comments can be made regarding Professor Slichter's criticism of the McGraw-Hill Index and particularly his assumption that "factory output in December 1956 must have been pretty close to capacity."

a. It is clear that *most* industries were operating at less than capacity—some by considerable margins—in December 1956, despite the high average operating rate. Only four of the twenty major industries in the FRB Index reached a level of output in December 1956 not attained or exceeded in prior months. In only two did production employees work longer hours than in any previous months of 1955–1956.

b. A high figure for average weekly hours worked would not necessarily indicate near-capacity operations in the sense measured by the McGraw-Hill Index. This is an index of capacity in terms of *plant and equipment only,* not in terms of the labor force or of materials.

c. The operating rate of 99.6 percent in steel, although high, is not quite as high as the figure suggests, for each year's theoretical capacity is rated as of January 1. The December operating rate disregards additions to capacity that were installed during the year—4 percent in 1956, according to both the McGraw-Hill Survey and the American Iron and Steel Institute.

The McGraw-Hill Department of Economics made a careful study of its Index of Manufacturing Capacity in 1958, to determine whether it did actually overstate the growth in capacity. The study included a special survey, in which companies were asked to report their aggregate increase in capacity since 1950 as a check against the cumulation of year-to-year changes reported each spring. It included also a comparison of the McGraw-Hill Index with other, more limited, measures of capacity—as described in the following paragraphs. As a result of this study, the index was revised, to correct statistical errors that had crept into some of the figures for individual industries. But the study confirmed the over-all index in indicating that manufacturing capacity increased by about 50 percent between the end of 1950 and the end of 1957.

OTHER MEASURES OF CAPACITY

Aside from indirect statistical approximations like that devised by *Fortune,* there is no over-all measure of manufacturing capacity other than the McGraw-Hill Index. However, there are a number of indices or other physical measures of capacity maintained for particular industries or groups of industries. By and large, these show the same trends as comparable segments of the McGraw-Hill Index.

Major Materials Capacity. The Federal Reserve Board prepares an index of capacity and output of seventeen "major materials." Capacity for this group of products increased by 43 percent between January 1, 1951, and January 1, 1959, compared with the 57 percent rise in the McGraw-Hill Index for all manufacturing capacity. It is a fair presumption, however, that capacity for producing finished goods has increased more rapidly than capacity for basic materials in the last few years.

Just as the McGraw-Hill Index has risen faster than total manufacturing production, the FRB Major Materials Capacity Index has risen faster than production of these materials. Thus, the FRB index shows a rise of 43 percent in capacity for major materials between 1951 and 1959, while the largest increase in output for any month since January 1951 was only 21 percent.

The following table compares the McGraw-Hill and FRB capacity indices for the years 1950–1958. To make the series more nearly comparable, the FRB index is converted from its usual 1947–1949 base to a base period of January 1, 1951.

End of Year *	Total—FRB Major Materials	McGraw-Hill All Mfg.
1950	100	100
1951	105	106
1952	112	113
1953	118	120
1954	121	126
1955	125	135
1956	130	143
1957	137	151
1958	143	157

* January 1 of following year for FRB index.

Trade Association Figures. A few national trade associations publish data on capacity of industries they serve, for the most part capacity for producing basic materials that can be measured in standard physical terms. The following table compares McGraw-Hill indices with indices based on capacity data published by the American Iron and Steel Institute, the American Petroleum Institute, the American Pulp and Paper Association (paper and paperboard) and the U.S. Pulp Producers Association (pulp).

End of	Steel		Petroleum Refining		Paper and Pulp		
Year	McGraw-Hill	AISI	McGraw-Hill	API	McGraw-Hill	APPA	Pulp
1950	100	100	100	100	100	100	100
1951	103	104	104	105	104	103	109
1952	111	113	109	117	112	107	116
1953	117	119	117	115	119	112	121
1954	119	121	122	121	125	115	130
1955	123	123	126	124	133	119	139
1956	128	128	132	128	140	125	150
1957	137	135	136	132	148	133	162
1958	144	142	141	139	155	141	171

In the cases of both steel and petroleum refining, the trade
association figures are in reasonable accord with the McGraw-
Hill Index. In the case of paper and pulp, the McGraw-Hill Index
has risen faster than the APPA data on paper and paperboard
capacity. But the McGraw-Hill Index in this industry covers a
broader field, including pulp—where the U.S. Pulp Producers
Association figures show greater expansion—and paper containers.

CAPACITY VS. PRODUCTION

Since December 1950, manufacturing production has increased
considerably less than manufacturing capacity. According to the
Federal Reserve Index, manufacturing production was only 16
percent higher in December 1958 than in December 1950, whereas
the McGraw-Hill Index reports a 57 percent increase in manufacturing capacity during these seven years. Even the high production rate of December 1956 was only 20 percent above the
December 1950 level.

It is reasonable that capacity should have risen faster than production during these years, because many industries came out of
the 1940s short of capacity for periods of really heavy demand.
The question is whether a gap of this magnitude between increases in production and capacity is reasonable.

The link between the two indices, which shows that the widening gap is plausible, is the decline in operating rate as a percent of capacity. The average operating rate as reported in the McGraw-Hill Survey reached a peak of 92 percent at the end of 1955 and declined subsequently, until it recovered slightly at the end of 1958.

A synthetic index of manufacturing capacity can be constructed by using the McGraw-Hill operating rate and the FRB Index of Manufacturing Production. (The trend in production divided by the operating rate should be the same as the trend in capacity.) The following table shows the course of the McGraw-Hill Index of Manufacturing Capacity and of a "Calculated Capacity Index" (based on changes in the FRB Manufacturing Production Index and the average operating rate as reported to McGraw-Hill) since the end of 1955. The "Calculated Capacity Index" is set up so that it agrees with the McGraw-Hill Capacity Index for the end of 1955; the two indices are thus comparable for measuring trends in manufacturing capacity since 1955.

Month	McGraw-Hill Index	Calculated Capacity Index
December 1955	135	135
December 1956	143	148
December 1957	151	150
December 1958	157	153

Over these three years of rapid expansion of manufacturing capacity, the McGraw-Hill Index shows an increase of 16 percent, while the "Calculated Capacity Index" shows a rise of 13 percent. Between the end of 1955 and the end of 1957, the two indices show almost identical increases.

COULD THE INDEX BE WRONG?

So far, we have recounted the various methods we have used to test the accuracy of the McGraw-Hill Index. The over-all index comes off remarkably well, and most of the indices for individual industries also seem reasonably close when compared with other measures of capacity. Are there any features of the index itself that might invite overstatement, or understatement?

1. Definition of Capacity. From early experience, the Department of Economics decided it would have to let companies set their own definitions of "capacity" and trust them to stick to their definitions. This leaves open such questions as number of shifts of operation, treatment of low-grade standby capacity, final assembly vs. intermediate capacity. But in general, companies seem to follow a common-sense definition of capacity as maximum output under normal work schedules. This is indicated by interviews the Department has conducted.

2. Mergers. Companies are asked to report only changes in capacity through new installation (or retirement) of plants and equipment, not changes resulting from acquisition or sale of facilities. Shifts in ownership do not represent changes in industry capacity. Questionnaires are carefully edited to eliminate inclusion, by mistake, of capacity changes through merger; but some may slip through.

3. Diversification. With few exceptions, companies are classified according to the industry of their principal product. Product diversification, however, has become increasingly important, and many companies are significant producers in two or more industries. Inclusion of a rubber company's new chemical plant in the rubber industry figure, for instance, would raise the rubber capacity index when it should be raising the chemical industry's index. Many of these errors, however, are offset by diversification moves in opposite directions. The over-all index is probably not much affected one way or the other.

4. Bankruptcies and Retirements. The McGraw-Hill Index probably does not fully reflect the withdrawal of facilities through scrappage, demolition or abandonment. 'Our inquiries indicate that most companies do try to take account of retirements and report *net* changes in capacity. But bankruptcies pose a difficult problem, for these typically affect smaller firms that have never been in the McGraw-Hill sample. Reduction of capacity through plant abandonments and bankruptcy has been a problem especially in the textile industry, where the Economics Department's check-up indicated that the earlier indices of capacity were too high.

5. *Big Company Bias.* The sample of participating companies in the McGraw-Hill Survey is dominated by large companies, though diligent efforts have been made to include a greater representation of small and middle-sized firms. Large companies, as a rule, account for a disproportionately large share of plant expansion, so their expansion rate may exaggerate the trend for the industry.

There are, then, several possibilities of bias in the McGraw-Hill Index, mostly in the upward direction. Besides those just described, there are a few of a technical statistical nature. However, through careful editing of questionnaires, continual broadening of the sample and study of industry developments, the Department of Economics has made every effort to minimize these possibilities of bias. At most, they may mean that the Index overstates the growth of manufacturing capacity by a few points during a period of eight years.

APPENDIX II

Special Problems in Income Distribution

For the most part Chapter 4 was concerned with the *average* consumer family. The average consumer is typical of the bulk of the families in the U.S. But there are special cases that deserve attention. These are the families at the extreme limits of the income scale and the particular regions of our nation where income changes have been especially great.

UPPER INCOME GROUP

In the case of the upper income group, incomes are in larger part derived from investments than from employment. During the past two decades, interest rates, rents and dividends have failed to keep pace with the increases in wages and salaries. Thus the upper income group has been losing out, relative to other income classes.

Progressively higher income taxes have also hurt the upper income group. The relatively higher tax bite on upper incomes results in a sharp cut in the number of families in the extremely high income brackets after taxes have been deducted.

A comprehensive study of the upper income groups was made a few years ago by Simon Kuznets.* He found that the share of income received by the top 5 percent of the population was cut substantially between 1929 and 1948 for the reasons just mentioned. He found that in 1929 the top 5 percent of the population received 31.9 percent of all income; by 1948, the share of this

* Simon Kuznets and Elizabeth Jenks, *Shares of Upper Income Groups in Income and Savings*, New York, National Bureau of Economic Research, 1953.

256

upper income group had been cut to 19.5 percent. Most of the decline in the share of income of the top 5 percent of the population took place in the 1939–1944 period. This was the period when labor's share of national income made the biggest strides forward, while taxes acted as a brake on upper incomes. Since 1944, however, the share of income in the hands of the upper 5 percent of the population has not been cut significantly. What evidence there is seems to indicate that very little shift has taken place in more than a decade.

LOW–INCOME FAMILIES

The January 1955 Economic Report of the President stated: "A small and shrinking, but still significant, number of American families have incomes under $1,000 per family. By current standards, most of them must be considered poverty-stricken." Many people are technically unemployable because of advanced age, physical or mental disability and various other reasons. Nevertheless, some portion of the low-income group could become more productive members of the community and thus move up in the income scale.

During the past decade, some changes have taken place in this low-income group. In the years 1955 to 1958 about 20 percent of all families had incomes under $2,000. In the three years 1949 to 1951 the share of families in the under $2,000 group ran over 35 percent of the total. Thirty years ago, in 1929, nearly half of U.S. families had incomes under $2,000. Thus, this group is gradually being reduced and is a source of continued growth for the middle-income group.

FARMERS: A SPECIAL LOW–INCOME GROUP

The income of farmers has long presented a special problem. This is evidenced by the history of farm price-support legislation as well as by events like the beginning of an agricultural decline in the midst of general prosperity in 1952. The continued weakening of farm prices and farm income from 1952 through 1956 when the rest of the nation was experiencing boom times points up this problem.

What has happened then to farm income in recent years? The income position of farmers compared with the rest of the population may be measured by the portion of total national income they receive. In 1958 farmers made up about 12 percent of the population. If they shared proportionately in the income of the nation they would have received 12 percent of the national income. Instead, farm income was less than 4 percent of the national income, or one-third of a proportional share. Back in 1951, farmers accounted for 15 percent of the population, while their share of income was 9.4 percent, or nearly two-thirds of a proportional share.

Income per capita of farmers in 1958 may also be compared with per capita income trends since 1951 to see how they have fared in recent years. In 1958, farm income per capita was over $1,000. This was the first new peak since 1951, when per capita income reached $983. (Per capita farm income declined steadily from 1952 through 1955.) Personal income per capita in 1958 was $2,060. This was considerably higher than per capita personal income in 1951. Farm income per capita has not kept pace with the growth of national income per capita. It also is much less than the national average.

The farmer's position, however, really is not as bad as these statistics seem to indicate.

1. Farm families have more children on the average than non-farm families. This helps to distort the farm income per capita figures.

2. An increasing number of farmers supplement their incomes from the farms by working part-time in industrial jobs.

The truth is that farmers recently have been doing much better than is generally believed to be the case. But their *share* of income —compared with that of the rest of the population—is still relatively small.

Commercial farmers, by and large, have shared in the rapidly rising incomes for the nation as a whole during the last decade. It is the two million or more subsistence farmers who have continued to drag average farm income down and failed to share in the over-all gains of the economy. The problem of these subsistence farm families is part of the general problem of low-income families. We may hope for a continuing shift from subsistence farms to larger, more efficient farms, or to industrial jobs, as one solution to this problem.

REGIONAL INCOME CHANGES

The trend toward income equality shows up in comparisons of per capita income in the different regions of the United States. Incomes per capita are becoming more nearly equal among regions. Without exception, per capita incomes in all regions of the nation are moving closer to the U.S. average. This means in areas where income per capita is at a lower level than the national average it is increasing faster over the years than the national average. And in areas where per capita income is at a higher level than the national average it is increasing more slowly than the national average.

People in some regions are still better off financially than those in other areas. But the region with lowest per capita income, the Southeast, has moved up to 70 percent of the national average from 52 percent in 1929. Per capita income in the Middle Atlantic region, which was 38 percent higher than the average for the United States in 1929, has moved down to only 18 percent higher than the national average in 1957.

Regional differences in levels of income per capita and in changes in income per capita have been determined by three major factors:

1. The type of industry within a region

2. The portion of people earning income in each region

3. Geographic differences in wage scales

Regions which have made faster gains than the nation as a whole in industrial activity, in number of industrial workers and in pay rates have improved their relative income position in recent years. The Southeast, where industry is replacing marginal agriculture and pay scales are rising in existing industries, provides

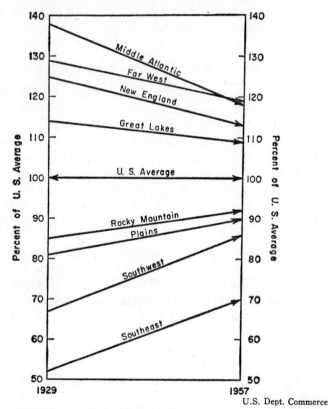

Regional Incomes Approaching U.S. Average

U.S. Dept. Commerce

All U.S. regions, with the exception of the Southeast, are now within 20 percent of the U.S. average of per capita income. Per capita incomes in the Far West, Middle Atlantic, New England and Great Lakes regions now range from 19 percent to 9 percent above the U.S. average. The Southwest, Plains and Rocky Mountain regions now range from 14 percent to 8 percent below the U.S. average. The Southeast has moved up to only 30 percent below the U.S. average. In 1929 per capita income in the Southeast was only about half the U.S. figure.

an outstanding example of a region with a rising income level.

In other "problem areas," such as the coal-mining sections of Pennsylvania and West Virginia or the old textile towns of New England, the hope for higher incomes rests on the development of new industries. In an economy characterized by large expenditures for research, there is a good chance this hope can be fulfilled, and the movement toward more nearly equal incomes continued.

APPENDIX III

Improvements in the U.S. Economic Intelligence

Happily, there is no room for debate on the proposition that we have both a far better economic intelligence service than we had a generation ago and far better machinery to mobilize effectively the intelligence acquired.

The machinery for mobilizing economic information that makes it vastly more meaningful is our system of national accounts.* This method of economic bookkeeping, which provided a way to piece together the myriad statistics on production and income, amounted to a great social and political invention. Economists can now look at a running report on the state of the economy, instead of the big blob they once had to face.

Back in the 1920s, just to get an idea where business was—let alone where it was headed—an economist had to sort through an undigested mass of statistics on such things as production or shipments in isolated industries, freight car loadings, bank clearings, stock market activity and commodity prices. These provided plenty of clues, but no real measure of the performance of the economy. And the clues often pointed different ways.

OUR NATIONAL ACCOUNTS

The National Bureau of Economic Research, with the leadership of Wesley C. Mitchell and Simon Kuznets, deserves a large

* For a detailed discussion of the various statistics comprising our national accounts, see William H. Chartener, "Too Many Statistics?" *Challenge*, Vol. VI, No. 5, February 1958, pp. 62–66.

measure of credit for showing the way to pull the available statistics together in a form that permitted an over-all view of the economy. The painstaking labor of the National Bureau in developing, during the 1920s, a comprehensive set of accounts that added up was the first necessary step to a better understanding of the way the economy functions. This work has since been carried on and refined by the Department of Commerce, which began publishing estimates of national income in 1933. It began with the year 1939 to report quarterly on gross national product.

With our system of national accounts, we cannot only measure the over-all performance of the economy but also assess the relative health of important sectors. The gross national product, for instance, is the most comprehensive measure of the performance of the economy. It represents the total dollar value of all goods and services produced. But the way the GNP is reported gives us a systematic breakdown of the demand for these goods and services, by consumers, business and government. Thereby, we can spot the places in the economy that are moving ahead and those that are faltering.

Experimental work has also been done on other methods of organizing statistics on the performance of the economy. Morris Copeland and economists of the Board of Governors of the Federal Reserve System have developed an analysis based on the "flow of funds" between the various sectors of the economy. And Professor Wassily Leontief of Harvard University, aided by economists of the U.S. Bureau of Labor Statistics, has worked up another approach, the "inter-industry" or "input-output" method of analysis. This approach takes off from the principle that what one industry produces (its "output"), another industry uses (its "input"), and tries to place every producing and consuming activity in a mammoth egg crate.

These methods of analysis are still relatively new, and their advance is held back by the lack of accurate or timely information. But, with further development, they will enable economists to learn even more about the vital forces that determine the course of the economy.

In addition to these methods of organizing our national accounts, there have been great improvements in the particular pieces of information we have to fill out the accounts and in the devices for forecasting. A considerable number of the statistical series now considered by economists as basic in gauging important areas of the economy were not even available on a regular basis in the early 1930s. There were no official figures regularly published on employment and unemployment until 1940. We had few figures on business inventories before 1938. Data on business expenditures for new plant and equipment were not regularly available until after World War II.

PLANS, INTENTIONS AND EXPECTATIONS

For help in forecasting, we have now an increasing battery of information on plans and intentions. In the important field of business' plans for capital spending, there are the quarterly and annual surveys of the U.S. Department of Commerce and the Securities and Exchange Commission and the surveys conducted each spring and fall by the McGraw-Hill Department of Economics. These surveys have given accurate indications, within a few percentage points in most years, of business spending for new plant and equipment. The National Industrial Conference Board has recently added a new survey of corporate appropriations for capital purposes, which may prove as helpful in providing information about business spending plans at another stage.

We in the McGraw-Hill Department of Economics have also within the last few years developed a series of indices of new orders for machinery other than electrical machinery and, using data from *Engineering News–Record's* reports on construction contract awards, an index of new orders for industrial construction. This approach has been carried a stage further with a regular survey of *expected* new orders for machinery as forecast by machinery manufacturers. This survey gives economists a look ahead at economic developments a couple of stages in advance, for new orders for capital equipment are generally considered one of the best advance indicators of business activity.

In the field of expectations, other work is now being carried on by Dun & Bradstreet, which queries businessmen quarterly on their anticipations of sales, prices and profits, and by the University of Michigan Survey Research Center, which conducts periodic surveys of consumer attitudes.

An indication of how generously supplied with economic information are the American economists and policy makers of the 1950s may be found in an envious article published in the (London) *Economist*.* In a table comparing economic indicators in Britain and the U.S., with respect to frequency of publication and the interval before publication, the *Economist* gave the benefit in almost every instance to the U.S. statistics. "On balance," the *Economist* concluded, "British economic statistics lag well behind the American ones, both in scope and timeliness." And Britain is a country that must have a wealth of economic statistics for the detailed planning of a semi-Socialist state.

OBSERVERS AND ADVISERS

Another great improvement in our organization to handle economic problems is the creation, since World War II, of special agencies charged with the responsibility of observing economic developments and of keeping our principal economic policy makers—the President and Congress—well informed. The Council of Economic Advisers, set up by the Employment Act of 1946, performs this job for the President. It prepares, for transmission by the President to Congress, an annual report on the state of the economy. And it is constantly available to provide information and advice to the President. For itself, Congress established the Joint Committee on the Economic Report (now called simply the Joint Economic Committee), which reviews the Economic Report of the President and conducts studies on economic matters, with its own full-time staff, for Congress.

In the 1920s and 1930s there was no agency, in the Executive or in Congress, responsible for surveying and reporting on the events that shaped the economy and led us, successively, through a

* Aug. 4, 1956, pp. 386–387.

treacherous speculative boom and the worst depression of our history. Now we have not only the Council of Economic Advisers and the Congressional Joint Economic Committee, but far better organized and less parochial economic advice in such important agencies as the Treasury, Commerce, Agriculture and Labor Departments and the Federal Reserve System. These improvements insure that the abundance of new economic information and the means of mobilizing this information that have become available since the 1930s will also be more wisely interpreted.

More recently, the Federal Statistics Users Conference, a nonprofit organization composed of representatives of business, agriculture, labor and nonprofit research groups, has become an effective force in asking for and getting Federal funds for improvements in Federal statistical programs. Because it represents the four important groups of users of Federal statistics it carries weight with Congressional committees.

The development of high-speed electronic computers in the last few years has resulted in some speeding up of the flow of economic information. These new machines have made it possible to apply more advanced statistical techniques in analyzing current economic problems.

There is still much room for further improvements. At the end of 1958, the President of the American Statistical Association said, "Appalling deficiencies in the quality of existing statistical series persist." * The statistics we have on such important fields as business inventories and some branches of construction are either so poor in quality or so late in publication—or both—that their usefulness in business forecasting is severely impaired. (Requests for small appropriations to enable the Commerce and Labor Departments to improve these statistics have been blocked repeatedly by the House Appropriations Committee.) But what we already have makes us vastly better off in knowing where the economy is and may be going than we were a generation ago.

* Presidential Address of Walter E. Hoadley, Treasurer, Armstrong Cork Company, at the Annual Meeting of the American Statistical Association, Dec. 29, 1958.

Special Aids for Small Business

Congress, which has for many years sought to devise an effective program to help small business, enacted during its 1958 session a promising series of tax and credit aids. This appendix describes and appraises the more important features of this new legislation.

THE SMALL BUSINESS INVESTMENT ACT

The provisions of the Small Business Investment Act* stipulate how investing companies are to be set up and indicate the rules under which they are to operate. The main points of the legislation are as follows:

A Small Business Investment Company (hereafter called SBI) can be formed by ten or more persons (as few as three if it is formed under a state charter) and must have at least $300,000 in paid-in capital. Up to $150,000 of this may be obtained from the Small Business Administration; the remainder must be provided by individual investors. However, additional loans up to 50 percent of a company's total paid-in capital can be made by the government agency.

Any individual or institution including commercial banks, national or state (provided the state laws allow it), may put up

* For a more complete discussion of the implications of the act see: Robert P. Ulin, "New Funds for Small Business," *Challenge,* Vol. VII, No. 6, March 1959. See also Eugene A. Meyers and Randall S. Stout, "New Federal Aids for Small Business," *Michigan Business Review,* The University of Michigan, Ann Arbor, Michigan, Vol. XI, No. 2, March 1959, pp. 11–15.

money for an investment company. However, a bank must limit its investment to 1 percent of its capital and surplus.

To be eligible for an SBI loan, a company must be a "small business," which is defined as a company whose total assets are less than $5 million. Another gauge of small business, according to the act, is that total after-tax income must have averaged less than $150,000 a year for the past three years.

The maximum amount which an SBI can invest in or lend to any single concern cannot exceed 20 percent of the SBI's paid-in capital. However, an SBI may join with other SBI's or financial institutions in making larger loans to a small concern.

SBI's are authorized to make loans for a twenty-year period, plus an additional ten-year extension. Loans are to be made primarily by the purchase of convertible bonds which can be exchanged for shares of common stock at any time. These bonds carry relatively low interest rates.

The Small Business Investment Act also allows the SBA to grant loans of various types to state and local development corporations for aid to small businesses. Such corporations, especially active in New England and the Southeast, are set up by local governments and financial institutions to attract business to their local areas. The attractions range from actual construction of plants which are rented or sold to private firms at very low prices, to exemptions from local taxes for a certain period of time.

To provide even further incentive for the establishment of SBI's, Congress furnished a new set of tax regulations (in addition to the reform measures which will be discussed later) in the Technical Amendments Act of 1958. These new tax regulations were set up to give a tax break to investors in SBI. The key provisions are:

An investor in a local SBI can deduct any loss on his investment directly from taxable income. Ordinarily, this type of loss would be deductible only from investment gains.

An SBI itself may deduct all its own capital losses directly from income. Also, it pays no tax on any dividends it receives from stocks in small companies (acquired through conversion of the original bonds).

TAX REFORMS

Small business tax reform measures included in the Technical Amendments Act of 1958 were designed to eliminate unintended hardships that turned up in the 1954 law and to provide greater incentives for direct investment in small business.

The most important provision directly affecting small business is the one authorizing greater depreciation write-offs on purchases of machinery and equipment—up to $10,000 a year ($20,000 in the case of a joint husband-wife return). It allows a special deduction of 20 percent of the cost of new equipment from taxable income in the first year, in addition to normal depreciation. (The rest of the cost must be depreciated by normal methods.) It applies to all types of equipment, new or used, with a useful life of at least six years. The allowance is available to any firm, but the $10,000 limit makes it of somewhat greater benefit, proportionally, to small companies.

Some of the other provisions of the tax revision act also apply to companies of any size, but were designed especially to help small business.

1. An operating loss may now be carried back three years, instead of two, and applied against previous years' income in claiming tax refunds.

2. Family-owned corporations may retain earnings up to $100,000 (previously $60,000) before paying dividends, without penalty for thus avoiding the tax on dividend payments.

3. Estate taxes, in certain circumstances, may be paid over a period of ten years—instead of fifteen months—if the estate consists mainly of investments in a family-owned corporation. Thus the heirs of a small business are given a better chance to avoid having to sell the business in order to raise funds for lump-sum tax payments.

4. Corporations with ten or fewer stockholders can elect to be taxed as a partnership. Owners can thereby be taxed only once on profits at the rates applying to their individual income

brackets, rather than twice—at the 52 percent corporate rate plus their individual tax on distributed profits. Partnerships also can choose to be taxed as corporations. If a partnership decides to take advantage of such an arrangement, it does so in order to have a tax advantage, and obviously is not in distress.

5. Corporations set up for a single, specific operation, such as making a movie, can apply the capital gains tax to profits, instead of using the regular corporate rate. They are allowed to use this method if the value of the corporation's assets increased by 15 percent or less.

6. As in the case of investors in SBI's who suffer a loss from the sale or exchange of stock, investors in small businesses also can deduct their losses directly from taxable income to a limit of $25,000 ($50,000 on a joint return). To qualify, the stock must meet these requirements:

It must be issued under a written plan adopted after June 1958 and calling for the issuance of common stock within two years. The stock must be issued for money or property rather than for other stock, securities or service.

At the time of issue, no prior stock offering may be outstanding.

However, if an investor purchases small business stock and subsequently makes an additional contribution to the business' capital, the amount he can deduct as an ordinary loss from the sale of his stock will be adjusted to the total amount he has invested in the company.

HOW MUCH HELP?

The question is: Will all these measures really work? To find out what businessmen think of the Small Business Investment Act, the *Harvard Business Review** recently made

* Problems in Review, "Small Business Financing," *Harvard Business Review*, Vol. 37, No. 2, March–April 1959, p. 6.

a survey among its readers. The survey points up the following conclusions:

1. There is a widespread consensus that small business needs additional sources of funds, although an outspoken minority argue that present sources are sufficient.

2. Reaction to convertible bonds as a means of financing is less than enthusiastic, largely because of the fear that they may limit the flexibility of financial arrangements between the investment company and the small businessman.

3. Many of those holding a negative view toward the act assert that government red tape has already seriously reduced the incentive for organizing a Small Business Investment Company.

In addition to the observations taken from the *Harvard Business Review* study, the following points have been made indicating that the Small Business Investment program may not be effective:

1. The government has not given the SBA enough money for the SBI experiment, since the total appropriation adds up to only $250 million for two and one-half years. Only $50 million, or one-fifth of the total, is to be used in the first six months of operation.

2. The prospects for making capital gains out of SBI investments are greatly exaggerated. How will an SBI shareholder be able to sell his stock? The doubters say few people will be interested in buying shares of these relatively closed, often obscure SBI companies.

3. The SBI program differs little from previous, generally unsuccessful efforts to provide venture capital for small business. SBI owners are not interested in losing money and will avoid risks inherent in loans to small, growth enterprises. If banks take the

lead in the SBI program, as is anticipated,* it could mean that their usual stringent credit standards would apply.

To such comments and criticisms, the SBI enthusiasts generally answer:

1. The special tax benefits make the SBI program significantly different from other small business development schemes tried in the past. They say that historically tax concessions have acted as a spur to venture capital.

2. The enthusiasts say large capital gains can be made. If there is no ready market for SBI stock, an SBI shareholder can dispose of his stock to a fellow SBI shareholder or sell it back to the SBI company itself.

3. The prominent role commercial banks will evidently play will not make the SBI's unduly conservative. A bank can tie up only 1 percent of its capital and surplus in an SBI. With so little at stake, a bank is unlikely to become overly cautious. In fact, bank participation in the SBI program will be a highly salutary development, for banks can provide SBI's with invaluable know-how and contacts.

Perhaps the number of businesses aided by the SBI program will be small. But this does not necessarily condemn it. The SBI program is set up to aid small *growing* businesses. If the SBI's give aid to these companies—even a few thousand of them—the new program will have substantial justification. For it will fortify the proposition that, even in this age of "economic concentration" and "corporate giants," there is still a place for the small enterprise—and a fair chance for each small business to become a bigger business.

* The fact that 23 percent of the returns in the Harvard Business School survey were received from financial institutions would bear out this conclusion, *op. cit.,* p. 148.

INDEX

Abbott, Charles C., 118
Accounts, national, 139, 262–264
Adelman, M. A., 168–169
Advertising, 90, 101–107
  dollar volume (charts), 103, 105
  impact of television, 107–108
  and research, 50
Advisers, economic, 265–266
Aging equipment (*see* Obsolescence)
Agriculture, 200–212, 242–243
  and research, 58
Aid, foreign, 211, 214, 220–222
Alderson, Wroe, 99
Allowances, depreciation (*see* Depreciation allowances)
Amortization, five-year, rapid, 38–40, 44
Anderson, Robert B., 174
Anti-missile system, 52
Antitrust legislation, 120, 149, 151, 156, 171–173
Arsenal economy, 125–132
Atomic Energy Commission, 126
Atomic research, 55
Automobile ownership, 84
Average consumer, 256

Backlogs, consumer demand, 85–86
Barger, Harold, 94
Barkin, Solomon, 189
Basic research, long-range, 51, 68
Basic resources, shortage of, 11
Beckerman, W., 91
Big-business competition, 151–156
Boom and bust cycle (*see* Business cycle)
Bottlenecks, 6–8

"Bracket system," 44
Brannan Plan, 211–212
Budget, governmental, 125, 134, 136–141
  deficits and inflation, 175, 185
  proportion for defense, 127–128
Burns, Arthur F., 77, 140
Bush, Vannevar, 50
Business cycle, 63–64, 66, 67, 237, 239
Business information (*see* Economic intelligence)
Business investment, equation, 45–47
  long-range planning of, 19, 35–37
  new elements shaping, 18–20
  as source of growth, 8–9
  sustaining high level of, 15–47
  (*See also* New plant and equipment)

Calculated Capacity Index, 253
Capacity, manufacturing, definition in indices, 254
  excess, 4–5, 14, 33, 67, 249
  indices of, 247–255
  and inflation, 186
  new, and research, 30–34
  versus production, 31, 252–253
Capital funds, availability of, 19, 37–40
  future flow of, 40–43
Capital expenditures, dollar volume, 17
  U.S. and U.S.S.R., 25–26
  (*See also* Business investment)
Caplan, Benjamin, 144

Car of the future, 52
Charge accounts, 76, 111
Chicago *Tribune*, 99–100
Civic salesmanship, 115–117
Colm, Gerhard, 136
Competition, 149–173, 191
  big-business, 151–156
  big- and small-business, 156–166
  in free markets, 227–231
  increasing, 172–173
  Russian economic, 216
Consumer credit, 10, 76, 111–114,
  187
Consumer demand, 44, 85–86
Consumer market, 70–89
  income and, 83–85
  problem areas, 79–80
  teen-age, 80–81
Consumer price increases, 176
Consumer Price Index, 193–194
Consumer research, 74, 88, 98–102,
  265
Consumer spending, 71, 89–90
Copeland, Morris, 263
Cost-cutting devices, 33
"Cost-push" inflation (*see* Inflation)
Credit controls, 178–185
Crop yields, 205
Crowther, Geoffrey, 93

Dealer education, 98
de Chazeau, Melvin, 66
Defense, Department of, 126, 132
Defense spending, 11, 58, 125–132
  charts, 126, 133
  and economic stability, 132–137
  proportion of Federal budget,
  127–128
Deficit financing, 140, 141, 184, 185
Depreciation, 68–69
Depreciation allowances, 19, 24*n.*,
  38–45
Depreciation reserves, 43

Depression, 1, 2, 3, 5, 7, 39, 67, 91,
  104, 137–139, 144–145, 201–
  204, 237, 238
  (*See also* Recession)
Development (*see* Research and de-
  velopment; Innovation)
Dial, Morse, 53
Dichter, Ernest, 101–102
Dillon, C. Douglas, 235–236
Discount houses, 109, 110
Distribution industries, 94–96, 215
  effect on corporate structure, 96–
  98
Dun & Bradstreet, 265
Durable goods ownership, 85

Economic intelligence, 262–266
Economist (London), 93, 265
Eisenhower, Dwight D., 139
Employment, full, 15
Employment Act of 1946, 10, 265
European Common Market, 217,
  226, 229, 231–234
Excess capacity (*see* Capacity, man-
  ufacturing)
Excess profits tax, 56, 162*n.*
Expansion (*see* Innovation; New
  plant and equipment)
Export-Import Bank, 224
Exports, U.S., 214–215, 234, 235

Farm income, 79, 200, 202, 209,
  257–259
Farm price supports, 4, 142, 193–
  195, 200–201, 204, 206–208,
  210, 211, 257–258
Farm prices, 191, 193–195
  and depressions, 201–204
Farm production cycles, 202
Farm surpluses, 205–206
Fears, economic, 2–6, 10–11
Federal National Mortgage Associa-
  tion, 187

Federal Reserve Board Index of Manufacturing Production, 30–31, 248, 249
Federal Reserve System, 76, 100, 175, 180, 184–185, 263
Federal Statistics Users Conference, 266
Federal Trade Commission, 101, 151, 158, 169
Finletter, Thomas K., 134, 135
Fisher, Joseph L., 244
Ford, Henry, 59
Fortune magazine, 84, 248–250
Free markets, U.S. competition in, 227–231
Funds, availability, 19, 37–40
future flow of, 40–43

Galbraith, John Kenneth, 12, 116
Government, economic role, 9–10, 119–123, 124–148, 241
support of industrial research, 48n., 56, 60
Gross National Product, growth (chart), 2
quarterly report on, 263

Hansen, Alvin H., 15, 16n., 17, 47, 197, 198
Hathaway, Dale E., 202
Hepner, Harry Walker, 90
Home of the future, 51
Home ownership, 84, 86, 88
Hoover, Herbert, 137, 237
Humphrey, George, 139, 144–145, 237
"Hydrogen process," 65

Import quotas, 223
Imports, U.S., 220
Income distribution, 76–78, 241
continuing revolution in, 85–87
low groups, 79, 257–259
and markets, 83–85

Income distribution, middle group, 74, 76–78, 84–85
problem areas, 79–80, 256–261
regional changes in, 259–261
teen-age, 80–81
upper group, 256–257
Industrial Revolution, second, 52–53
"Industry of discovery," 48
Inflation, 42, 86–87, 120, 174–199, 237
consumer reaction, 195–198
"cost-push," 188–191, 193–195
early postwar, 178–181
and farm prices, 193–195
Korean War and after, 181–185
1956–1958, 187–191
Innovation, industry of, 19, 49, 56–61
technological, 54–55
Installment credit, 85
Intelligence, economic, 262–266
Internal Revenue Code (1954), 39, 40
International Bank for Reconstruction and Development, 224–226
International Monetary Fund, 224–226
International trade, 213–236, 243
new institutions for, 222–227
in 1968, 233–236
Investment, depreciation as stimulant, 43–45
estimates of, 36
formula, 45–47
long-range planning of, 19, 35–37
and research, 34–35
sustaining high level of, 15–47
(*See also* Amortization; Capital expenditures; New plant and equipment)

Keynes, John Maynard, 139
Khrushchev, Nikita, 214, 216
Kuznets, Simon, 256, 262

Labor, forced, 219
Labor force, 2, 7, 20–22, 86
  (*See also* Population; Technical
    manpower)
Labor unions, 3, 149, 177, 190, 198,
    242
Leontief, Wassily, 263
Life magazine, 76
Lindsay, Franklin, 11
Long, Huey, 123
Long-range investment planning, 19,
    35–37
Low-income groups, 79, 257–259
Low-income regions, 79

McGraw-Hill Index of Manufactur-
    ing Capacity, 31, 247–255
Management, corporate, 12
Manpower (*see* Labor force; Popu-
    lation; Technical manpower)
Manufacturing capacity (*see* Ca-
    pacity, manufacturing)
Marginal utility, 87
Market research department, 97–98
Marketing, 90–123
  arts of, 74
  consumer credit and, 111–114
  impact of television, 107–108
  mass, 108–110
Markets, agricultural, 211
  consumer, 70–89
  free, 227–233
  growth of, 72–74
  mass (*see* Mass markets)
  new American, 75–76
  saturation of, 87–89
  world, growth, 213
Marshall Plan, 213, 214, 224
Martin, William McChesney, Jr., 175
Mass markets, 63, 161
  European, 232
    (*See also* European Common
      Market)
  U.S., 98–99

Merchandising (*see* Marketing)
Mergers, corporate, 151, 166–172,
    254
Middle-income group, 74, 76–78,
    84–85
"Middle management," 77
Mitchell, Wesley C., 262
Monopoly, 3, 149, 150, 190, 242
Motivation research, 99
  (*See also* Consumer research)

National Bureau of Economic Re-
    search, 100, 201, 262–263
National Defense Education Act,
    131
National Industrial Conference
    Board, 100, 264
National Planning Association, 136
National Science Foundation, 154–
    155
NATO, 214
Natural monopolies, 150
New materials from research, 50
New plant and equipment, 4–5, 9,
    16*n.*, 18, 22, 24, 25, 33–34, 66,
    133, 192–193, 240
New product (*see* Innovation)
New-style inflation, 187–191
Nuclear energy, 53, 55

Observers, economic, 265–266
Obsolescence, 19, 22–26, 28, 44, 64,
    240
Office of the future, 53–54
Old-age insurance benefits, 146
Optional consumption, 73–74, 76,
    89, 91
Output, per capita, world, 219, 222
  per manhour, 190–192
Overseas business (*see* International
    trade)

Packaging, 50, 95–96, 98
Passer, Harold C., 59

Payoff lag, research, 62, 64
Peloubet, Maurice E., 43
Petrochemicals, 53
Planning of investment, long-range, 35–37
"Point Four" Program, 220
Pollution control, 19, 27–28, 115–116
Population, shift of national center of, 82–83
Population growth, and productivity, 20–21
  U.S., 72–73
  world, 218–220
Population mobility, 81–83
Poverty, 78, 79, 257
Pre-selling, 98, 107, 109
Price inflation (see Inflation)
Price supports, farm, 4, 142, 193–195, 200–201, 204, 206–208, 210, 211, 257–258
Productivity, 1, 20–22, 61–64, 96, 191–193, 252, 253
Profit incentives, 19, 39, 68
Profit margins, 34–35
Progressive taxation, 78
Public works programs, 141
"Pure competition," 150
Pusey, Nathan, 115–116

Rationing, 178, 179, 181, 182
Raw materials, 26–28, 53
Recession, 18, 30, 31, 37, 66, 71–72, 105–106, 133–134, 136–140, 142–144, 147–148, 181–182, 184, 185, 191, 192, 203
  (See also Depression; Inflation; Stabilizers)
Regional income changes, 259–261
Relocation of workers, 7
  (See also Population mobility)
Replacement program (see Obsolescence)

Research and development, 8, 9, 48–69, 154–155, 162
  advanced, 53–54
  consumer, 74, 88, 97–102, 265
  and investment incentives, 34–35
  and new capacity, 30–34
  pressure on investment, 29–30
  problems arising from, 68–69
Retained earnings, 41–42
"Revolving credit" plans, 111–114
Reynolds, Lloyd, 177
Romney, George, 150, 156
Roosevelt, Franklin D., 125, 138

Safety, worker, 28
  (See also Pollution control)
Sales as research stimulus, 61–63
Salesmanship, civic, 115–117
Savings, 13, 113–114
Schumpeter, Joseph A., 64–65
Schweiger, Irving, 159, 160–161
Scientific manpower (see Technical manpower)
Securities and Exchange Commission, 158
Selling (see Marketing)
Sherman Act, 149, 172
Shift to suburbs, 82
Shopping center of the future, 52
Shopping centers, suburban, 83–84
Slichter, Sumner, 48, 66, 146, 155, 173, 248, 249
Small business, 58–60, 151, 155–166, 267–272
  definitions, 158n.
Small Business Administration, 158, 160, 162, 267
Small Business Investment Act, 164, 267–268, 270, 271
Social security payments, 142
Spending units, 75, 76
Stability, defense and, 132–137
Stabilizers, automatic and nonautomatic, 10, 44, 125, 141–145

Stabilizers, improving present, 145–147

"Supermarket merchandising," 109, 111

Supermarkets, 83–84, 109, 110

"Supplemental unemployment compensation," 146

Surplus, farm, 205–206
(*See also* Agriculture)

Survey of Consumer Finances (1958), 76, 78

Survey Research Center (University of Michigan), 100, 101, 195, 196, 265

Swedish Federation of Labor, 190–191

Tariffs, 214, 223, 228, 229, 233

Taxation, 4, 38, 119, 127, 137–138, 241–242
income, 10, 56, 141, 162, 256
reduction of, 122–123, 130, 137–141, 143, 146–147
reform of, 44, 56, 268–270
and small business, 163–164, 269–270

Technical Amendments Act (1958), 269

Technical manpower, 68, 127–129, 131–132

Teen-agers, economics of, 80–81

Television, impact of, 107–108

Time-payment plans, 114

Trade barriers (*see* Import quotas; Tariffs)

Trade unions (*see* Labor unions)

Trade, world (*see* International trade)

Undeveloped nations, aid to, 211, 214, 220–222

Unemployment compensation, 7, 10, 125, 142, 145, 146

Unions (*see* Labor unions)

Upper-income group, 256–257

Veterans bonus, 141

Wage increases, 120, 177, 190, 192–194, 198, 241, 242

Wage scales, 38, 86–87, 259

War, role in American economy, 3
(*See also* Defense spending)

Warburg, James P., 3

Warfare, economic, 217

Working hours, 95

Workweek, 21, 22

World trade (*see* International trade)

World War III, 10–11, 244

ABOUT THE AUTHORS

DEXTER MERRIAM KEEZER is a Vice-President of the Mc-Graw-Hill Publishing Company and Director of the Economics Department. A former professor, newspaper editor, and college president, Mr. Keezer has also served in various government positions and is the author of several books.

WILLIAM H. CHARTENER, with a Ph.D. in Economics from Harvard, and later a teaching fellow there, worked in Washington on the staffs of Editorial Research Reports and for the Wage Stabilization Board. He has been a member of the McGraw-Hill Department of Economics since 1953.

DOUGLAS GREENWALD, Chief Statistician of the Department, is President of the New York Area Chapter of the American Statistical Association. He is the McGraw-Hill member of the Federal Statistics Users Conference, and serves on the National Economic Accounts Review Committee.

ROBERT P. ULIN, M.B.A. from Harvard Business School, a senior economist in the Department, was co-author with Mr. Keezer of the book *Making Capitalism Work*. In addition to work as a consultant for several large industrial corporations, he has written numerous articles in publications on business forecasting and business finance.

E. RUSSELL EGGERS, an American Rhodes Scholar, was with Mc-Graw-Hill's Economics Department at the time *New Forces in American Business* was being written, and is now on the staff of the Chase Manhattan Bank as a consultant on the European Common Market.

MARGARET K. MATULIS, assistant economist, joined the McGraw-Hill Book Company in 1951, and a year later moved to the Department of Economics. She received her B.A. degree from Middlebury College in 1948, and has done graduate work at New York University.